First Edition published 2019 by
2QT Limited (Publishing)
Settle, N. Yorkshire

Printed in the EU on behalf of Latitude Press Ltd

A CIP catalogue record for this book is available from the British Library

ISBN 978-1-913071-09-7

BLOOD, SWEAT AND SMEARS

GARY GIBSON

2QT (Publishing) Ltd

Mum and Dad:
Miss you and love you always

Contents

Acknowledgements

Writing acknowledgements is never an easy task as you are always likely to miss somebody out and offend them, which is never my intention.

What I have tried to do throughout my narrative is to try and identify those who I have climbed with and those who I am indebted to for putting up with me through some of my tantrums, bizarre sense of humour and not least my obsession for new routing, although I would like to single out a few: Derek Beetlestone and John Perry for being there when I set out on this mission; Adam Hudson for being a mate; Geoff Birtles for giving me a chance, and my drinking mates, Howard, Steve, Nick and Mick for fun nights out and the arguments that invariably ensue: politics and football eh?

I am indebted to Gordon Jenkin, Matt Ward, Tony Penning and Martin Crocker for the support they gave my wife and family through the stress following my almost fatal accident. You have my utmost respect.

To everybody that helped with the minutiae of this book: Ian Carr and Charlotte for their proof-reading ability, Graham Hoey and Jim Perrin for their support, and Chris Parker, Josh Dawson and Andy Birtwistle for a bit of advice, help and encouragement. I am indebted to Mick Ward who supported me through the process, edited my work, directed me and, more than anything, gave me positive feedback when I most needed it. Mick, you are a star and I couldn't have done this without you.

To Mark Radtke for helping with advice and pointing me in the direction of 2QT, my publisher. To Catherine Cousins and Hilary Pitt at 2QT for their support and advice.

I have to thank Roy Thomas for his endearing friendship, his trust in me when things went wrong ... and they did, many times ... and for just being a mate.

To my brother Phil. You took me climbing, taught me so much about it and were always reliable, despite my argumentative nature and me just being me.

My final thanks go to one person and one person only, Hazel my wife. I have put you through so much, you have supported me when I have been down and we have enjoyed plenty of good times together as well. Long may it continue.

Gary Gibson

Foreword

By Mark Pretty

'A bit mad.' 'Grumpy.', 'What a laugh!', 'Crap routes', 'He's a bit of a hero of mine', 'Does he ever shut up?', 'A character!', 'Have you seen the size of his hands?'

Those are just a few of the comments which have been elicited when I've mentioned Gary's name over the years; this is someone about whom people have an opinion, one way or another. For me, if put on the spot, the key words in describing Gary are energy and enthusiasm – he simply bubbles over with the stuff and his new routes record (getting perilously close to five thousand) stands testament to that.

While the elite of British climbing have consistently ignored or dismissed his achievements (due to some inherent snobbishness about mid/lower grade climbing?) they cannot be so easily ignored. Here is someone who, more than anybody else, has advanced easy to mid-grade sport climbing in this country – not to mention the trad routes.

He was (and is) a rule breaker, something of a maverick who had the vision and the nerve to change the nature of the game in the UK.

Look at it like this: if, out of those five thousand, one percent is three stars, then fifty are classics and if ten percent are three stars, then five hundred are! That places him in the all-time list of great climbers in the UK.

Gary is 'a character' in a pastime where personality seems to be fast disappearing; climbing is becoming a sport in the eyes of many and climbers increasingly see themselves as athletes. In such a culture, stepping out of line or having an unconventional world view may well jeopardise your sponsorship potential. Ironically, British climbing athletes may well owe their careers, at least in part, to Gary. Without the massive investment in time, effort and money which he's put into UK climbing, many of the businesses which make a living out of it might not exist. And if they didn't exist, they certainly wouldn't be sponsoring our modern heroes!

Of course, as you will learn, he's made mistakes and has definitely raised the hackles of more than one climber; however, when you tell people what you really think and you challenge their conceptions, this is bound to happen.

Gary has been a major player in UK climbing, without being one of the 'best' climbers and as it is in an elitist culture, this has proved difficult for some to cope with. Never unhappy to have his say but happy to listen to others and, with enough stories and escapades to fill five books, his is a voice of how climbing used to be. Whether you like it or not, climbing in the UK wouldn't be what it is if Gary wasn't who he is. Read on!

Prologue

'Muggle he ain't: climbing wizard he is. Always a great sense of humour, and fiery, steely determination (that's why he's a wizard). The legacy he has left UK rock climbing will speak for itself, long after we've gone. The routes, and the traffic they get, shout out loud.' Nadim Siddiqui

Before you read this – my story, yes, my story – not one portrayed by the media or other people's writing (rewriting?) of history – you need to know a few things about me. I am not a great climber, and never professed otherwise. I am not some hero who needs worshipping. I am not perfect. And I am definitely not the same as anyone I know.

The simple truth is that I am obsessed by many things: my climbing, my profession – even though I am now retired – my musical tastes, my football team and, most of all, my love for my wife, my friends, and for life itself.

This is a story like no other story. It is not one based on reaching the highest levels of climbing ability, nor the training needed to get there, nor the talent required to achieve it. No, mine is a tale of relentless obsession mixed with passion, drive, determination, all tinged with a modicum of madness sprayed about the edges.

The obsession is the beast still within me. It burns relentlessly inside.

To sit down and begin to collate the information, stories, memories, facts and photos seemed an arduous task. Over the years I've kept a series of diaries, listing my routes, events and memories, the joy of climbing with friends, tales about my childhood and stories about my parents and family. However, reducing them to a meaningful history, while avoiding getting bogged down in a multitude of side issues, was no easy task. It conjured up some magnificent memories though and had me chuckling to myself along the way.

But how could I make my mark and be the best climber in the country, the world, when I wasn't even the best climber in my own town, street or house? No, I made a mark in another way: by challenging the boundaries of the establishment that were promulgated by those who felt precious about climbing. They had laid down 'the rules', but their rules weren't necessarily my rules. And, of course, I have courted controversy; it has followed me around like a bad smell. But was that always the intention?

Early on, I decided that my path would be new routing. I had read about my heroes in the magazines, and new routing became my 'route' (!) in. You didn't have to be the best to climb new routes; you just had to find them and do them. I redefined the boundaries of what a new route could be. I didn't necessarily need a line, such as a crack, a groove or corner; I just needed space, and to hell with what grade it was. A new route mattered, come what may, and that was how I decided to make my mark. And as for ethics, well, you'll see ...

Now I may well be as mad as the proverbial hatter but at least I delivered. As soon as I made my decision, I set out to implement it. I was never going to stop. In the end, of course, it became an obsession. Whether you love me or loathe me, you've probably heard of me – so perhaps I've achieved my goal after all. Almost certainly you will have climbed at least one of my routes – there are so many! My mark is scratched in history for all to see. Whatever the quality of those routes, you will undoubtedly have passed by and recognised them. For better or worse, I've chosen my path and this is where it has taken me.

I didn't want to write this book, but someone told me I should. They told me to get my life story on paper, to right some of the wrongs that have been foisted upon me. And so now you have it: my life – and heart – on a plate. Believe it if you will but if you don't, it won't make any difference. I am what I am. I do what I do. My mission isn't over until I'm finished.

Chapter 1

My Childhood

'*WE BOTH HAVE to be thankful to our parents for the rich and wonderful childhood they gave us at our home, and the weekends in the countryside and during holidays. This, I believe, gave us a love of adventure and the outdoors, and never once did our mum and dad hold us back from our climbing exploits, even when things went wrong, with life-threatening accidents.*' Phil Gibson

I had a wonderful childhood, full of knocks and scrapes, trials and tribulations and even a few successes. I wasn't an above-average kid education-wise, nor was I thick. I had plenty of friends; we all knocked around together. The occasional difficulties with which I was confronted taught me how to deal with setbacks: just learn from them and move on. This set me up perfectly for adult life in the complicated and enigmatic world of rock climbing.

I was born into a hardworking family in Newcastle-under-Lyme in 1960. My brother, Phil, was five years older than me. My mum and dad both worked hard to earn a reasonable living so they could keep the house they owned and provide for their family.

By trade, my dad was a hairdresser, not the fancy kind that you see in almost every town nowadays but your straightforward, no-frills barber. For all of his working life, my dad operated in Burslem. He plied his trade from the early age of thirteen, firstly tutored by Burt Heywood, then later setting up his own business in the centre of the mother town of 'the Potteries'.

My dad was one of seven, a large family by today's standards but a very happy one all the same. Their background was coal mining. I have little memory of my grandad who died when I was young, but my grandma was a wonderful woman, always resilient and friendly, and always keeping a close watch on the local community from behind her net curtains.

My mum had a different family background, very much the opposite of my dad's. She lost both her parents to illness when she was very young. Subsequently she was adopted by her aunt's family. Her cousin, Ruth, became her 'sister'. Throughout my life, I have regarded Ruth as my auntie. When I was young, I knew little about my mum's upbringing. She was a quiet, somewhat reserved lady, almost reticent about her past.

My dad was something of an enigma. Throughout my childhood, he was a very caring and loving man, always focussed on supporting his family. He loved my mum very much and, looking back, it's clear that they had a very close relationship indeed. Everything he did in life was for the benefit of his family.

But my dad also had an awkward, almost belligerent side, one that seems to have been passed on to me. If he didn't like you, you'd know it very quickly indeed. He would do his best to shun you and he wouldn't even speak to you. He didn't set out to be blunt or rude; he just liked his own space and his own company. Many were the hours, later in life, that he would happily sit alone in the conservatory of our house and listen to music or the radio. He wasn't a reader; he would never stick his head in a book, but he was well-versed in the ways of the world and taught me so much throughout my life.

My dad had many redeeming qualities. However, one trait, which I disliked intensely as a kid, was his disciplinarian tendency. His belt was his weapon of choice, and, due to my mischievous nature, I felt this in a physical sense on more than one occasion. I don't despise my dad in any way, shape or form for how he chose to discipline me. It was a very old-fashioned method which, for some of the things I used to get up to, I probably deserved.

My mum, on the other hand, was the bedrock of our family, always supportive of my dad but always sensible about how to bring up my brother Phil and me. I don't think my mum ever really raised her voice to me, although its tone would send shudders down my spine when I'd done something wrong.

When my mum passed away in 2015, having lost my dad in 2004, I felt that a part of me passed with her. She was such a wonderful lady.

My older brother

So what can I say about my brother Phil? When we were kids we were so different that we had little to do with one another. I don't mean this in a negative sense, but my being five years younger than Phil meant that his circle of friends was always different, his school was always different and his career path, mainly because of his focus on art, was always going to be different. Unlike me, getting involved in school sport and watching football, he wasn't the athletic type. Ironically, looking back, I can't say, hand on heart, that I remember clearly what Phil did when I was young. How that was to change when we discovered climbing!

As kids we didn't sit watching television all day long, and you couldn't play on a computer; that wasn't in our parents' plan. Instead, we had Sunday outings and family holidays to places that my parents could afford.

I remember with great fondness all our holidays, most of which were at Butlins holiday parks. It was a perfect solution for our parents, as both of them loved dancing. This was a twice-weekly tradition that they upheld until my dad died in 2004. At Butlins they could dance as often as they liked. It was also the perfect entertainment solution for me as a kid. I could go off each morning to the fairground by myself and while away the hours to my heart's content.

As I recall, the entire place was a rabbit-warren of entertainment. There were daytime and evening shows, there was self-catering accommodation, dancing for my parents and no shortage of other things for me to do.

I would occasionally make friends with other lads of similar age. I remember when we were on holiday at the Skegness 'campus', I met up with a lad named Tim and we thought we'd try some golf. There was a putting green at the front of the site and Tim thought he'd try a full-on swing at the ball, rather like a Jack Nicklaus or Lee Trevino shot, as we'd seen on television. Sadly, he missed the ball completely and hit my jaw instead. I've little doubt that he broke it, as it swelled up to three times its normal size. Naturally my parents were really upset, but one benefit was that I couldn't talk. My dad always said that I must have been vaccinated with a gramophone needle.

I'll take a dare

I went to the local primary school at Ellison Street where I met most of my early mates, some of whom would follow me through many of my school years, and I spent most of my time playing the fool; there was no pressure. My dad always used to tell me, 'Make the most of your childhood: these are the best years of your life.' Of course I took no notice but, looking back, how right he was.

At the age of eleven, we were all set an end-of-year test, about which I knew very little. I just sat down and did the best I could. What I didn't realise was that this was the famous Eleven Plus which decided the destiny of your subsequent schooling. Depending on the results, you went to either a grammar school or a comprehensive. Phil was at the latter; naturally I assumed that I'd be joining him. To my surprise (perhaps even more to my parents' surprise), I did rather well in the exam and ended up going to the grammar school. Maybe I was bright after all?

Meanwhile, I was constantly getting into trouble with some lads down the crescent where we lived. They would hatch a plan, and I would be the only one who would carry it out. We would dig dens and if they collapsed, which they quite often did, I'd be the one under the rubble.

One idea, I remember, was to steal some vegetables from the back garden of a neighbour. As a deterrent, he had constructed a narrow fence and some netting round the garden. This wasn't an insurmountable problem; I simply dug a hole under it, crawled through and pinched as many of the neighbour's vegetables as possible. Naturally we had absolutely no idea as to what we were going to do with the plunder. It was just something we could do, so I did it.

Unfortunately, I had bright red hair, just like my dad when he was young. I couldn't have been easier for the neighbour to spot. He didn't need an identity parade; sure enough he was round at our house in minutes, asking my mum where I was. My mum didn't need anything other than, 'Wait till your dad gets home!' as a warning, and I was sent to my room to wait for the belt.

I was that mischievous child everybody knew and talked about but it was something to be proud of, rather like a badge of honour. My mates knew that I would meet any dare they threw at me, within reason.

All tarred up

On another occasion, with some local kids, Adrian and Brian Lucik and David Morris, I was wandering around Ravensdale when we stumbled across an old tar pit, close to the new A500 that had been built about four hundred yards from our house. The tar had been left over from when the road had been built. A heavy scab had formed on its surface. The pit was about sixty feet in diameter and I came up with the idea that we could have a game of football on it. I was told to go in goal – I wasn't regarded as a good footballer by my mates – and we played a group of other lads from up the road in Bradwell.

Now the one thing you shouldn't do when you are on a tar pit is stand still, something I didn't think about at the time. Inevitably I began to sink, so much so that by the time I realised it, I was knee-deep in tar. At first, my mates thought it was hilarious but the more I tried to get out, the more I sank. Finally they woke up to the fact that it was serious and, all pulling together, they managed to drag me out of the pit. I couldn't clean the tar off my legs and the lower part of my back, so I went home. I knew my mum was at work, as it was the middle of the school holidays, but thankfully my brother was at hand. He pulled out a small hand basin, stood me in it and tried to scrub the tar off with the kitchen scourer.

By the time my mum came home, I was still standing in the hand basin with Phil scrubbing away at my legs, red-raw with discomfort. It must have been the funniest scene imaginable. Mum reminded me of it a few weeks before she passed away. Even dad thought it was funny. Perhaps that's why this was the only misdemeanour I ever got away with.

Schooldays

My first days at my new, 'big' school were, as I recall, an intimidating experience. A few of my friends had also passed the Eleven Plus and ended up at the same place. I wondered if I'd ever again see other friends who had moved on to different schools. However, making new friends has never been a problem for me and at the new school it wasn't too long before I had a whole bunch of them.

My priority at school was sport. I loved football, even though I wasn't much good at it. However, at this school it was quite firmly not on the agenda. It was rugby for two terms and then cricket or cross-country for the other. I knew nothing about either of them, but was happy to give them a go, and quickly found out that I was quite good at rugby. By the end of the first year, I was in the school team, something I'd never achieved in football at my old school. How could this be? How could a chunky little kid be any good at this sport? Of course, rugby can suit all shapes and sizes, and I was uncomplainingly thrust into the scrum.

I actually became more than just good in my school team and had the opportunity to travel with some of the best players in the year to a selection process for the Midlands Colts. Sadly, I didn't win through.

Throughout my school years, despite making some good friends, I began to feel more and more isolated from their social circles. I took maths O level a year early, achieving a grade A at the age of fourteen and went on to learn A level maths in my final year.

For my dad, success in my exams was everything, and I did quite well, with six passes, which pleased both of my parents immensely. Nevertheless I was becoming more and more unsettled at school and felt the need to move on. I had no desire for more A levels. Instead I moved to the local college of further education in Newcastle-under-Lyme to extend my education and, perhaps more importantly, my social life; well, you have to understand your priorities in life.

By this time, I had discovered climbing. While I still did some fishing and went to watch my local football team, for most of the time I could think of nothing else but going climbing with Phil and achieving something great in the future.

Port Vale

When I was a kid, my dad introduced me to a number of things. His notion was that if I could sample as many things as possible in life, I would have a clear idea of what would interest me when I grew up.

I had the delight of being introduced to religion through Methodism, the enjoyment of going to the Boy Scouts, the pleasure of being introduced to fishing by my uncle Jim, and the joy of being introduced to my local football club, Port Vale.

Every other Saturday, at one o'clock in the afternoon, my dad would shut up his barber's shop in Burslem, so that he could go to watch his beloved football club. He never went to the away matches; it wasn't really the done thing in those days. Anyway he couldn't do so because he had to work in the mornings and tidy up the shop after everybody had left.

The Port Vale passion was inevitably passed onto me and, on 22nd October 1966 (exactly eleven years to the day before I would do my first new route), he took me to my first Vale match against Wrexham. My memory of it is extremely vague but I do recall being lifted over the turnstiles and standing on the ash banking at 'the Hamil end', watching the players far, far below. Goodness knows what the score was but I was totally hooked.

Having said that, going to matches wasn't a regular event at first. Perhaps I needed time to get to love my dad more deeply, despite his disciplinarian traits. As I grew older, I began to cherish our Vale visits more and more. I would get the chance to go to 'work' for Dad at his shop on a Saturday morning, when there was a game on – work being a very loose term when it comes to just brushing up. Then he would lock up, take me for a brew and a sandwich next door at Toni's café and off we would head for the match.

If my dad was unable to take me when he and my mum were off somewhere else, he would ask Ted Shirley, a neighbour of ours, to give me a lift on the back of his scooter to go and watch what today I still regard as the 'Mighty Vale'.

For me it was a seminal experience. It wasn't like watching a football team on the telly and picking the best of the bunch, rather like glory hunting and perhaps swapping sides if they weren't doing too well. This was part of what every football fan should feel: a sense of belonging, a sense of comradeship and a sense of community. I could never desert the Vale.

Today still, after so many years, I always look for their score, even if I'm on holiday. My heart yearns if I don't go to as many home matches as possible and even some of the away matches. I never boo the players if they play poorly or the team loses; what's the point? I support my team with all my heart. They are a part of me and I am a part of them, unconditionally, save of course that they take money off me for the pleasure – I've spent money on many worse things in my life, believe you me.

Club chiropodist

In 1982 I qualified from college as a chiropodist, and in 1983 I approached John Rudge, the then manager, to see if they had a chiropodist working for the club. They hadn't and I was fortunate enough to be appointed as their 'foot specialist' in October 1983. It was a humbling experience.

I got to meet and work with the staff and players, some of whom I had idolised from the terraces. Now when I say 'idolise', obviously I mean idolise as a fan, but when I met them as people, they turned out to be a great bunch of blokes. Over the years, one or two have become good acquaintances, through mutual professional respect.

I also got to work with one of my all-time footballing heroes, Alan Oakes, who used to play centre-half for Manchester City in the 1960s and became the first team coach at the Vale. Now here was a truly wonderful bloke, of huge stature as a person and imbued with a sense of dignity and respect. I don't doubt though that he would have had a rough edge when he was on the football pitch or training ground.

Both John Rudge and Alan were great to be around, and on a number of occasions I was allowed to travel to away matches on the team coach along with the team and physio, my good friend, Martin Copeland.

It was such a friendly place that in 1986, when the Vale were on the verge of promotion, I got to travel with the team to the Shay, the home of Halifax Town. Vale needed a draw to be promoted, or Leyton Orient, the team in fifth place, needed to lose and we were 'up'.

When we got into the dressing room, Alan asked me if I would like to sit on the bench alongside him, John, Martin and the substitute – there was only one in those days. How could I refuse?

What a different place it was to watch a match! A ground-level view where you could hear every moan and groan on the pitch, every instruction from the bench, every communication between the players – the word 'Odessa' from Phil Sproson, the Vale's centre-half, meant to move up to catch people offside – and every roar of the fans. It was both scintillating and nerve-racking.

As Halifax scored two goals and Vale none, the atmosphere was growing increasingly tense, but in the end it didn't matter. Orient had lost, and as the final whistle blew the Vale fans ran onto the pitch in celebration. I was hugged by a few of them and even asked for my autograph; not that they had a clue who I was, and I certainly wasn't going to tell them.

Old Trafford, here we come!

Another cherished occasion was when the Vale were drawn against Manchester United in the League Cup in 1986 and I had once again been invited by Alan onto the team coach for the away trip; I had the chance to go inside the dressing rooms at Old Trafford.

Manchester's team was full of superstars with the likes of Brian Robson and Gordon Strachan, and they beat the Vale, just as they should have done, by two goals to nil. It was hardly a surprise that the minnows would come away with nothing but a loss.

After the match, as Martin and I were tidying up the kit, the players went off to socialise in the bar with the United players. It was then that Alan came in and asked us to follow him.

We were led down the corridor into the Manchester United manager's office, and there was the manager, Ron Atkinson, and Vale's management team. I was stunned. Ron offered us a glass of whisky each, which we accepted with glee – it would have been rude not to. What an honour it was to sit and chat with the three football greats in the theatre of dreams. Ron was really down to earth, without any edge or arrogance whatsoever.

Mistaken identity

In 1988 the Vale had sneaked through to the second round of the FA cup by playing Macclesfield Town at Vale Park – promoted as the Wembley of the north when it was opened in the early 1950s – and winning, through a late Kevin Finney goal. The Vale were on an awful run of form, struggling in the league, and it was rumoured that the soon-to-be 'great' John Rudge would have lost his job had we lost.

In the next round of the cup, we drew Tottenham Hotspur at home but we first had an away match at Southend United on the preceding Friday night.

Luckily for me, again (!), I was invited to travel on the team coach for the Southend trip and we set off around lunchtime. As usual, there would be a pre-match meal at a local hotel before we headed off to Roots Hall, the home of Southend United.

As the bus pulled up, we could see that a few members of the press were circling around, waiting for us to disembark. They would be trying to chat to some of the players about the forthcoming cup-tie against Spurs; it was a big event for our little club.

As usual, Martin and I were first off the coach and headed off into the hotel. All of a sudden I was confronted by the BBC reporter Tony Gubba. He launched into a barrage of questions: 'How do you think you'll do against Tottenham?' 'What's the atmosphere at the club like at the moment?' 'Do you think there will be a big crowd?' He then asked me what position I played. When the reply came that I was the club chiropodist, he didn't stick around long before making a beeline for the manager and genuine team members.

Stoke to Llandudno to York to Stoke

That same season, my girlfriend Hazel and I had decided to go climbing at Pen Trwyn on the Great Orme in Llandudno. Naturally we were there early and had done about four or five routes; well, I had, because it was absolutely freezing and there was no way Hazel was going to climb in such dire conditions. Despite being wrapped up well, she was shivering with cold. Suddenly, out of the blue, she asked where the Vale was playing that day. 'York City,' I said. There was a mischievous glint in her eye. 'Shall we?' I asked. The answer was obvious and just before 1 p.m. we set off for York for a 3 p.m. kick-off.

We had a Ford Fiesta XR2 at the time and the roads were fairly quiet as we hurtled, at around 100 mph when possible, along the A55, then the M6 and finally across the M62, to arrive at York City FC ground a little after 3 p.m.

As we went through the turnstiles, I asked the guy in the booth what the score was. 'One-nil,' he replied. I said that I thought the Vale would win. 'To York,' he retorted.

What a bizarre reason to support your football club! Go out for a day's climbing, with a two-hour drive, get cold and decide to go and watch your team, some 150 miles away in the opposite direction and they're losing when you finally get there!

It turned out to be worth it though. Vale wrestled it back to two-all, and with a few minutes remaining we scored and won three-two. To cap it all, we were promoted at the end of the season, away to Halifax Town.

A supporter, to the end

As the years rolled by, my support for the team grew to the point where it would be a group of mates – my cousin Howard, Nick, John and a few others – going to the away matches in our VW van. We would pile in and troop off to away grounds, such as Bolton, Bury, Nottingham or Mansfield.

Such incidents highlight the trials and tribulations of many a football fan supporting a lower league team. I have witnessed the highs (including visits to Wembley and the Millennium Stadium, great cup successes against Tottenham Hotspur, Derby County, Everton, Arsenal [almost!] and Southampton) and the lows of relegation, administration and watching my beloved football team almost go out of business.

But this is what you have to expect – to enjoy and to suffer at the hands of your football team. There are the delights of success, the woes of failure, and the camaraderie with your mates. You only hope that your team will be back to fight again, and win another day. Port Vale is a part of me, and I am a part of them. They mark my identity; they are from where I belong. I would never support another team; no amount of money, success or failure could make me do that.

Chapter 2

Boys Will be Boys

'I LOOK BACK through my diaries in amazement at all the climbs and love for the things we have done together. It all seems like yesterday and somehow bizarrely so surreal – a quixotic adventure. Things were so different, back then.' Phil Gibson

The start of my climbing life was a relatively low-key affair. I had been drifting around at school with no real sense of direction. I didn't know what to do for a career; who does at the age of thirteen? I enjoyed sport but preferred football to rugby. As my school didn't provide football, I had to make do with rugby, even though I wasn't bad at it. I did cross-country running, but I was a bit of a tub, so could never compete at a decent level.

My other interests were more diverse. I enjoyed painting model soldiers, and one day a week my dad would get up at five o'clock in the morning to take me fishing. The following week he would take me after work to watch my local football team, Port Vale. I loved all these activities. To help fund them, I had a newspaper round. Both my parents were very encouraging, thus giving me an understanding of money from a relatively early age.

I had no problem with getting up early, whether for the newspaper round or for fishing. I was like a whirling dervish, full-on for everything outside of school and studying. One morning I got up so early that when

I arrived at the paper-shop, usually at around 6.30 a.m., it was still only 5 a.m. My parents were amused by my exaggerated notion of timeliness. Even today, I am annoyingly early for almost everything I do.

When I was thirteen years old, my brother Phil had already left school and was studying for a degree in ceramic design at North Staffordshire Polytechnic. Phil was by no means an academic, but when it came to illustration and design he was, and still is, an utter genius. If he was a Rembrandt, I was more an Etch-a-Sketch.

At college, Phil went on some walking and scrambling trips. Around that time he met Alan Sherlock, a Liverpudlian, who did a bit of climbing. This meeting was a game-changer for Phil, who accompanied Alan on a number of climbing days, and he would alternate with our cousin Robert. Robert had an old Fiat 500, and many were the times that I remember Phil coming home brimming with enthusiasm for the day he'd just had. He would read about his then heroes, Joe Brown and Don Whillans and, inevitably, I stumbled across Phil's books, not that I understood what they were all about.

About six months after Phil had started climbing, I became fascinated enough to hassle him into taking me along with him. I suppose, in some way, it had to happen. The problem was that Phil and I weren't very close, not because we didn't get on, but because of the five-year age gap. Nor did we really share any other interests. Phil didn't play football or go fishing and had already developed his own social circle with a bunch of like-minded mates. He was most definitely into Motown and Ska, and I hadn't yet discovered music, save for a bit of glam rock and my first single, 'Ernie the Fastest Milkman in the West'.

The fateful day finally arrived in the autumn of 1973. Phil had arranged to go climbing with Robert, red Fiat 500 and all, and asked me if I wanted to come along. I could hardly refuse; in fact, my recollection of the event is one of huge excitement. I was almost 'wetting my pants' at the thought.

Robert turned up and off we went to our nearest cliff, the Roaches, where both Phil and Robert had cut their teeth. I remember the tension and excitement as they discussed the day's plan, with me in the back trying to join in, like the adult I thought I was. I think they must have thought, 'what have we brought along?' Well now they knew – a kid who could never shut up. Robert was talking about *The Sloth*, teasing me somewhat with its description. I just said, rather immaturely, 'Oh I'll climb that for you ...'

We arrived at the crag and walked up through the maze of boulders and steps. When they pointed out *The Sloth*, a route they clearly revered, I understood the stupidity of my comments.

When I look back, I feel a little embarrassed about what I thought was my first climb; however, having consulted my brother and his ever-meticulous diary (he has always been the most puerile of tickers – probably a Gibson trait), I found out that my first outing on rock was *Inverted Staircase*. Now my memory is pretty damn good, and I thought my first climb was *Prow Cracks*, but heyho, who cares? I had made my first climbing foray, and suddenly I had another hobby to pursue. Despite all the stress and nervous energy, I just loved it and wanted more as soon as I could get it.

It's worth pointing out that this was traditional climbing; there were no sport routes in 1973, and there was no 'official' bouldering. The latter was something you did at the end of the day for a bit of fun, goading each other on, with only our mates to land on. The traditional style of climbing was what I had been brought up on, because back then there was nothing else.

Naturally, I was completely reliant on Phil. He provided the support and encouragement, the transport (or access to transport via other people) and, crucially, the gear: ropes, harnesses, nuts. In fact, he made some of his own nuts at college. All I provided was an old pair of Hush Puppies, kindly donated by my dad for footwear, and a questionable belaying ability.

As we began climbing together more and more, Phil became reliant on me to hold his ropes, very much in the vein of Dennis Gray holding Joe Brown's ropes. Dennis had written a book entitled *Rope Boy*, which was exactly what I was becoming. This suited me just fine. It was a great bonding experience. Phil and I became more than brothers; we became friends and partners in our chosen pursuit. Looking back today, I owe him so much for getting me into climbing and for the wealth of knowledge and experience he passed on to me; I trusted Phil implicitly.

Great Chimney(ing)

The trials and tribulations of my early climbing years were plentiful and added to the charm of my learning experience – not that I always thought so at the time.

I had only been climbing for about six months when Phil, Robert and I went up to Hen Cloud for some classic ticking. One route on the agenda was *Great Chimney*, on the right-hand side of the Cloud. The route began in the crack in the left-hand side of the chimney, all relatively straightforward, and then transferred to the wider, right-hand crack at about half-height.

Robert climbed the pitch, and then it was my turn. I managed the initial part quite easily; however, once I had transferred to the right-hand crack, I jammed my right knee into it, lacking any form of technique. I sat down on my knee, fully bending it, and when I pulled up it was jammed – well and truly stuck in the crack.

I was distraught. I couldn't move, and if I put weight on my knee it started to get really painful. What to do? I carried on struggling. Robert realised the gravity of the situation and tried to pull me up on the rope but that didn't work either.

The only solution was to summon help. Two guys abseiled in to offer assistance. After about half an hour of failed attempts, with much pushing and pulling and a lot of stress on my part, my knee was finally freed. I battled up the reminder of the route with a great deal of relief and vowed not to go back in a hurry. In fact, to this day I've never done *Great Chimney* again.

My mountain apprenticeship

As the months passed and we became more competent, Phil and I began to travel further afield. My parents would lend Phil the car, and off we'd go, inspired by the tales of Joe Brown and Don Whillans.

One of our first forays was travelling to the eastern gritstone edges, bringing Stanage, Froggatt, Curbar and surrounding crags into range. Today it seems rather bizarre that I would regard such places as a faraway land, but to us at the time, and for the world in which we lived, it really was quite an adventure. However, that was Phil's mantra: get to the crags where Brown and Whillans climbed. It was like following the bible of climbing.

Somewhat unceremoniously, we would tick off the lower-grade routes. As we improved, *Valkyrie, Brown's Eliminate, Avalanche Wall* and a whole host of other classics became reachable, despite their difficulty. While I was on the 'blunt end' HVS was our limit, yet Phil still encouraged me to try leading. While I was in no way near his standard and, believe it or not, I really was quite a shy and timid lad, but I managed to lead a few V Diffs, some Severes and even the odd VS. My first lead was *Gamma* at Froggatt, of which I was inordinately proud.

As spring rolled into summer, Phil teamed up with Alan and his mate Bob for a few trips to North Wales. Strangely, at the time and perhaps something that I've carried with me to the present day, the Lakes were never an objective. I don't really know why.

On Friday nights Phil would pack our dad's car with his enormous scout tent – it would probably have housed about ten Karrimats laid next to each other, if we'd had them – a couple of camp beds and associated sleeping kit and all the cooking equipment. Off we'd troop to Liverpool to pick up Alan and Bob.

Alan lived in Childwall. My recollections of the journey are vague; even today I couldn't find the place without a map. If I remember rightly, it was quite a poor area, but Alan's family and friends were so friendly and enthusiastic that it became almost a rite of passage.

From Liverpool, we would travel down past the old soap factory in Speke; you could never forget the smell of the place. Then we'd go through Denbigh and out onto the Denbigh moors. This really was a memorable trip. We'd pass by the Sportsman pub, which is still there today, above which stood this great edifice of a house on the skyline.

My childhood memories of this place were harrowing. I always imagined it as some great haunted house, full of wailing ghosts and ghouls. If you dared to venture inside, they'd trap you forever. Of course, Phil and Alan did absolutely nothing to dispel this notion; if anything, they probably accentuated the myth, so it scared me even more. Many were the nights where I would be wrapped up in my sleeping bag, wide awake, in dread. Recently I travelled this route once again with Hazel; the house is now gone, its remnants scattered across the hillside. Perhaps it was a mental-health institution?

Alan and Phil used to have a wonderful little hidden nook in the Ogwen Valley where we could camp, right away from the hordes around the Milestone Buttress or Ogwen Cottage. We were never bothered by anyone. It was quiet and tranquil. Best of all, it was free.

The first trip of many introduced me to the multi-pitch style of climbing for which the area is well-known. For a kid of thirteen going on fourteen, doing these routes, despite their lowly V Diff or Severe grades, was a frightening yet utterly rewarding episode. The experience was enhanced by the company of Phil and Alan. It took me away from the monotony of school, from boring studying and from the bullying to which I was becoming accustomed. Let's face it, a lad with ginger hair and a tubby waistline stood no chance.

My first multi-pitch, as I remember, was *Pinnacle Ridge* on Brach Ty Ddu – not an outstanding climb but an unforgettable experience. Even better was to follow.

The next day I was introduced to the rigours of Dinas Cromlech. Now, when I say rigours I mean not only the route we were about to do but the walk up to the damn thing. We drove round from our camping spot and down into the Llanberis Pass, not that I knew its name at the time, and parked up under this incredible cliff. Its most identifiable feature was a striking open-book corner. I didn't know what it was, but Phil was talking to Al about climbing it one day. For my part, I dismissed the idea out of hand.

And so we set off. I still remember that slog, even to this day. As you read these pages, you may be grinning at my torture that almost had me in tears. I wanted to turn back, but there was no way Phil was going to let that happen. He would never tell me off, rather just ply me with encouragement, while Al helped me out physically as we battled with the scree slope to reach the foot of our route. It was now possible to glance across at the open-book corner, still thinking it ludicrous that anybody could climb it.

Hush little puppy?

My memories of *Flying Buttress* are vague, though I do remember it being fairly straightforward until we reached the final belay – a lofty perch high on the right-hand side of the crag. People on the road, far below, appeared as tiny dots.

The last pitch sticks in my mind as a defining experience in my life. As ever, I was wearing my faithful Hush Puppies. The friction they provided was almost nil; my parents weren't prepared to spend money on a pair of proper shoes for me until I'd shown that I was really interested in climbing. I remember trying the first few moves off the belay, but the rock was so polished and shiny that my boots, frictionless as they were, kept slipping and I didn't have the strength to pull up without some footholds.

With a bit of cunning, Al, still giving me loads of encouragement with Phil giving me plenty of snug on the rope, put his finger under my Puppy. It held firm; well of course it would, and I managed to scrabble up the rest of the climb without more ado. I was blown away by what I'd done. The aid was irrelevant. What mattered was the achievement of climbing what to me was such an intimidating piece of rock. All those people whom I could see down on the road far below couldn't do that – but I could.

More than anything, it was such experiences that inspired me to take up climbing seriously. The company of Phil and Al meant so much to me. I didn't have any real friends back then and it was as though climbing became my true companion. I probably didn't realise it at the time, but when you sit down and retrace your memories you start to realise just why you became so enamoured with climbing in the first place.

Come fly with me

Phil had a yearning to climb on Clogwyn Du'r Arddu, having read the superb climbing book *The Black Cliff*. It was inevitable that the time would come for us to venture up there. Sure enough, one summer's day in 1975, Phil and I made the fateful decision.

In truth, I knew little about the place. I was guided by Phil's enthusiasm and drive. We parked at the normal spot at the end of a narrow road running up behind the Snowdon railway in Llanberis. We walked up to the cliff at a relatively brisk pace, very much aware that others might be heading for the same route. After a brief stop, we passed the Halfway House and continued up to the edge of the plateau from where we could get our first proper look at the cliff. Previously, you could see it brooding on the brow of the hillside, but you couldn't really tell what you were letting yourself in for. The magnitude of the cliff didn't frighten either of us in any way, shape or form. In fact, looking back, I think it was quite an inspiring sight for both of us.

We passed below the East Buttress, heading for the West. Phil had chosen *Great Slab* as our first foray on the cliff. This seemed about right to me. A tricky entry pitch followed by an easier series of slabby walls to the top. If I could get past the low crux we'd be fine, and Phil would be 'made up'.

He led off up the first pitch, dismissing the crux traverse across an inset slab with little ado. He continued relatively quickly up the long slim groove, placing very little protection – which presumably meant it was relatively straightforward. Then it was my turn.

Getting up to the start of the inset slab was easy. Phil had placed two good runners to protect himself for the delicate moves left. I took the two nuts out and committed myself leftwards onto the slab. Suddenly I was in difficulty. I shouted for Phil to give me some slack, so that I could step back right, but he was about 120 ft above and couldn't hear me. I tried to step back right anyway, but couldn't, so I committed leftwards with my Hush Puppies pedalling, and then ... off I came.

I felt a great whoosh of air as most of the climb swept to my right, and I went hurtling leftwards. Phil hadn't put any gear in to stop my flight, and I think I swung so far that, for a moment, I saw the East Buttress in front of me before coming back to end up hanging in mid-air somewhere around *The Arrow*.

Phil realised what had happened and lowered me to the ground. I was in shock, hollering back up to him. He abseiled off. Our first visit to Cloggy had ended in defeat.

Here, there and everywhere

The great thing about climbing with Phil was the diversity of crags that we visited. Initially our intention was about gaining the summit, particularly on multi-pitch routes in North Wales; however, we had to start somewhere, and that somewhere was gritstone.

When we moved onto the longer multi-pitch routes which, in fairness, didn't take us long, we'd go to the mountains one weekend and then a lower crag, usually Tremadog, the next. In the Peak we ventured onto limestone as we climbed better, and it came more into vogue. At the time, limestone seemed a radical departure, perhaps because Joe Brown and Don Whillans didn't climb on it so much.

The variety of climbing was fantastic, and it was all traditionally based. Many people seem to forget my background and even today I love to do trad climbs. People just assume I have always been a sport climber, but my roots go back to way before sport climbing was even invented. In fact the odd bit of aid was quite common on some of the harder routes; we also used to go aid climbing in the winter, at places such as Raven Tor. Phil would aid up *Mecca* and I would sit belaying until he had finished; then it would be my turn. I can therefore lay claim to have done *Mecca* more than once – and flashed it at that!

I was still at school, and Phil was at college; however, there were no issues about petrol money. Because of my paper round, I could contribute to costs. When I didn't have any work, Phil was happy to pay. Phil had a method of calculating whether he'd had a good day's climbing or not. He would divide the costs of the journey by the number of routes he'd done. The target was 50 pence per route, or less.

The 'washing line' affair

My father was a strict man when it came to my upbringing. Early on he had decided that I was destined for danger, and he wasn't prepared to let me have a bicycle of my own. Of course, when I was a toddler, it was *de rigueur* for me to have a small bike to learn how to ride, but when I got into my teens it really was a no-no. Dad had decided I'd already done enough damage to myself, and a bicycle wasn't going to contribute to any more accidents.

I had a problem when a friend of mine from school, one Roman Lytwyniw, wanted me to take him climbing. We walked into school together almost every day and, although I wasn't one for boasting, he was aware that I went climbing with my brother and he fancied a go. He knew I went somewhere nearby, and he asked me to take him 'for a climb'; in fact, he hassled me no end.

There were two major issues. How would we get there, and what would we use for gear? I hadn't got a bike, a rope or any nuts, so what would we do? Roman had the solution to one problem: his brothers had bikes, and he had his own, so he offered to lend me one, and we could cycle to the nearest cliffs for our adventure. The other problem was less easy to solve: the rope.

Phil had told me tales of Joe Brown in his early days and how he used to use his mum's washing line for climbing. My mum had a washing line which she didn't use that often. Problem solved.

So Roman and I hatched a cunning plan, and sure enough I 'borrowed' my mum's washing line and also 'borrowed' one of Phil's Moac nuts for protection. Roman provided the bike, and early one Saturday morning, off we went like a pair of intrepid explorers.

We cycled up to the Roaches. I chose to take Roman up *Pedestal Route*, which sits tidily under the watching eye of *The Sloth*, on the Upper Tier. I had climbed it for the first time a few weeks previously; I was 'experienced'. In my dashing Hush Puppies, I led off up to the top of the pedestal, using my Moac to protect me on the short layback section. Roman was the competent belayer – not! I belayed on top of the pedestal and brought him up. I have to say he climbed very deftly indeed for his first time out.

The rope wasn't long enough to get to the top so I did the traverse and used Phil's Moac to belay under a small overhang on the far side of the slab. Roman tiptoed across, and we finished victoriously. Roman was now a fully-fledged climber.

We cycled home in high spirits. I ditched the borrowed bike at Roman's and then faced one final hurdle: returning my mum's washing line. I must have arrived home at about five o'clock. I remember carefully replacing the clothes line on the wall where it belonged. Mum wasn't in sight. I scurried into the house to switch on the television and settle down sheepishly to my pre-tea viewing.

But my mum had the last word. About twenty minutes later, she came into the lounge and tartly commented, 'I see the washing line has returned.' To this day I still don't know if she realised what I'd been up to.

The Italian job

Phil was well versed in mountaineering literature; he was very much into the ethos of multi-pitch climbing, and the emphasis was always on the summit experience. He constantly spoke about Alpine peaks such as the Matterhorn, the Eiger and the Tre Cime di Lavaredo and we knew people who were heavily involved in Alpinism, making ascents of some of the lesser but still quite demanding peaks.

We'd been to see Whillans and Doug Scott do their national talks, focussed on their Himalayan activities, and they were nothing but inspiring. We travelled up to Wigan for a Whillans lecture, and he was the best raconteur I've ever heard – absolutely inspirational. His humour was infectious, calling someone 'Harpic' for 'being clean round the bend'. Phil was captivated by his aura. I was similarly impressed, though, at my tender age, such far-flung ascents seemed little more than a pipe dream.

Sure enough though, in July 1976, Phil had conjured up a plan to go to the Dolomites in Italy. I'd only been abroad once before, on a school trip to eastern France, yet to me it may as well have been the other side of the world. I was spellbound by Phil's wonderfully enthusiastic imagination. He designed the trip, and his baby brother was happily, albeit nervously, coming along for the ride.

I'd just finished my O levels; not a bad set of results, except for maths and physics, which I was particularly good at, scoring a grade A in each. At least I had the summer free to myself, to do with as I pleased. Previous summers had revolved around going fishing or playing stupid antics with my mates – upsetting the neighbours and my parents. I felt as though I'd reached a hiatus in my life; maybe I was starting to grow up. Phil had organised the trip in the microscopic detail to which I had become accustomed. Off we set, two young lads, Phil aged twenty-one and me just fifteen, on what was to be the trip of a lifetime and a truly memorable experience.

We took two rucksacks in which were climbing kit, camping kit, enough clothes to last a month, including the obligatory 'woolly pully', some maps and guidebooks, around £40 and two train tickets to Italy.

We were deposited at Stoke station by our parents, and off we went for the month, not really knowing when (or if) we'd be back. Mountains and summits awaited the Gibson brothers.

I don't remember much about the first stages of our journey through England and across the English Channel by ferry. My sole abiding memory of travelling across France was my rising unrest. We had been sitting around in automobiles, trains and boats for quite some time, trying to get what rest we could but always with an overpowering sense of nervousness and excitement about our destination. Sleep was at a premium as we finally rolled into Milan railway station for the next leg of our journey to the Dolomites.

Phil had it all worked out. I sat in the grandeur of Milan station as Phil went to source our tickets. Neither of us could speak a word of any foreign language, so you can imagine the likely problems if we'd lost each other.

The next stage of our journey to Cortina d'Ampezzo involved a train journey to Calalzo di Cadore and then a bus ride up into the mountains. This would give us our first sight of the majestic landscape that we had dreamed about. However, at one of the stations the train was due to split into two halves, with the front half going to Calalzo and the rear half disappearing into oblivion. We were on the rear half. We heard various announcements, all in Italian, and realised, more by luck than judgement, that the front half of the train was pulling away, and we needed to be on it.

We grabbed our stuff and scampered desperately down the platform, with some Italian guard furiously waving his flag. Phil leapt onto the train before me. As the train hurtled off, he grabbed me and dragged me aboard before I almost dropped off the end of the platform.

At Calalzo we sorted ourselves out. The coach for Cortina was waiting by the station entrance. We shuffled aboard as it crept off up into the mountains, providing our first sight of the stunning beauty of the place.

For two lads used to the Peak District and Wales, this was a whole new experience. Though we had certainly found a new beginning, the climbing remained a completely unknown factor.

The bus dropped us off in Cortina at around 8 p.m. It had been a long journey, and all we had to do now was to find a campsite. We had a look at the local map and set off down a road heading for one of a number of campsites marked on it. It was getting late, we were completely worn out by the experiences of our journey, and all I wanted was to find somewhere to sleep. My familiar bed at home was as enticing as it was unavailable.

I could rely on my big-brother Phil. He was as strong as the proverbial ox, both physically and mentally. Sure enough, we trudged in the right direction and, with our heavy sacks and weary bodies, found a huge campsite just out of town.

It was dark by the time we arrived, so we hurriedly unpacked our rucksacks, hauled out our trusty two-man Vango Force Ten, pitched it, rolled out our sleeping bags and bedded down for the night.

The next morning we awoke to a vibrant Italian campsite with huge trailer tents, caravans and tents the size of houses. They dwarfed our little abode.

Phil went off to find the facilities, while I stayed by the tent and put on a brew. I'd been used to camping rough in places like the Ogwen valley, and this campsite was a revelation. As I sorted out our morning rations, other happy campers were vacuuming their caravans with electric gadgets the likes of which I'd never seen before. Some were barbecuing their breakfasts on great roasting pans. One bloke was even cutting the grass outside his caravan. Even today, it still makes my brother smile when he remembers the look of astonishment on my face.

The next day we had to find the route to our first destination, the Tre Cime di Lavaredo. As ever, Phil had it covered; I think he'd sussed it out the night before when we were at the bus station in Cortina. We folded the little mansion of our two-man tent, tidied our campsite detritus away, packed up our kit and headed back to Cortina, which seemed so much nearer than it had on the previous night.

At the bus station we bought two tickets for the Refugio Auronzo, and off we went, passing through the beautifully tranquil village and mirror-lake of Misurina, to the series of hairpin bends that led up to our destination.

Normally this would have been a truly majestic way to get to the hut. Unfortunately it seemed as if our driver had been watching the film *The Italian Job* too many times and decided that he'd have a go at mimicking it on the winding, hairpin road.

My idea of driving around horseshoe bends, even today, is to take it nice and easy, using my gears to best advantage. This bloke threw his coach into every bend and, at the very last moment, dramatically swung it around. Bear in mind, these weren't horseshoe bends in the Peak District or some Welsh mountain hillside but ones on the edge of vast Dolomite precipices. Phil and I, who just happened to be on the outer side of the bus, had great views of the scree below. And there were moments when that's where we thought we were heading.

The driver was howling with laughter as each bend approached. It all added to the atmosphere. I wasn't looking forward to the journey back.

By some quirk of fate, we arrived in one piece at the Auronzo Hut. Unfortunately all we could see were the backsides of the Cima Grande and Cima Ovest; we had to wait another day to view them in their magnificence. We trudged, in *Sound of Music* style, up the long path past the Arunzo and a little chapel to find our destination for the next few days: a small camping area alongside the Lavaredo Hut. There were a number of other tents dotted around here, with a scattering of climbers relaxing in the paddock below the profile of the *Spigolo Giallo.*

The next day we were up early for a proper look at the Cima Grande and Cima Ovest. The weather was fine, and, as we scrambled up the path to reach the col, the atmosphere was still. We topped out on the edge of the col to see one of the most iconic views in the pantheon of world rock climbing. The Cima Piccolissima, in the foreground, was dwarfed by the vast precipices of the Cima Grande and Cima Ovest.

In awe, we contoured around to the foot of the cliffs, overwhelmed by the impending walls above. There was no noise and hence, we thought, no climbers. But wait: Phil with his beady eye spotted two dots high up on the North Face of the Cima Grande. Those two tiny dots, as Phil worked out from his guide, were on the *Hasse-Brandler*, which still, even now, reminds me of the magnitude of those faces. And Phil and I would be on them, well, on the edge of them, the very next day. But these Dolomite walls were as intimidating as hell. Frankly, I was terrified.

Cima (not so?) Grande

Phil had chosen the south-east arête of the Cima Grande, the *Dibona Arête*, as our first venture onto these magnificent pinnacles, probably because of its grade and accessibility. I wasn't agreeing or disagreeing; I trusted him implicitly to be my guide, as had been the case for the previous three years.

The next day, all I saw at the base of the climb was this incredible, rambling edge disappearing into the skies. We prepared well. Big woolly jumpers (pullys), mountain boots (not my Puppies), some standard nuts – of course the essential Moac – and a little rucksack with water and provisions. We were true mountaineers! Phil had marked the ropes at the half way point and I suggested that I call up to him on each pitch when he reached it. Looking back, my shouting up on every pitch he led must have been a right pain in the arse. Nevertheless it quelled some of my anxiety.

Rambling pitch followed rambling pitch. Eventually, it started to get not only boring but very tiring for a couple of lads used to sixty-foot gritstone pitches and a few Welsh mountain multi-pitches. As the day wore on, I began to wear out. I started to feel sorry for myself each time we approached what I thought was the top. Upon reaching the aforesaid top, above us would rise another mighty section of cliff. And so on and on it went.

We finally reached the Rigband Terrace, with the summit dipping in and out of the mist just above. I pretty much burst into tears of relief, thinking that was it, and we could finally go down. It must have been around 5 p.m., but Phil had to reach the top – it was always his mantra: 'the summit experience'. Luckily he found a ridge off to the left, and a little later we reached the true summit. But how would we find our way back down? We only had the vaguest of ideas. Dusk was approaching, and we needed to be down – or at least on the scree slopes leading down to the hut – before dark. Picking a route at night was out of the question, and we had no bivvy kit. Remember, we were just two lads from Stoke on a holiday jaunt to the mountains.

We had seen the backside of these giant monoliths a couple of days before. From below, they looked like great rambling jumbles of blocks pierced by chimneys, buttresses and cracks but from above, they looked like a chaotic mess. We couldn't even see the scree slopes below, never mind work out how to get down to them.

Moving quite quickly, we picked what looked like the best way down, via chimneys and little scree runs in gullies. We came across numerous bits of fixed gear but never chose to abseil, instead just taking what seemed to be the correct route. It was all going swimmingly. In fact the thought of a brew and something to eat was more in our minds than failure, as we could see the hut and slopes below. But – and with me there's always a 'but' – we suddenly hit a dead end. The line we'd taken simply disappeared and we seemed to be on the edge of an abyss, with a buttress covering the view of the scree slopes below. There were some old pegs and slings attached. Phil decided we should roll the dice and abseil off. I wasn't about to argue with him.

About thirty minutes later, we were tumbling down the scree slopes below as twilight became darkness, and we finally reached the haven of our tents. That cup of tea tasted wonderful!

The next day, we wandered around to look at the Cima Grande and savour our success. However, our attention was overtaken by a much more prosaic concern; our provisions were starting to run low.

Cabbage and potatoes

While we had been on the route, an army training camp had been set up about a hundred yards from our tent. That evening we were hungry and one of our 'neighbours' told us that the previous night he'd gone over to the army billet to see if he could scrounge some of their provisions. Sure enough, we tried that on and got some leftovers. All I can remember was a little meat and masses of cabbage, which I loved but Phil wasn't so keen on.

The next day we went down to Misurina for supplies. We returned for more rest as well as more army meat, potatoes and wonderful cabbage. We were fuelling up for the next day's exertion – an attempt at *Spigolo Giallo* (Yellow Edge), which winked down at us from high above the campsite.

Phil knew this route's history in minute detail. A steady climb with a little bit of aid at mid-height; well within our capability, he informed me.

The dawn was crisp and clear. We both felt regenerated by our rest and the army supplies, so we went for an early start. We knew what the route entailed, and we knew the descent from the top was much easier – numerous abseils from fixed abseil stations. After our previous descent from the Cima Grande, I was much happier about this. Off we set, up the paths contouring the scree slopes, to reach the foot of the climb.

Phil's plan was for us to alternate pitches until we got to the harder stuff higher up where he would take over. I led off up the first pitch, which was quite easy, and Phil joined me at the first stance. As he started up the next pitch, I wasn't feeling too rosy. My stomach was beginning to gurgle, but I didn't want to stop Phil from pursuing his goal. He pressed on and quickly reached the next belay. Unfortunately I didn't think I was going to last the pace, so I told Phil I'd have to go down. He abseiled back to my stance and, as quickly as possible, lowered me to the base of the route. In a mad rush, I untied from the rope, pulled off my harness and dashed behind the nearest boulder. The cabbage had certainly worked its magic.

We agreed it wasn't a good idea to go back up, so we set off down the slopes with the most wonderful scree-running I've ever done. I needed to rest my stomach and allow it to settle for the following day.

Sure enough, the next day we were back again. This time Phil suggested I lead the second pitch. As I set off from the first stance, unfortunately it was now Phil's turn to feel unwell. It was a mirror image of the day before with Phil, instead of me, squatting behind the boulder, suffering the effects of the army billet food. Another day's rest was taken at the hut.

We agreed that *Yellow Edge* would have to wait for a future encounter. The next few days were spent walking, with a view to climbing *Preuss Crack* on the Cima Piccolissima as our last climb at the Tre Cime. The army billet had departed, and we now had enough provisions to serve our needs. If we needed to replenish, Misurina was only a short bus-ride away, assuming we could survive the antics of the mad driver.

We settled for a long walk around the ridges facing the Tre Cime, into Austria, via the Locatelli Hut. This was one of the most amazing experiences I can ever remember. The walk to the hut was straightforward, but the return leg along the ridge involved wandering in and out of old disused tunnels and caves dug out by the army in the First World War. It was a fantastic encounter with rugged terrain.

Sure enough, a few days later, we were at it again; this time on the aforementioned *Preuss Crack*. I am told that these days it's a very polished affair; however, back then it was a truly great achievement for us, up the huge chimney-cum-crackline. The pitches varied between face climbing and chimneying and they culminated with Phil and me joyously reaching the top. I loved every minute of it. Perhaps I was getting into this Alpinism lark after all.

We abseiled off the back of the pinnacle via a series of fixed rings, something I'd never done before, and we were safely back at the hut well before sunset.

By the time we reached the Sella Towers, after a wonderful coach journey from Cortina to Bolzano, our appetite for climbing these big peaks was even greater, although, inevitably, we were tiring from our exertions.

I really don't know why Phil had planned to go to this area, but he was confident that the Sella Towers were the ideal destination to test our abilities on another series of pinnacles and summits a little less daunting than those of the Tre Cime. I suppose he had picked the most iconic venue first. Now we were at a place with a significantly less intimidating atmosphere.

Flapjack, Johnny!

Our campsite was alongside the Sella Hut, a lovely grassy glade with a few other tents and climbers there to sample the delights of the crags. I remember one group of climbers led by Dave Briggs, who entertained us of an evening with their tales of derring-do and Dave's particular desire for flapjack. His regular shout 'Flapjack, Johnny!' remains a fond memory. Our little Vango tent was in good company, and so were we.

We loved the place: easy access to the crags, a friendly environment and the nearby hut from which we obtained provisions. A comforting bar of chocolate was rationed as our £40 was coming to an end.

How not to use your billy can

For two likely lads from Stoke, our tent was surprisingly luxurious. We had enough room for the pair of us to sleep, we could brew up inside the flysheet if the weather was inclement, and we had good sleeping bags. Well, they were good in that they were warm, but we each had to pull them tight at night with a drawstring to create our own little haven and keep out any marauding flies.

We had one set of billy cans, which we cleaned out every night. Our diet continued to unsettle our tummies, and there were a few more frantic dashes to the toilet. There was one particular event that I will never forget, and that Phil wishes he could bury. Naturally I won't let him!

Our low budget meant that we could hardly dine like kings. We had sourced a cheap alternative with the army billet at the Tre Cime di Lavaredo, but we had no such luck at the Sella Towers. Instead we ate cheaply and relied on beans and inexpensive meat such as sausages. Drinks of tea supplemented every meal, and the local water supply was free.

One evening, after a good day's climbing, and after we had finished the cooking, I washed out the pans, and we packed everything away for the night. We went to bed and Phil did his habitual knot-tying of his sleeping-bag strings after he'd drawn them up tightly. I can remember seeing just his nose peeping through as he switched off the torch.

In the early hours of the next morning, I heard Phil wriggling around trying to get out of his sleeping bag. I thought nothing of it at first, but then his cries became increasingly frantic as he realised he'd tied a knot which he couldn't undo. Those beans were certainly having an effect. He thrashed about until he finally made it out of his sleeping bag, but far too late to undo the zip on the tent. He just had to go, and one of those billy cans proved very useful! Of course it received a thorough cleaning in boiling water before we used it again the next day.

Every holiday comes to an end, and this one has lasted long in my memory. I have to thank Phil big time for that. We arrived home on 3rd August to one of the hottest and longest summers on record.

Off to college I go

For me, the trip to Italy with all our adventures had further bonded our climbing partnership. We had experienced the joys of success and the bitterness of failure. We had come through a lot together. On our return home, that relationship wasn't going to end.

By now I had left school, which didn't mean I was done with education; there was no way my dad was going to let that happen.

When we arrived home, I had a job waiting for me at Jo Royle's, the local climbing shop, which, if I remember rightly, Phil helped me secure. I also had a place at my local college of further education in Newcastle-under-Lyme to do a foundation course for a computing degree. Although I was useless (i.e. not bothered) at many things at school, I was particularly good at maths and physics, so computing seemed a logical choice.

Climbing had well and truly become part of my life. Inevitably, Phil and I would be off on another trip somewhere else before too long. If my dad, and particularly my mum, had known what we got up to, I would never have been let out of the house. Thank goodness they trusted Phil implicitly.

The Long Reach

Phil had been reading about climbing in Scotland, and he planned a trip over the 1976 August bank holiday weekend, to the Etive Slabs. He had probably been influenced by a chapter in *Hard Rock*.

Late one Friday evening we packed our dad's car, the old Cortina, and set off for Glen Etive. When we arrived, we hurriedly pitched our tent by the light of a single torch. It was a particularly muggy night, what locally we would call 'puthery', and we wanted to get into our sleeping bags as quickly as possible.

What we hadn't accounted for was that we'd pitched the tent alongside a nearby stream, and, for the remainder of the night, we were plagued by clouds of midges. Phil would normally have tied his sleeping bag up as tightly as possible to keep them out, but after his experience in the Dolomites, that wasn't going to happen again. The midges were so bad that after an hour or so of failing to fend them off, we got out of our sleeping bags and climbed back into the car where we slept for the rest of the night. By next morning, the windows were so steamed up that surrounding campers must have woken up thinking that a rather loving couple had arrived!

The first thing we did after getting up was move the tent to a much better spot before setting off to the crag.

I discovered that I just loved the place. At that time, slab climbing really was my forte, but these days, with my flab, I can't see my feet or where to place them. I had already led my first E1, and the idea of padding up those slabs just seemed idyllic.

Swapping leads, we quickly dispatched *Swastika.* Then we did *Pause* free, which really lit my fire about the Etive slabs. Before we packed up our gear for the day, we had a play around on the first pitch of *The Long Reach.* After a much better night's sleep, we were back with renewed vigour and determination. Sure, we knew that it was a poorly protected route, but so what? We had climbed the Cima Grande, and this thing was more of a pimple than a route compared to that.

I led the first pitch up to the overlaps, and we pressed on up the slabs above. A couple more daring pitches led me to a poor belay on tiny wires, with only one more pitch to do before we were off the slabs and onto the shorter headwall that finished the route. Unfortunately, when I belayed, I was unsure as to whether I was in the right place. When Phil joined me, we managed to convince ourselves that it was correct after all.

By now the weather had closed in, and we felt that it wouldn't be too long before it started raining; not a particularly good thing when you're on friction slabs.

Phil set off on a very poorly protected pitch, and when he got about halfway it started to spit with rain. The problem was that Phil still hadn't convinced himself that he was on the right route, and he hesitated too long before coming to a decision that he couldn't go any further. He wasn't going to reverse such a slippery pitch, so decided the best course of action was to shout for help, as loudly as he could, down to the climbers in the camping area.

After numerous calls for assistance had brought scant response, the rain abated and Phil managed, by the skin of his teeth, to creep his way up the rest of the slab and reach the haven of a safe belay above. I followed the pitch and continued on up the headwall to the top of the route. We scrambled back down, packed up our gear and headed along the path towards our tent. There seemed to be a lot more people and cars around than before.

As we approached our tent, it became obvious that the Mountain Rescue team had been called out, led by local legend Hamish McInnes. As we passed him, he muttered something to Phil which I didn't quite hear. I did heard Phil's response though, and it left Hamish in no doubt as to what he felt.

Due to the clouds of midges and encroaching weather, we decided that we'd had enough of the place. We packed up all our camping kit, loaded it into the car and headed for the Lakes for more midge action. Sadly, neither Phil nor I have been back to Glen Etive since.

Thank you, Crags

In March 1976 a new climbing magazine had arrived on the scene, one which would have a highly significant influence on me over the rest of my climbing life. *Crags*, the brainchild of Geoff Birtles, was a radical departure from existing magazines. It focussed on the rock-climbing playgrounds, such as the Peak District, rather than snowy summits in foreign parts. It took an irreverent look at the scene around the best rock climbers of the day. When it was first published, I wasn't really aware of it; however, when I started my job at Jo Royle's climbing shop in the autumn of 1976, I became an avid reader. I would thumb through every page, forensically reading every paragraph, every sentence and every word. It was like a drug – sensational to an easily influenced boy of sixteen. And, like a drug, it had a profound effect.

The pages of *Crags* were littered with tales of the heroes of the day, alongside photographs of their new routes. How could a young lad like me not want to be like my new-found heroes?

I wanted to be on the pages of *Crags*. I wanted my name there. I wanted fame. To achieve this, I would have to delve into the new route scene. But was I good enough, did I have an eye for a line, and did I have the dedication and the drive?

Then, *Crags 4* arrived with my hero of heroes, Ron Fawcett, on the front cover alongside the provocative caption 'Can this be Britain's first 6c?'

For me, that was it. I had to find my first new route and hoped Phil would join in; he probably would if I nagged him enough.

Then one day in late 1977, we were climbing at Willersley Crag in Matlock, when I noticed a piece of rock that, according to the guidebook, didn't have a route on it. It was a vague line on a relatively neglected face, via a series of grooves, short walls and a gully/chute top-out. I suggested it to Phil, and he agreed to do it.

Today I have only a vague recollection of the route, and yet it was a huge milestone for me. I named it *Boot and Run*: partly a critique pertaining to the style of play of Port Vale's opposing football team, Stoke City, but really more about the debris that I kicked off during my ascent.

I wrote the route up in my best English and sent a letter to Al Evans, who was the news editor of *Crags*. I wish I still had a copy of that letter. I probably wrote up *Boot and Run* as one of the best new routes in the Peak, such was my naivety. But you have to start somewhere, and I had started on the road to what I fondly imagined was success, fame and stardom. Somehow I don't think it has quite worked out that way, has it?

Chapter 3

A Ceaseless Tide...

'*GARY AND I were notorious for having arguments or 'bust-ups' on the crag. I wanted to do "this" and he wanted to do "that": "this" being climbing and "that" being new routes*'. Phil Gibson

By the end of 1977 my life was to move in a completely new direction. I had left school and moved on to the local college of further education where my social life proper was to begin. I had claimed my first new routing scalp with *Boot and Run,* and I had passed my seventeenth birthday, which meant I could finally learn to drive.

My dad had taught Phil to drive at a local industrial estate before he was seventeen, and he was happy to do the same for me before I got my official provisional licence in order to go out onto the roads.

Look out, world!

Now, Phil and I are the complete opposites when it comes to temperament. Phil is calm and controlled where as I, certainly when I was in my teens, was like a bottle of fizzy pop.

My relationship with my dad during my school years had, to say the least, been a little fraught, but his attitude towards me had softened somewhat once I succeeded in getting a number of O levels at school – though I have to admit that this was more through luck than judgement, rather like collecting tokens on a Kellogg's packet.

However, when I got behind the wheel of a car, all hell broke loose.

After an hour of 'test-driving' his beloved red Ford Cortina around what I regarded as my personal version of Silverstone race circuit, he blew enough fuses to put the lights out over all of north Staffordshire, and we'd arrive home without speaking.

My mum always played the mediator and managed to pacify my dad despite his 'never again' attitude. Sure enough, a few days later we'd be back at the 'test-track' again.

It was fortunate that I now had more than a paper round to adequately fund my hobbies. Working at Jo Royle's in Hanley on Saturdays and the occasional bank holiday gave me enough money in my pocket to help pay for the petrol costs on our climbing trips. It also funded my social activities at college.

Early the following year, Phil and I were about to climb a route named *Wazzock* at Burbage South and, as usual, a massive argument erupted. That wasn't unusual, and it was probably fuelled by my teenage foolishness and fieriness. I refused to climb with Phil again (or was it the other way around?). What I should have realised was that not only had I lost my long-term climbing partner, I had also lost my mode of transport.

To find new climbing partners and transport at my age wasn't going to be easy. None of my college mates went climbing, and I didn't know of anybody, other than Phil, who had transport. I had managed to create more than one problem for myself through my own stupidity.

The Valkyrie

'*Checking and writing the guide was hard enough in itself without extra distractions. Most of the routes were short and verging well into the crap variety but some were quite good. At this time, 1978, Gary had the ambition and foresight but the ability hadn't caught up. It was to plague him for the next few years.*' Dave Jones

Luckily for me, around this time, I had been going down to one of the local pubs close to where I lived, to meet up with the local climbing club, the Valkyrie. Strictly speaking, it wasn't really a climbing club, as such, as it didn't have a hut or an official membership. It was just a bunch of mates who'd go climbing together and meet in a pub once or twice a week.

The group revolved around three close mates who shared a house together: Dave Jones, Bob Cope, and Dave Astbury. They welcomed me with open arms. I couldn't help but look up to them.

There were also some younger climbers, one of whom – Ian 'Hotshot' Johnson – had been in the year above me at school. Ian was an interesting character. Very clever but when it came to driving, nobody wanted to share his car with him. Everybody else would arrive at the crag, and Ian would arrive about an hour later. It wasn't that he got lost, but he really was 'Mr Slow'.

Another interesting development for me was that not only did they have a laugh, go to the pub, go climbing together and enjoy all the other social revelries, but they kept a club logbook of all their activities. I had never come across a situation like this where people logged their routes, and everybody passed their own sarcastic critique. There were also the jottings of some new routes that a few of the club members had done. When I managed to get my hands on the logbook, I just revelled in all the banter and competitiveness.

'Hotshot' got his nickname from the competitive attitude he had towards the rest of the group. Even though he was much younger, he had a particular technical talent for climbing, so much so that he led the first ascent of a new slab route at the Roaches, which he had called *Chalkstorm.* I rather liked this route, as well as the notion that you could log your routes and compete with other members of the group; not that I could really compete with them at the time, as they were all significantly better. In fact, Dave Jones once commented of me, 'His ambitions are much greater than his talent'.

I now had the magazines, guidebooks and the local logbook to fuel my appetite for climbing new routes. What more could I need?

The weeks following the divorce between Phil and me were spent doing the only thing I could, which was hitching up to the Roaches on a Sunday or joining forces with some of the Valkyrie team, most notably Dave Jones.

Dave had started to identify some of the remaining lines at the Roaches and was intent on tackling them himself. He was happy for me to tag along and I wasn't going to complain about that.

At around the same time, a group of lads led by Jim Moran were also looking at the potential of the crags in the Staffordshire gritstone area. With the magazines focussing on the new route scene of the eastern edges, the western edges had become somewhat neglected. This made for a friendly and competitive atmosphere. One team was undoubtedly concerned about another stealing its potential lines, which led to all manner of secretive midweek raids.

My first trip out with Dave Jones and Roger Bennion was up to Hen Cloud for a line that Dave had seen on the left-hand side of the crag. Dave also had an affinity for soft American-style rock and he named the route *Slowhand*, after Eric Clapton's style of guitar playing. Now, before you start, I know Eric Clapton ain't American, but from where my musical background was coming at the time – the fast, heavy, raucous beat of punk rock – this all seemed anathema to me, and it still does. Zzzzz!

Having seen how Dave had found his line, I started to scan through the guidebooks looking for my own inspiration: I looked for gaps – any gaps – long, short or narrow. What struck me was the amount of unclimbed rock to go at. Triviality wasn't an issue; the sole incentive was to get my name in my beloved *Crags*, alongside the legends of the climbing world: John Allen, Steve Bancroft, Tom Proctor, Pete Livesey and my hero, Ron Fawcett.

Over the next few weeks I remained obsessed about new routes. I scoured the crags with my microscope. In truth, many of the lines that I climbed were completely irrelevant. But that wasn't the point; they served my desire for fame. For a young directionless kid, this was pure inspiration.

'*The first time I climbed with Gary was when we did the first ascent of* Slowhand, *in 1978, with Roger Bennion. This was a competitive time and the route was literally snatched from under the noses of the Glossop lads. Gary had no problem with the route and later in the afternoon he did the first ascent of* Face Value. *Five new routes were put up that day.*' Dave Jones

Sleeping at the Ritz

As we slowly moved into spring, and while I was working on Saturdays at Jo Royle's, Brian was only too happy to give me a lift up to the Roaches on his way home.

As dusk began to settle, I would amble up to the cliffs, maybe do a few boulder problems or even spy a new line, then settle down for the night under one of the huge boulders below the Upper Tier. For some reason or another, the place where I slept had been ironically christened the Ritz.

Now the great thing about climbing on the Roaches on your own was that you would bump into a whole host of people. I never minded asking people if I could climb with them and, by a quirk of fate, I bumped into two brothers who had just started climbing. Fred and Ken Crook were much older, but very friendly to be around. I was fair game to take the piss out of, and they indulged in their game as much as they could.

Luckily for me I was a much better climber than both of them at the time, and they appeared quite enthusiastic about the uncontrolled idea of new routing, so much so that they were happy to play along with my amusement. We'd revel in banter. Fred supplied the occasional beverage and biscuit, and Ken would just take the piss. I had to name one of my routes in their honour – a trivial little one that came to be known as *Fred's Café*.

The Perry clan

'OCD, he's definitely OCD. I had a week in Wales with him in 1978 with only the Stranglers Black and White *Album to listen to, and we never did an established route all week. 40+ years later, the sounds remain the same and he's still an Obsessive Climb Developer.'* John Perry

Things in my life have a way of panning out for me. Sure, I seem to be prone to numerous mishaps, but in hindsight, things just happen to land right. I had started to plough my own furrow in life, but felt I still needed the company of some like-minded individuals, and, sure enough, that happened.

One day, knocking about on the Upper Tier, I bumped into a really affable group of lads led by the very likeable John Perry. This ragbag bunch of reprobates, and I say that in the nicest possible way, included Derek Beetlestone, Mark 'Ralph' Hewitt and Keith 'the Oblatron' Edworthy.

They too were fuelled by the desire for climbing, even new routing, and what I really liked about them was their unbridled energy and laughter. They had begun to enjoy the music that I liked, and they had the naivety of youth and the joy for anything stupid that I liked as well. The companionship of youth blossomed into a wonderful, yet slightly fractured, friendship.

I had also just passed my driving test, which helped still further as, on the odd occasion, my dad would let me borrow his car. Even though I'd pop up to the Roaches for a day's climbing, my world had begun to expand and other areas of the Peak were becoming significantly more accessible.

'I first met him in 1978. He was bivvying at the Roaches. Driven by the desire for publicity, both good and bad, new routing was his bag. It was fun to see your name in the magazines – the climbing equivalent of your name in lights. With Ralph (Mark Hewitt) and John Perry sometimes in tow, every square yard (inch?) of Peak District rock was scoured for a new line.' Derek Beetlestone

Stoney, here I come!

At the time, the centre of the climbing universe, as extolled by *Crags*, was a little grimy café in Stoney Middleton where the stars and groupies of the day would hang out. Afterwards they'd congregate in the local pub, the Moon. I'd heard and read many a vaunted tale about Stoney café and, when transport became available, I had to pay the place a visit and announce myself to the climbing scene.

To my complete amazement, this chocolate-box of an emporium was far less salubrious than I could ever imagine. But that wasn't the point. It was THE place to be.

My first trip there was memorable in more ways than one. It was the very first day my dad had let me use his car. I raced like James Hunt across the Peak District in search of the fabled Stoney café. As I shot down the valley, I took little interest in the oncoming traffic. Such was my brazen haste that I overtook a line of parked cars right outside the café. More interested in the bystanders on the pavement, only too late did I realise that a car was heading straight for me. To a raucous cheer from the crowd of climbers, it ran into the side of my dad's car and dented the wheel-arch. I'd certainly arrived at the place with a proverbial bang.

Unperturbed, I sauntered into the café, full of my own self-importance, and viewed the motley bunch of climbers sat about the place. I was so let down by the faces in the crowd; where were Ron, Tom, Geoff, John, Pete and Steve, I wondered? I'd read they were always here, but all I could see was a load of scruffy climbers sat in little groups, bent over cups of tea and the occasional bacon butty, jabbering and chattering away.

After a few visits, it didn't take me long to realise that this was the scene, and a myriad of climbers amongst the crowd became known faces and friends. I still see a few like Chris Lawson and Jim Burton even today. I loved the place and just had to make my mark and become one of them. New routing fame was the only way, or at least that's what I thought. I wanted to be Ron, Tom or Pete.

My new route 'interpretation'

'Al Evans was complaining that he was receiving letter after letter off a school boy who kept claiming 'new routes' at the Roaches. These were often shoehorned in between existing routes where gaps, at the time, simply didn't exist.' Dave Jones

Consequently, I continued to plough a furrow of new routes on my local crags with the occasional trip to Stanage, Burbage or Froggatt for the occasional 'space to be filled'. At the time, my perception of new routes was purely my own interpretation. In my head, I had designed the parameters of what a new route was: it didn't have to climb a crack or a groove or an arête or a corner or a prominent feature. It just had to be a bit of rock that hadn't been climbed before.

Today people climb every gap imaginable. Back in the late 1970s, that wasn't the case, or at least it wasn't until I came onto the scene. I may well have created the practice of gap-filling, but I didn't just leave it at that. My view was – and still is, to a degree – that if you couldn't touch the holds on the route to the left with your left hand and couldn't touch the holds on the route to the right with your right hand, it was a new route. But of course, me being me, I took this to the extreme. Now I might have long arms, but on some of the routes my left hand would be on holds on the route to the left and my right hand would be on holds to the right. Criticism inevitably followed but, to me, new routes were just that. Moreover, they fulfilled my need to get my name in the climbing magazines.

Now, the magazine editor of the time, one Al Evans of *Crags*, must have wondered what the hell was going on when a plethora of letters hit his mat with my new routes itemised one by one. I'd bull them up no end, thinking them to be the best routes since climbing was invented. I thought of myself as the new Joe Brown with my piles of new routes. My naivety must have shone through no end, but I was so determined to make my mark that I just kept sending letters, one after another. It must have driven them to distraction. Nevertheless, slowly but surely, the odd route of mine would appear in *Crags* and other magazines. I was beginning to make my mark.

As the new route tally increased, I began to compile list after list of my routes: my ten best new routes, my ten hardest new routes and my ten best route names. It was a complete deluge of nonsense. But at the time I didn't think so; it was serving my dream to become famous. The tide of events had completely engulfed me. I was so buried in my obsession, not realising that nearly all of my new routes were almost completely worthless.

I'd drive back with my new group of mates, completely enveloped by the series of events. In either in my dad's car or Ralph's Corsair, we'd bomb around the countryside, to a loud halo of music blasting from the radio or cassette player. We'd pump out a Stranglers' song or a Buzzcocks' song or a Sex Pistols' song to satiate our enthusiasm. It was just so great to be alive, with the seemingly limitless energy of youth and with such wonderful, like-minded mates.

The book of truth?

At around the same time, a new route book was placed in Stoney café, in which it became almost *de rigueur* for people to write up their latest offerings. It was much like the route book at the Valkyrie climbing club, except that potentially the entire climbing world could see it.

I vividly remember my first encounter with the said book. I was mesmerised by the handwritten entries. Of course, I got my chance to write up my own new routes in it, but I was unnerved by some of the graffiti that followed. Back then, graffiti was very much part of the social scene as opposed to the faceless chat rooms of today. Sarcastic critique was aimed to belittle new routes and their 'owners', in a typically British way. Why applaud something that was the bedrock of the sport when you could make fun of it and knock the perpetrators?

It was similar to some of the graffiti that adorned the toilet walls of the café. Such classics as '*Oh Oedipus, ring your mother*' and '*Flush hard, long way to cafe*' were infamous then and have since gone into climbing folklore. To be subject to the amusement of the new routes book, you had to have your name in it. I followed suit with my catalogue of pointless climbs.

Back to the mountains

As I began to find my feet, we decided to travel a little further afield, to the Llanberis Pass, a place I knew from my exploits with my brother. The slabs of Dinas Mot had a particular attraction as I knew them quite well; as a lad, slab climbing suited me more than anything else. Derek and Ralph accompanied me on my 'adventure'.

I had seen this line which put together three sections of unclimbed rock. I chose not to abseil down and clean it, probably for the first time. Instead, we just climbed it on-sight, each leading a pitch. There seemed an obvious conclusion to our efforts by naming it after the three intrepid heroes who had climbed it, ha ha: *GBH*, after Gibson, Beetlestone and Hewitt.

Putting up a new three-pitch route was something completely new to me and gave me the encouragement not only to tinker on my local cliffs, but to spread my wings even further afield. Over the ensuing weeks, we paid many more visits to Welsh crags such as the Mot and Tremadog, another area I knew well from my winter trips with Phil. Admittedly, we were only filling relatively insignificant gaps, but this grounding gave me a firm platform for the future. It felt good to use the experience that Phil had passed onto me.

Good old Staffordshire gritstone

Throughout my climbing career, I've always gone back to my climbing roots and the gritstone cliffs of Staffordshire. Many's the day I've popped up to the Roaches or the Skyline or Hen Cloud for a new route. One pleasant Sunday with my brother gave us a batch of three worthwhile little routes on the right-hand side of Hen Cloud. Phil led one and I led the others. I couldn't wait to get back to the Valkyrie new route book to write them up with the almost arrogant self-confidence – or stupid naivety – which I had recently developed. Usually this meant a complete over-exaggeration of the quality of the routes, to say nothing of their (lack of) importance.

I was just trying to impress Dave Jones, who knew the area very well indeed. He took a look at the descriptions and, to my disbelief, complimented me on the routes. I was so surprised that I asked him if he wanted to go up there and do them again with me. It was all in an effort to gain some credibility.

I just couldn't wait to get up there, and one midweek evening gave me my chance. Youthful bravado put me on the sharp end of the rope of a route I had named *Jellyfish.* Wanting to impress Dave, gung-ho, I went for it. On the tricky upper wall I had placed a small wire, in which I had ultimate confidence.

No sooner had I got above the wire than the friction somehow disappeared, and I went cartwheeling down the wall, ripping out the wire and almost landing on Dave, about 25 feet below. I'm not sure how bewildered he was, but I wasn't having any of it. I just got back on and went for it again. This time, success came by the smallest of margins. I'm sure Dave won't forget that little episode!

That old competitive spirit

During the bank holiday week of August, I once again teamed up with Derek Beetlestone, and we headed off to the Lake District, having read in *Crags* about the scene up there. The climbing scene was well and truly alive with new routes, and I felt we just had to go and stamp our mark on it.

I knew very little about Lake District climbing, as Phil and I were more interested in climbing in North Wales. However, one crag I had visited with him was White Ghyll. I knew it had an impressive wall that, according to the guidebooks, didn't seem to have any routes on it. I decided that this would be our objective for the weekend.

After a little bit of cleaning and a closer inspection for some fairly sparse gear placements, I led the pitch, arriving at the top in quite an exhausted state. But the fun couldn't end there. On their most recent album, my beloved band, the Stranglers, had named one of the tracks *Dead Loss Angeles,* which was about their impressions of the city when they visited the USA. So I used this as a route name. It was intended to be an ironic comment on what I thought of the place. Actually, I knew very little about the Lakes scene except for what I'd read in the magazines, but I just couldn't resist the temptation to have a jibe at them.

The Lakes climbers got their revenge by putting up a route next to it called *Dead Loss Gary Gibson* – probably something I deserved!

But our trip together wasn't over as we headed back down to North Wales, specifically for a line that I had seen overlooking the Idwal Slabs. I had little focus about where I wanted to climb unless I had spotted a new line.

We trudged up to the crags and wandered up the slabs to below an impressive thin crackline that I'd seen on a previous visit. I cleaned it from abseil with an old wire brush I had and then proceeded to try to climb the thing. When I got to the top of the crack, I couldn't unpick the technicalities of the finish; I tried repeatedly, but I just couldn't unlock the sequence needed.

Now Derek was a competitive sort, and on more than one occasion he has outdone me. There was no way we were going to leave the line unclimbed, and Derek was itching to get one over on me. I lowered off the pitch and handed the lead over to him.

In the blink of an eye he passed the sequence with which I had been struggling, truly putting me in my place – something he's done on a number of occasions before and since. He named it *Demetrius*; I have never been quite sure where that name originated.

My brother, Phil and me.

Together with our mum on top of the Dewerstone.

Five years old and ready to shoot from the hip …

Just look at the name of our house!

All photos Arthur Gibson.

Phil and me at the top of the Cima Piccolissima, boots and woolly jumper *de rigueur.*

The Tre Cima di Laverado hut without the army billet.

My old mate Adam Hudson.

Already a style guru? The first ascent of *Rattus Norvegicus*, Lawrencefield Quarry.

All photos Gibson collection.

Derek Beetlestone and me at Willersley crag.

Photo Gibson collection.

My attempt at the Incredible Hulk.

Photo Gibson collection.

Left: *Homo Sapien* at Craig Pen Trwyn. Long reach me? Nah.

Photo Dave Summerfield.

Phil made his own 'hexagonal nut' - great fit, big weight ... about 1.5 kilos!

Great Arête, Millstone. I reversed down in fear from the ledge just above even though I had done all the hard climbing!

Great Wall, Clogwyn D'ur Arddu.

All photos Phil Gibson.

The first ascent of *Smear, No Fear*, Lundy.

Photo Hazel Gibson.

The first ascent of *We've Got the Honeymoon Blues Two*, Wintour's Leap, the day after our wedding.

Photo Hazel Gibson.

The Pillar of Judgement, Nth Cloud, Staffordshire - a notoriously bold lead.

Photo Hazel Gibson.

Repeating *Jermyn Street*, Millstone Edge in 1981.

Photo Paul Heyliger.

A Widespread Ocean of Fear, Lundy island. One of my most seminal climbing moments. Andy Popp and John Codling climbing.

Photo Gary Gibson.

The Great Chimney, Hen Cloud moments before I got my knee stuck in the crack.
Photo Phil Gibson.

The wonderful *Private Targets* at Hall Moor Quarry. First ascent.
Photo Gibson collection.

The first ascent of *All Roads Lead to Rome* at Houghton Quarry.
Photo Hazel Gibson.

My first guidebook publication.

Our family together in 1983. *Left to right*, mum and dad, Phil and his wife Ruth, Hazel and me.

Photo Gibson collection.

My first (of five) London marathons.

Two escaped convicts(?) after the first ascent of *Fitzcarraldo* in Pembroke in 1983.

Photo Ruth Gibson.

Mum and dad.

Photo Phil Gibson.

A ceaseless tide ...

I continued to push hard with the magazines, perhaps most notably my beloved *Crags* and its then editors, Geoff Birtles and John Stevenson. I wanted them to let me write an article about the recent activities on Staffordshire gritstone. Of course, my sole intent was to glorify my own somewhat trivial additions that I still perceived to be the best things since sliced bread.

I wrote letter after letter to John about what I wanted to do and how important my efforts were. With a torrent of my letters landing on his editorial desk, he finally conceded.

When I had written the article – an amateurish effort by any stretch of the imagination – John said he would come over to the Roaches in a couple of weeks' time to meet up with me and take some photos. I was finally getting there. I had always wanted my name up in lights. My ultimate goal was that fabled mugshot in the climbing magazines, usually accompanied by a little ditty about the achievements of the person they were portraying. They had done it for so many other climbers, so why not me?

John took some photos and, sure enough, a few weeks later the article was printed in *Crags* number 18, but there was no sign of that thumbnail mugshot of me. In my mind's eye, my name was headlining the article. My climbing companions were reduced to bit-part players in a play which I had written and in which I was the star. But I still craved that thumbnail photograph.

One evening, while sitting in the pub on a Valkyrie Climbing Club meet, sure enough I heard a rumour that my photo was going to be in *Crags*. Actually, it was more than just a rumour. I knew that Mike MacDonald, a friend of Dave Jones and others at the club, had been asked by John Stevenson for that mugshot of me to be put in the next issue, and he had one that he'd taken at Curbar. I couldn't believe my ears! My heart was racing at the very thought of my achievement. My peers mocked the idea but, to me, my day in the sun was about to arrive.

I knew the next *Crags* was due in ten days. Accordingly, I planned to get my hands on the first copy as it arrived through the door of the local climbing shop where I worked.

Two days later, when I was working in Jo Royle's, I asked Brian Royle, the owner of the shop, when he thought the next issue of *Crags* would arrive.

He checked his books. 'Next Saturday,' he replied.

I just couldn't wait. I was in a state of euphoria.

I walked into work, about a three-mile trek down through Middleport, along the canal towpath and up through Etruria to arrive at the shop early for Brian's arrival. He didn't normally arrive until around 9.30 a.m., the shop's opening time. I was there, pacing up and down at least fifteen minutes early, tension steadily building in my stomach.

Brian duly arrived, opened up the shop and in we went. I sped to the back of the shop where the guidebooks and magazines were shelved but there was no new *Crags* to leaf through. My heart sank. I took my jacket off and started organising some rucksacks for display, i.e. stuffing them with polythene bags to make them suitable for presentation – a job Brian knew I thoroughly disliked.

Just then I heard the front door bell go. The postman came in with a medium-sized package which looked as if it might be a batch of *Crags*; I signed for it and opened the package to reveal just that.

I put the magazines in their rightful place and, like an expectant child with a Christmas present, thumbed through the pages to find the Peak area news. Sure enough, there was my photo, complete with caption, '*Above: Gary Gibson. A ceaseless tide of crap new routes or a futuristic eye for a line? Worried about his escalating bad reputation* (see Letters)*, he promises to be more selective in his new route activity in future.*'

The first part of the caption passed in a flash. All I could see was my name up in lights. I'd achieved my dream. I was famous. I didn't notice the critique or the irony of the comments, I had achieved fame.

I now felt I could roam the crags, and everybody would know who I was.

I was so proud. Finally, I had arrived. Now all I had to do was push on towards my fate and secure my rightful place – whatever that be – in British climbing history.

What a pillock.

The Stranglers

By now, pretty much everyone who has read about me and my route names knows that I'm a Stranglers' fan. In fact, I'm more than that. I have followed them around for over forty years, never missing a tour, buying all of the paraphernalia, attending conventions, doing quizzes on them, wearing their emblems – the lot. I've now seen them live 180 times, and I have more gigs booked in the future. To me it's a communion: I go to hear my band, meet friends and together 'the family', as we are known, celebrate the life, times and music of the 'Meninblack'.

How did it all begin? Well, as a kid I was subjected to – and that is in no way meant as a derogatory word – the music that my brother, Phil, liked: Motown, a bit of Ska and generally music with soul. Phil would play his music on a regular basis on Thursday and Saturday evenings, when my parents went out, and I really enjoyed it – to a point. It wasn't my choice, but I liked it all the same. Occasionally, Phil would have his mates round, and they would enjoy a beer or two; of course I wouldn't miss such an opportunity. I would go around trying to get the last dregs of each can they had purportedly 'emptied'. It was my first introduction to alcohol at the tender age of thirteen.

However, by the mid to late 1970s, things began to change for me musically. I had started college and begun to meet a bunch of mates who, while having a bit of a rebellious streak, were older than me and had taken up an interest in a different type of music. They went for a drink – they were old enough – and had started to go to the odd concert. I didn't even understand the concept of going to a concert, but I was willing to give it a bash. In early 1977 they invited me to my first concert at the Electric Circus in Manchester. I had no idea about the band we were going to see; I assumed it was some long-haired rock group, as all my mates had long hair and the image fitted. The long hair thing was never going to happen to me for two reasons; the first being that my hair grew more into a Stylistics-type bush, and the second was that my dad wouldn't allow me. I went along all the same, just to see what the fuss was all about. It might even be a Motown night. The band was named the Ramones. Motown it was not.

It was an altogether bewildering experience. They came on stage with some sort of banner, chanting, 'Gabba Gabba Hey!' and went into overdrive, playing something like twenty-two songs in just over an hour. They didn't even come up for air. It was a complete departure from what I was used to in my brother's world, as well as the glam rock bands such as Gary Glitter and The Sweet, who I had seen on Top of the Pops. It was fantastic!

A couple of months later, on 21st June 1977 to be precise, we all went off to see another band that I quite liked the name of. They hadn't really been heard of that much, although I'd seen them on Top of the Pops, performing a song by the name of 'Go Buddy Go'. They just seemed to be like another rock 'n' roll band to me. I certainly didn't understand Punk Rock before I went.

Again I was blown away by the whole experience. People thrashing around with gay abandon. Everybody dressed up in skin-tight jeans, ripped T-shirts and altogether wayout clothes. There was abuse, spitting, complete vulgarity and absolutely no restraint. I came home begging for more of the same but not necessarily from that particular band. It was the wholesale rebellion that I loved – people doing their own thing and not really caring what anybody thought. I hadn't given any real thought to the music.

Over the next few weeks we went to see a number of bands, such as: Siouxsie and the Banshees, the Buzzcocks, the Clash, 999, and Magazine. It didn't matter who they were, I just liked the idea of a bunch of kids going wild at some venue nearby.

As kids of seventeen and eighteen, it felt right to be part of this new Punk Rock movement. I started wearing as wild a set of clothes as possible, and so that my dad couldn't see me in them, I'd sneak out of the house, or even hide my clothes in the garage and get changed there. No way could I let him see me dressed like that!

Finally, in the autumn of 1977 we made a commitment. One of the lads at college had a car, and he suggested we go and see as many concerts of one band as we could. There was no plan to it, and we weren't bothered about which band to go and see; we just happened to choose the Stranglers. We travelled the length and breadth of the country to about a dozen gigs – on one occasion driving to Bristol one night, going to college the next morning and then driving to Cardiff the following night. It was their 'No More Heroes' tour.

For me, at the time, it was all about the new music 'scene', not really the Punk movement, as I didn't dress up in the same way and Kons, the guy I travelled with, was more of a heavy rocker than anything else. For us it was about the whole idea that kids could go out and have a wild time, come what may.

At first, we didn't buy any of the albums that these bands were putting out. But then, in 1978, I decided to buy a couple: one was by the Buzzcocks and the other, by the Stranglers, named *Black and White*. I went home and played them on my parents' stereo and found myself slowly becoming addicted after listening to the latter. It wasn't immediate, but the driving bass, swirling keyboard arpeggios and the lyrics all had me wanting more. The Stranglers became the band I had to go and see again. I was being reeled in.

And so we planned to go again, this time to Bingley Hall in Stafford where they had a sell-out crowd. It was a Tuesday, and we decided to go early in order to get to the front of the queue. 'Bobbing' college had never been an issue for me.

As I remember rightly, it was a blisteringly hot day. The tension grew and grew, until we were finally let into what was more like a cattle-shed than a venue. In fact a cattle-shed was probably more appropriate, considering the mobs that were there!

I can remember very little about the gig, which is unusual for me, except that every song was belted out at full decibel level and, for some strange reason, the Stranglers were now all wearing black – no other colours whatsoever. This was something I didn't understand at the time, but in later years it marked the fact that they didn't want to have a fashion identity associated with their music such as the Punk movement.

The band, specifically JJ Burnel, was in a menacing mood and the whole thing captured my imagination completely. They played almost their entire new album live; it was a gig to behold. Now the Stranglers were *my* band, no ifs no buts. I decided at that particular gig that I would follow them for the rest of my life.

Now, if anything sits in the pantheon of live gigs for me, Battersea Park has to be it. It was another warm and sunny afternoon, and we had arrived at the gig by coach, drunk rather too many cans of cheap lager and joined in at the front with all of the moshing. Hugh jibbed and jousted with the audience, as usual, JJ prowled about the stage in his low-level pose, and the whole shebang was fantastic. And then, yes then, to the roars of the crowd and the thundering baseline of 'Nice 'n' Sleazy', came the strippers – not one, but four – onto the stage. It was a dream come true; the Stranglers up to their old provocative tricks.

That evening, as we drank more and more, we decided not to catch the bus back, but to sleep in the park and return home the following day. We or at least I – the others' interest seemed to wane a few months after – had to enjoy the event for as long as we could, and the whole thing sticks in my memory so clearly, even today.

The idea came to me that whenever I climbed my first new route on a particular crag, it would be named after a Stranglers' song. It would be my calling card, my personal commitment. If there's a cliff near you with any of my routes on it, then there will be a Stranglers' name somewhere. Some may be obscure, but others like *Always the Sun*

(Pembroke), *Golden Brown* (Cornwall), *Feline* (Wintour's Leap), *Peaches* (Birchen Edge) and *A Midnight Summer Dream* (Chee Tor) are not.

I suppose that one day I should run a competition for people to name every Stranglers' song title I've used, including the lyrics, and on which crag they are.

Another thing that I liked, and still like about the Stranglers, is their wonderful ability to upset people by just being themselves, no holds barred, telling it how it is. Many are the stories of them upsetting journalists and punters. They gaffer-taped a journalist to the Eiffel Tower and gaffer-taped another to a chair on an Icelandic glacier. They've stripped naked people who had the audacity to invade the stage. They've jumped into the audience to accost and even attack people who dared disrupt their gigs. And yet their music is straightforward, about real-life events, not your normal lovey-dovey stuff that I still completely detest.

Over the ensuing years, the ritual of going to see the Stranglers has become a regular one that is built into my psyche. I have never missed a tour and have only failed to be at one convention. In fact, at the last convention at the Camden Centre in 2011, we had the opportunity as a team (Doug Kerr, Claire Kelly, Colin Mace, Simon Kent and myself) to enter the national Stranglers quiz hosted by John Robb. It was a strange evening, following on from one of the live sets, filled with numerous extremely difficult (anorak-style) questions. But we won by three clear points. I now own a trophy and a signed copy of a photo of the band.

Today I remain proud to the core that I am part of the 'family' of fans that has never missed a Stranglers tour, excluding of course the early days when they were making a mark for themselves around the London pub scene, and I have no intention of stopping now. Sure, Hugh Cornwall and Jet Black have exited stage left – one for personal reasons and the other because of ageing. But even if people still seek to criticise or admonish them, they are still mine, and like a Catholic needs communion, so do I at least once yearly, and I won't stop until they stop.

Chapter 4

The Obsession Bites

'*JOHN CODLING INTRODUCED us to the enigmatic John "Fritz" Sumner and his beloved Craig Cowarch. After a couple of weekends spent at Bryn Hafod, resulting in a crop of good new routes, "Fritz"quipped afterwards to Codling, "You should never have brought these two down here!"*' Phil Gibson

After three wasted years ducking in and out of lessons at the college of further education, I had finally decided on my career path. I had spent enough time considering doing a degree in computing, back then a relatively new field. Computers were the size of elephants! It just wasn't for me, though.

When I had left school, I had it in my head that I was suddenly grown up and that going to college involved extra-curricular activities. I was never a womaniser; my interests lay elsewhere. Of course, climbing was my main leisure pastime, but I had discovered music, mainly being engulfed by the Punk Rock movement and, all of a sudden, alcohol came onto the agenda. We would often spend our lunchtimes in the pub across the road from college, playing records on the jukebox and getting up to all manner of stupid activities, usually resulting in our not being seen at college for the remainder of the day.

So I jacked in the computer course and my dad got me jobs in a few of the local pot banks – a colloquialism for pottery factories – to earn some money and pay my way in life. I started at Middleport Pottery – now the home of the Great Pottery Throwdown – moved onto Grindley's in Tunstall and finished at Barrett's, just round the corner from my dad's barber's shop in Burslem.

In his oh-so inimitable way, my dad enlightened me that I needed to find a proper job. He was right, of course, but I didn't have a clue what to choose. My dad's guidance was, as ever, astute. He knew a local chiropodist who had a shop within walking distance of where we lived and suggested I speak to him. So one day I popped in to have a look round, and I was stunned to find that I quite liked the idea of being self-employed, just like my dad.

As I looked into it a little more, I found that I had all the necessary qualifications, except for biology – something which I'd never done at school – to apply to one of the colleges in Manchester or Birmingham. I also discovered that jobs were really easy to come by, as chiropody was a developing profession that was beginning to blossom in the National Health Service. At college, instead of applying for an O level course for human biology, I blagged my way past the enrolment officer, straight onto the A level programme.

Twelve months of hard study at evening class followed. In the meantime, my application to the Northern School of Chiropody in Salford was accepted, with the proviso that I passed the end-of-course examination. The door was open for me to start in September 1979 and begin a career that I wasn't quite certain was right for me. I passed my yearly project and final exam with flying colours. It was a peculiar feeling.

I had chosen to go to college in Salford for obvious reasons. Some of my climbing mates were already 'studying' at Manchester Polytechnic, the crags were within easy access of Manchester, and I could get home at weekends with my trusty bag of clothes for my mum to wash.

My first visit to the college was a lonely one. Mum and Dad weren't able to join me, as they were always at work, and I decided that at first I'd stay in a bed and breakfast in Prestwich within reasonable walking distance of the campus which would help me get acquainted with the city.

Some months prior to starting my course in Manchester, while still studying at Newcastle College, I thought it would be wise to get my own 'wheels'. My brother Phil put me in touch with a mate of his, Geoff Davis, who owned a car repair/spraying centre in a garage just down the road from my dad's shop in Burslem.

Geoff helped out by putting me in contact with a butcher friend of his who was selling a Morris Thousand van for fifty quid. What a buy – despite the smell of meat in the back.

When I first got it, we used to 'kidnap' fellow students from college, bundle them into the back of the van and disappear off to a place unknown to them and just dump them there: some back street, a park and even, one day, the road below the Roaches. You wouldn't believe the mayhem we caused!

Of course, it ended in tears. Steve Keeling, a chap whom I'd met shortly before, told me his parents had a house in North Wales, near Trawsfynydd, and he asked if I fancied a trip out there in the summer of 1979. How could I refuse?

I picked him up, and we raced out through Llangollen and down the side roads into Bala, where we munched on a chippy tea. As we headed out of Bala for Porthmadog, we hurtled – a bizarre word for a Morris Thousand van, I know – round the side of the large reservoir and found ourselves behind a car which was wavering along the road, completely unaware of our presence. I took the opportunity to overtake him and, just as I accelerated towards him, he hit the brakes and we hurtled into the back, smashing my beloved van to pieces, with both Steve and I ending up in Wrexham hospital.

My dad had to do the honours of picking us up at about three o'clock in the morning. I remember the despair on his face and in his voice, as we drove the long, weary journey home.

College days

My first few weeks at college were very commuter orientated. We didn't have lessons on a Monday morning because we had an evening clinic on a Thursday. I would catch the train up to Manchester and, for the first three or four weeks, walk from my accommodation to college and back again. Each weekend I'd return home with my bag full of dirty laundry. As this got more and more irritating, I decided to spend some of my hard-earned money on a new car. I bought a little Triumph Herald, my 'Triumph of the Good City', to facilitate my travel requirements. I also had a mandatory grant, which provided me with enough money for my B&B, as well as petrol and other sundries.

And so my life changed dramatically. I had found my feet in Manchester, had enough mates in the city to go out climbing with and started to make friends with a number of my colleagues for the odd night out.

We would go to this pub and that pub. One night I sauntered down from my bed and breakfast to a strange-looking little pub on Prestwich Road named The House that Jack Built. As I walked in, I couldn't believe my eyes. Sat on a stool, propping up the bar, was the unmistakable figure of the great John Cooper Clarke, a local inhabitant of Salford. The 'Punk Poet' was at the forefront of the lyricism of my beloved Punk movement, and I couldn't miss the chance of saying hello.

What a wonderful, wonderful bloke, so grounded, so pleasant, so unassuming. It was a great honour to sit alongside this legend and sample the wares of The House, as well as his wonderful irony and friendliness. Even to this day I can recite at least four of his poems verbatim, although not with his classy Mancunian style and charm. Hazel ain't too enamoured with my poetry reading ability, though.

The thumbnail

In climbing, it would have been so easy to have been chastened by that small thumbnail photograph and report in *Crags*, but instead it was just the fillip that I needed. To be there, alongside the names and images of my peers and heroes, was fulfilment.

What I had failed to appreciate was the satirical tone of the comments made about me. As far as I was concerned, my image, my fame and the path that I had chosen seemed right. It would be easy to look back and say I had chosen the wrong path, but it has led me to where I am today, and I can't say I have too many complaints.

Over the winter months, I happened on some acquaintances in the Matlock area. I'd started to look around the crags in Matlock Bath, specifically Wild Cat, with the odd foray onto Willersley Castle Crag. One evening in November, when I had soloed a couple of mediocre new routes, I popped into the local shop, the Bivouac, and happened upon its owner, Jim Ballard. Jim was very much of the old guard, but there seemed to be some mutual respect and many an hour was spent chatting about our respective exploits.

Jim was the epitome of encouragement. He asked if I was interested in climbing with a young lady he knew. Of course I was up for anything, and Jim introduced me to Alison Hargreaves, who, unbeknown to me, had just moved in with him down the road.

It's fascinating to look back and remember that lovely young fresh-faced girl, who bubbled with enthusiasm for climbing, at an even younger age than me. How could one believe that years later her passion would turn her into such a great mountaineer?

Throughout the winter, I kept visiting Wild Cat and Jim, in his Bivouac, and he would talk to me about hidden gems of crags that he knew about: this quarry here, that quarry there. It wasn't until a little later that I would test myself at these new venues. Some esoteric but wonderful routes were done, such as the immaculate flake line of *Private Targets* in Hall Moor Quarry and the bafflingly bold arête of *Outside Edge* at the now sadly filled-in, Birchwood Quarry.

These, though, were isolated gems. I had become consumed by the desire for new routes of whatever quality. The continuous stream of routes emanated from every opportunity I had; some I would solo or back-rope, some I would climb with my regular partners and with others I would simply grab anybody on the crag who was willing to climb them with me. It was a deluge of whatever I could find and report to the magazines. I certainly hadn't taken much heed of their comment that, 'he promises to be more selective in his new route activity in future.'

Strolling along, minding my own business

At Tremadog, Ron Fawcett had just made the first ascent of an iconic new route which he had named *Strawberries.* It was so named because it was alongside a route called *Cream.* Most people had nicknamed the line *Peaches,* but since Ron hadn't used it, that was OK by me; it was, after all, a Stranglers' song name to which I had sole possession.

A little while after Ron had done *Strawberries,* I was messing about at Birchen Edge and discovered a superb little wall below the monument which hadn't been climbed. I just had to do it. I abseiled down it, cleaned it and worked out all the moves, but I had no-one to belay me. There were a few novices around; well, in my arrogance, I considered them novices. I asked one of them, a guy called Steve Wilson, if he would belay me. He seemed quite happy at the thought – though his mood changed, shortly afterwards.

I got stuck into climbing the wall and did a tricky rock-up to a small break where I hung around and fiddled in a Hex 4, a placement I knew very well from abseil. I moved up past the protection, and suddenly my foot slipped off. Steve wasn't ready for my unexpected retreat, and nor was I as I hurtled down, stopping mere inches from the ground. Steve had never belayed anyone before; in fact, this was his first day's climbing.

Luckily for me, his more experienced mate came along and belayed me on my next, thankfully successful, effort. The name *Peaches* seemed just perfect – a new route on a new crag and, also, a Stranglers' name. Thanks Ron, for not using it.

The Thin Air

As spring turned into summer, my climbing ability, confidence and boldness began to improve. Such an upturn in ability brought me on to better fare, but I was still trying (and failing) to compete with the big boys and thereby getting myself into trouble for my antics.

The Thin Air at the Roaches was one such event. Phil Burke used the crag as his local haunt, and his rivalry with Ron Fawcett resulted in him doing some cutting-edge first ascents. In trying to muscle in on his supremacy, I'd noticed a super little slab line on the right-hand side of the Lower Tier, next to the now iconic Johnny Woodward route, *Piece of Mind*. I played about on the slab for a while and managed to top-rope it with one of my mates, but I couldn't pluck up the courage to solo it.

Two days later, back on my own, I got on the line from abseil and worked out the rock-over onto the narrow vein of rock. This time I decided to go for it, leaving the rope in place as a safeguard, should I wimp out. I set off up the route with the rope alongside me but hadn't realised that you moved right, off the line, to the crux, with the rope about six feet to the left. As I committed to the moves, it offered no solution should I slip or decide not to go for it. It was fortunate that I got the crux on my first try.

I wrote it up and mentioned the hanging rope in my description. I was stunned by the response. I was accused of using a knotted rope, of pulling on the rope and even using it as a form of protection. The mistrust that accompanied the route was shocking, to say the least, but it wasn't as though I hadn't brought it on myself with some of my previous, occasional malpractices. I suppose sometimes you get what you deserve in life. Phil Burke came along a little later, reporting a 'more ethical' ascent. However, considering where the rope was on my soloing of the line, I don't think that my ascent was much worse – gripe, gripe.

Clean, clean, clean ...

This brings me around quite naturally to my cleaning antics, and what I perceived at the time to be appropriate – although this has changed considerably over the years.

My original interpretation of cleaning came from what I'd read in the magazines, how the 'greats' of climbing had prepared their climbs before an ascent. I was so engrossed by the magazines of the time that every little nuance of an ascent was measured in my brain as being acceptable. My heroes were cleaning their new routes prior to an ascent by abseiling down them first, brushing off lichen and, in the cases of limestone and the mountain crags, removing any loose rock that was on the route.

Of course, until then, I hadn't really got into the limestone scene, so the loose rock issue wasn't on my agenda. I would simply abseil down most of my prospective new lines, scrub them with a wire brush and tidy them up as best as I could. It goes without saying that I would try the odd move on abseil as well, but that didn't develop more fully until a few years later; I would, put quite simply, copy the antics of what everybody was doing at the time in the Peak. I certainly wasn't into the 'ground-up' style of ascent.

I started my limestone 'career' in a similar fashion by brushing the lines that seemed suitable, such as those at Staden quarry. I'd strip off any vegetation on the line (I hope the nature gestapo aren't reading this) which, in some places like Wild Cat and Willersley, may have meant rather large sheets of ivy and other vegetation that got in the way. On the mountain crags, I just did what I had to in order to get the route clean.

As the years progressed, and certainly much later in my climbing career, I got myself into some really big cleaning sessions on places like Lundy Island, and in some of the esoteric limestone quarries that I sourced for my new route activity.

Lundy calling

'I look back on our time spent climbing together with great fondness. My best memory of a new route was on the Diamond at Lundy – a fine lead by Gary on Smear or Disappear.' Derek Beetlestone

The summer of 1980 provided me with one of the most important climbing experiences in my life: a visit to a climbing area that I have become synonymous with – Lundy Island.

If I were to choose one place to go back to, time and time again, through sheer compulsion, love and affection, it would be this magical isle; to me at the time, it was the best climbing venue I had ever come across.

I fell in love with it purely by chance. I had been climbing a bit with Steve Keeling, who had moved north to study at Edinburgh University. Early in the spring he asked if I fancied going on a climbing trip to the island; it was being organised by Andy Cairns, from the Edinburgh University Mountaineering Club. You were supposed to be a member of the club, but allowances were made, why exactly I don't know, and the two spare places were taken by Derek Beetlestone and me.

For sure, I had read all about the place: the iconic *Devil's Slide*, Pat Littlejohn's masterpieces of *Antiworlds* and *The Promised Land*, and, of course, I had heard about the potential mentioned in Littlejohn's recently published *South-West Climbs*. New routes were certainly going to be on the agenda.

Getting there was an experience that made the place even more enchanting. We went down a couple of days earlier to climb at Baggy Point, where we spent the night before we travelled to the island sleeping in the carpark by the harbour in Ilfracombe. It was quite a strange experience waking up next morning with tourists wandering past and looking at us disapprovingly, as though we were a bunch of dropouts.

The boat trip out was fantastic. We hauled our kit aboard *Polar Bear*, an old fishing trawler, now commissioned by the island authorities to ferry people to and from its shores. It was like being aboard the *Black Pig* in *Captain Pugwash,* a merry bunch of students, of different shapes and sizes, trying not to be sick on this rock 'n' roll ride to Lundy. The ship pitched in every direction the sea pushed it.

We stayed in two old bunk-houses alongside the Old Lighthouse, named East and West. This lighthouse was built at the island's highest point in order to signal to nearby boats the island's whereabouts in fog. Ironically, when it was foggy, the lighthouse was usually covered in fog and ended up being completely useless.

Our first week on the island was truly one of discovery. Sure, we had done our research, but that was hardly helpful when it comes to finding where you want to climb, especially when you're on top of the island looking for the crags at sea-level. We managed a couple of new routes, but most of the entertainment that week was spent watching Steve trying to climb a line he had cleaned on the *Wolfman Jack Wall.*

On two occasions he reached the last moves of the route, the crux, only to run out of strength and fall off. As we came to the last day, we baited Steve that he had one last chance or we'd have to do it for him, if, of course, we could. With the necessary incentive, he summoned up the determination needed and managed, by the skin of his teeth, to get past the crux.

Needless to say, this first week was little more than a taster for Derek and me. We returned the following year for far more important routes in a fortnight that turned out to be rather turbulent in our friendship.

A Widespread Ocean of Fear

By this time the mode of transport to the island had changed, and we were in for the even bigger treat of going there by helicopter from Hartland Point. It was a memorable experience. We had chosen to camp. With all our baggage and our cleaning equipment, I don't know how the helicopter got off the ground.

The year before, we had spied a line up the huge diamond-shaped wall behind the Devil's Slide. It had no routes on it, although someone had brushed clean a huge swathe of rock through the field of sea grass which adorned it. We'd come prepared with our own equipment for the cleaning of such lines, but, in this case, almost all the work had been done for us.

I had brought an extra-long rope, somewhere in the region of 100 metres for this purpose, and I decided to give the line a look. Sure enough, the person who had been there before us (whom we later found out to be Pete Thexton) had not only cleaned the line but placed nine pegs in it as well. I tinkered around on the line and knocked most of these pegs out as I thought they were unnecessary: something of an anathema to me nowadays with my 'in-situ protection attitude'. Actually, I thought the pegs might come in useful on any other new routes we might choose to do.

I remember relatively little about the first pitch as I stood belaying Derek. It was a very bold lead, with little in the way of protection, to a belay in the striking diagonal break that cut across the cliff. He did it in admirable style. The second pitch is, even today, indelibly imprinted on my mind: beautiful intricate climbing, good small wire protection and a sheer joy to climb, even though I had to push myself to my absolute limit to do it. Derek breezed up the thing and passed me by in a flash, heading for the top of the cliff. I had toyed many times with the idea of naming such a route. I would sit in anatomy lessons concentrating on route names rather than what I was being taught. I had come up with *A Widespread Ocean of Fear,* which felt entirely appropriate.

Even today, when I consider which lines would be at the top of my best new routes, this one usually heads the pile, even though that may not be for the climbing itself or that we did it with no other climbers on the island. No it's for the sheer pleasure of remembering it, and of the enjoyment that I had in climbing it with Derek. It was also a landmark ascent in my climbing development.

Controlled Burning

As we sat atop the newly christened *Diamond*, we looked north, and spied, in a cove opposite the cliff, a striking zig-zagging hand crack piercing the cliff. We examined our guide and saw that the area was named Torrey Canyon, but there was no mention of this crack being climbed, although a route named *Desperado* climbed the flake below it, before skirting off to the right. We had to go and have a look.

Once we had managed to get to the place, we were absolutely stunned by what we found. I later wrote in *Extreme Rock* that I had always hoped to find such a line one day. This was it.

A few days later we were back, with a young Marc Brown who was keen to accompany us and take some photos.

The morning was blisteringly hot as we abseiled in, barely giving a second thought to cleaning such a striking line. Thanks to my brother's initiation, I was good at crack climbing; such a line wouldn't be too difficult for me, or so I thought. Much to my annoyance, Derek won the proverbial toss of the coin and had first go at it.

He quickly climbed the crumbly flake-line of *Desperado* to arrive below the main crackline. He set off up it with me belaying, thinking how disappointed I was going to be not to get the first ascent. Then, all of a sudden, a large block in the crack wobbled loose and worried Derek so much that he sat on the gear. My turn had come; I wasn't going to miss this opportunity.

With an audience of seals bobbing up and down in the clear water of the bay – which we'd been entertaining by clapping as they dived beneath the ocean – this wonderful climb, with its not so wonderful rock, was to be mine. I had already named the climb *Controlled Burning* before I set off, as the sun angled across the wall in the heat of the day. It didn't all go so easily, though. I managed to get to the large roof and pull over it, as my arms started to wilt. There was the worry that I too would have to sag on the gear. I battled on with conviction and roars of approval from Derek below and Marc off to the side, taking photographs.

Ironically Derek had won a similar battle of wills a few days earlier when he bagged a line that I had been trying without success. I was far more pleased with this one though.

Increasing tensions

Throughout our fortnight of climbing together, tension between Derek and me was rising. I don't know whether it was cabin fever or our red-headed fiery temperaments, but, looking back, it saddens me to think that such a wonderful week became somewhat tainted by our arguments. Sure enough, we were competitive with each other and probably climbed at a similar standard, but something was brewing as the holiday drew to a close.

We had made friends with a couple of guys who were visiting the island, and Derek wanted to leave early to cadge a lift home. Of course, we still had lines to finish, and our last offering was one that was to change my mindset about climbing on Lundy over the following years.

While we had been climbing on the *Diamond,* I had seen a superb line on the large sweeping slab over to the right of *A Widespread Ocean of Fear.* I decided to have a look. I cleaned the line – not that there was much to clean – but was challenged by the boldness of a large section of the slab that was devoid of protection. Similarly, the small belay ledge above the pitch had no solid nut placements to belay from.

I'd taken a bolt kit to Lundy and, in a fateful moment, I decided to take the plunge and place one bolt on the run-out slab and another bolt for the belay. It seemed so obvious to me. I wasn't cognisant of the ethics of the place and decided that this was the way forward for such unprotected pieces of rock. I wasn't thinking I should leave it to someone else; I just decided to bring it down to a level that I could climb without the consequences of hurting myself should I slip off.

Smear or Disappear, as I decided to name the route, became perhaps a metaphor for change on the island over the next few years – a metaphor that wasn't supported by other climbers in the southwest, but one which meant I could do what I wanted to climb new routes. Greed yes, acting against the establishment yes, rebellion yes – but none of those things even crossed my mind. It just seemed to me to be the right thing to do at the time.

The two-week holiday that Derek and I had on the island was a marker for my involvement with the place over the next twenty years. Sure, these years had their controversies, but the island was certainly going to be a major part of my climbing life until well into the early 1990s.

'*The parting of the ways was on a journey back from Lundy. We'd had a falling out for some reason which I honestly can't recall, and Gary stopped his Triumph Herald in the middle of nowhere to inform me that the money I had contributed to the petrol kitty had run out at that point – did I want to contribute more or continue the journey on foot.*' Derek Beetlestone

My first bolt

Having referred to my first bolt placement, it seems appropriate to trace the story back to where it happened – at Staden quarry in the Peak District on a cold Wednesday in March 1981. I was out climbing with Hazel and had arranged to meet Derek at the quarry.

When we got to the place, I cleaned a couple of lines, one of which seemed way too bold for my liking. Having recently read stories of some of my heroes – perhaps most memorably Tom Proctor and Ron Fawcett – and their placing the odd bolt here and there to protect their ascents, I had invested in a bolt driver, should I ever need to use one. My intention was always clear: if my peers, or more appropriately my heroes, were investing in such ironmongery to procure their new routes, why shouldn't I?

It didn't seem controversial to me. I didn't really understand why you couldn't place a bolt for protection; it just seemed the elite generally deemed it 'wrong, old chap'. I had certainly spent many a happy hour with my brother hanging on the things when aid climbing was an appropriate winter alternative in the mid-1970s. So why not place them to protect yourself on some outrageously bold limestone pitch? Well, some 'outrageously bold' limestone climb, to my mind.

So there I was at Staden, cleaning this completely protectionless pitch, and I decided the time was right to place a bolt about halfway up it. I didn't intend to provoke controversy, it just seemed right. Similarly, I never even considered the fall-out. After all, this was an obscure quarry, one which people didn't really frequent too much at the time, and one that certainly wasn't deemed to be at the forefront of Peak District climbing.

Bang, twist, blow ... repeat

At this point it seems appropriate to reflect on how you put these things in. We didn't have rotary hammer drills back then. All we had was the bolt sleeve, which you threaded onto the end of a piece of iron rod, about eight inches long. You hammered it into the rock, twisted it a little bit and then continued the process. Every now and then you'd blow the dust out and continue until the hole was the same depth as the bolt. You would then clean out the hole completely and push a small, wedge-shaped piece of metal into the end of the bolt sleeve and hammer it into the hole. The bolt sleeve would expand and the whole thing would jam. Then you'd screw your bolt, already through the hanger, into the thread inside the bolt until it was tight and, hey presto, you were done. Incidentally, these bolts were eight millimetres in diameter and around one centimetre in length – none of your thick, heavy duty bolts; but, wow, did you trust them!

If you still did this process today, obviously with the thicker diameter bolts that came along a while later, you would be there all day equipping a sport route and not many would get done. Now we have rotary hammer drills, stainless bolts, glue-in bolts, the whole kit and caboodle. Quite often I carry a forty to fifty kilogram rucksack filled with such gear when I'm equipping (and re-equipping) lines. How times (and ethics) have changed!

Wintour's Leap

Throughout the early eighties my drive for new routes continued at the same maniacal pace with routes on Peak gritstone (from my local crags to the eastern edges) through to the occasional limestone route, and into North Wales and even the south west, where I had developed a particular liking for Lundy Island. I was also developing an interest in some of the bigger gaps at Wintour's leap.

Previously, Phil and I had climbed at Wintour's, as it was within a day's drive of where we lived, but when I was at college in Manchester this wasn't so simple. Sure enough, I had a car, but a trip of just over three hours each way would be overdoing it a bit. Luckily I had met up with a couple of great blokes, Neil Harvey and Bruce Miller, who were studying at the local university. I'd done a couple of new routes in Wales with Neil and asked them if they fancied a weekend at Wintour's Leap, my sole objective being some new lines I'd spotted on Fly Wall.

They seemed to be well up for it, so we set off one Friday night in June. When we arrived, we pitched our tent in the quarry at the top of the wall: an ideal place from which to climb on the crag and retreat for food, drink and then some sleep.

The only problem was that the routes I wanted to do had yet to be cleaned. I didn't want to take up prime climbing time cleaning them and then not have time to do them. My solution was simple: I got up around 5 a.m. on the Saturday morning, leaving Neil and Bruce in their sleeping bags, and went off to clean the routes.

About three or four hours later I was back. I encouraged them to get out of bed – I use the word 'encouraged' loosely – sorted out breakfast and plonked them at the bottom of my new lines to belay whilst I climbed. This was all very self-involved stuff on my part of course.

By the end of the weekend I had bagged what I thought to be three absolute classics in *Flies Aloft*, *Whip Lash* and *La Folie*, but sadly lost two good mates, who chose not to climb with me again after my selfish antics. This was a real shame and seems to have been a persistent theme throughout my climbing life.

University life

While all my climbing activities were going on, my world was shaped by friends at college, my bed and breakfast in Prestwich and a new, almost independent life in Manchester. Studying went with the territory – well that was the intention. Whether I ever really took it seriously was a matter of opinion.

I met many new friends at college, although I was lucky enough to already know a number of climbing buddies who attended Manchester Polytechnic and UMIST, and who were also residing in various parts of Manchester, including Whalley Range and Moss Side. The latter area was close to the Factory, where I had already paid a number of visits to satiate my desires for my Punk Rock musical tastes.

My friends who went to Manchester Poly used to have Wednesday afternoons off for 'sporting activities'. Well that's what they said and, as I didn't get Wednesday afternoons off, I decided to do something about it. I was timetabled on that afternoon to do life science, tutored by a lecturer named Graham Pashley. On my first visit, he explained the curriculum very clearly to the class. He was going to get everybody up to high O level standard in physics and chemistry and A level standard in biology. As I already had the required grades at the appropriate levels, I decided that I could surreptitiously miss the lessons and go out climbing with my mates instead.

Towards the end of the year, I thought it would be prudent to attend a couple of the life science lessons again before the exam took place, just to show willing. When I walked in, Graham Pashley told me that I was in the wrong room. I replied, 'Oh, I've been to this class before.' He said he didn't remember seeing me. So I said I had been at the first lesson. They failed me in the exam, despite my getting a high enough mark to pass. They must have thought the idea of my re-taking the exam in the summer would change my attitude, and I would revise for it. No chance; I passed it anyway.

Therein lay my attitude to college: get through by doing just enough, and perhaps a bit of extra work towards the end of the third year to show I meant it.

And so a whole itinerary of dodging lessons here and going climbing there ensued, not to say attending a few concerts, visiting a few pubs and getting up to no good as well.

After spending two terms at my bed and breakfast, a college mate, Paul Meredith, suggested that I could share his rented apartment/ bedsit. Paul was a great bloke, who I still see every now and again with another ex-colleague Gary Foley. His idea seemed sensible, especially considering that the shared expenditure of the bedsit would only cost me about £6 a week. Now you might get the impression from the £6 that it was more a den of iniquity than a fully furnished modern apartment, and you would be right. Paul had his own room and I was be in the bedsit proper, never really alone, as I was often accompanied by the scurrying feet of a mouse or two; but I just loved it.

One evening I had an unfortunate episode with Derek Beetlestone, who was studying nearby. We had been down to the Priory pub for a couple of drinks and Derek, sensible chap that he was, decided to stop over rather than drive back to Whalley Range in his Escort van.

When we got up the next morning, his van had been nicked, hardly surprising considering the area in which I lived, so we reported it at the local police station.

To our horror, Derek's stolen van had been used in a burglary, and the two 'culprits', who were seen escaping from the scene, were conspicuous by their ginger-coloured hair. Now, if you knew us both at the time, our hair was ginger (mine has now turned almost silver and Derek has none). Indeed, mine was the brightest ginger imaginable.

Upon reporting the theft, the police added two and two together and got five by assuming, quite incorrectly, that we were the culprits. They separated us and put us in different interview rooms. The tone of the questions put to me was extremely aggressive, and I think Derek was subjected to similar questioning. It wasn't exactly fun. Eventually, though, the police came to the conclusion that it wasn't us after all, and they let us go. Derek got his van back from the pound, and off we went.

'Perhaps the funniest thing I can recall was when I was couch surfing at Gary's flat in Salford. The Mark 1 Ford Escort, my current mode of transport, was stolen from outside by Salford's finest, and Gary and myself ambled along to the police station to report the theft. Unbeknown to us, the vehicle had been used in a robbery at Burtons and abandoned by two toe rags after a police chase. The local CID obviously thought we were the culprits, and we were only released after several hours' interrogation.' Derek Beetlestone

Pork scratchings, anyone?

At 'training' at college, we had a number of clinical sessions including the opportunity, in the first year, to study some basic foot pathologies. One of these was the condition of extremely long and thickened toe nails resulting from years of neglect, known as onychogryphosis.

I happened to have a patient come into the surgery one day with this condition. With careful treatment, I managed to cut back the toenails and make the lady more comfortable.

However my mission hadn't ended there. With a few of the lads in our group, I'd realised that such nails when removed look like pork scratching. We thus hatched a cunning plan. I saved the nails, and a couple of days later we were in the pub across the road from the college. Someone had bought a bag of pork scratchings, and, after finishing them between us, we filled the bag back up with the toenails and then passed them round the pub as an offering to some of its local clients for a laugh. To our amusement, surprise and no little disgust, the bag came back empty, and to this day I've assumed that our offerings, the extra long toenails, were happily digested by said locals.

Chance encounter

On 2nd October 1980, Paul and I decided to go out for a beer at the college, where, unbeknown to us, there was a party in the student bar. We weren't quite sure what was going on, but the turn of events which followed was to change my life.

I had never had a girlfriend. I was quite a shy character back then, and I wasn't really looking out for a girlfriend. I thought I had enough in my life, what with my obsessive attitude to climbing while living the life of a university student.

We arrived in the bar, bought ourselves each a beer and plonked ourselves down in one of the comfy chairs scattered around the room. There was music playing, some disco stuff, most unlike our preferred type, but it was good fun all the same.

Then, all of a sudden, this lovely young lady dressed in a grass skirt came whizzing by, with some guy in hot pursuit. I hadn't really noticed what was going on, except that the pint I was holding suddenly disappeared from my hand as it was grasped by said young lady, and thrown over the chap in pursuit. It had the desired effect, halting him dead in his tracks. It certainly cooled his ardour – but what about my pint?

This chance encounter proved to be one of the most important events in my life. The lady in question, Hazel Carnes, knew of me through one of her friends at college. She also knew of my climbing exploits. When I realised this, I asked her if she fancied coming along with me the following week. When she said yes, I was absolutely bowled over. I couldn't wait to take her out climbing.

We went to Windgather Rocks: not the greatest climbing venue in the world, but one which led to a relationship that has lasted all these years.

Off comes the wheel ...

By the middle of the second year at college, my climbing life had changed significantly. I was still climbing with a few of the lads from the Poly and, of course, Derek, but I would also have the occasional Monday afternoon going out cragging with Hazel and Elaine Rowe, who was in the same class.

Unlike me, there was no way Hazel or Elaine would skip a lesson, but in the second year they didn't have lessons on Monday afternoons. So I skived off college one day in May, and we paid a trip to Wharncliffe Crags on the northern limits of Sheffield. We had a good day's climbing and were on our return journey over the Longdendale Pass, Elaine sitting in the back knitting and Hazel in the front.

Just as we were coming to the top of the pass, moving at quite a pace (well, for a Triumph Herald) we approached a sharp left-hand bend. I felt the car jolt very slightly. As I hit the brakes more firmly, I heard a loud thud as my little car clunked and started to turn into the bend. Unfortunately it didn't stop turning and, just then, the right offside wheel, complete with tyre, came hurtling past the window of the car, and we did a 270-degree turn, heading backwards down the road. Hazel's first comment was, 'I'll get that when we've stopped.' As the car came to a shuddering halt, I realised the gravity of the situation. We were on the wrong side of the road at the highest point of the moors on a Monday evening, with dusk fast approaching.

Luckily there was an AA box within fifty yards of where we were. Unfortunately, when we got there, we found it had been vandalised and the phone wasn't working. I had to trudge down to a telephone in Tintwistle to contact the AA to recover my car. It was towed home and I had to incur the wrath of my dad once again. At least this time it wasn't my fault.

I rebuilt my car over the following few weeks and was soon back with wheels to pursue my beloved obsession.

The Incredible Hulk

College really was a blast, away from home with my own flat and every opportunity to have some fun and study, all at the same time.

Every year we had a college party, usually at the end of term, just before Christmas. It was organised by the third-year students. Towards the end of 1981, Hazel, Elaine and I decided to take the opportunity to have some fun at the forthcoming disco; it was probably Hazel's idea. We hatched a plan to go as cartoon heroes. Elaine chose Wonder Woman, Hazel chose Tinkerbell and I chose the Incredible Hulk – which was a bit of an irony at the time, as I was only twelve stone wet through.

You could easily sort out the fancy dress for Wonder Woman and Tinkerbell, but in those days you couldn't get a green blow-up suit as the Hulk, like you can today. I had to improvise. I found some green poster paint and just plastered it all over. I wore a pair of old cut-off jeans, no shoes and just went like that. And, of course, I roared, at every opportunity.

The whole thing went swimmingly. Afterwards Hazel and Elaine made their way home; I think Hazel's dad picked them up. When I got back to my digs with Paul, I thought it best to remove the poster paint before I went to bed. I concluded that a good bath would do the job, so down I went to the communal bath to scrub myself clean. That's when the fun ended.

The more I scrubbed, the more I realised that the stuff just wasn't going to come off. I tried a cloth and a stiff flannel, but it wouldn't budge, so I turned to the scourer from the kitchen in our bedsit. Sure enough, with a good bit of scrubbing, the paint finally began to come off, and, after about forty minutes of hard work, I was clean enough to go to bed. When I woke up the next morning, almost all my body was bright red, and I was sore all over. Let it be said that I never tried to impersonate the Incredible Hulk again.

More recent developments

I had always dreamed of the idea of writing my own book, similar to Steve Bancroft's classic *Recent Developments* from 1979. My notion was to update Peak District activity, as well as writing something even better than Bancroft's wonderful tome. My real reason, though, was to publicise my 'masterpieces' to the world; in my rose-tinted view, the magazines just didn't do my routes justice.

Even before then, I'd had the opportunity to be involved in a number of Peak District guidebooks on a limited basis, but this I thought, was the perfect opportunity to branch out. But who could I get to publish it?

All of a sudden, completely by surprise, I had a phone call from Geoff Birtles, the editor of my beloved *Crags* which had almost single-handedly influenced the direction of my climbing life from 1977 onwards. I was stunned by the thought of actually speaking to him. He informed me that *Crags* had run its course, and he was moving on to bigger and better things. He had decided to branch out into *High* magazine, which would also become the voice of the British Mountaineering Council (BMC).

To my amazement, Geoff was inviting me to be the news editor of this magazine, and he also offered to publish my booklet. Without even thinking about it, I accepted his offer, and, in its first edition in March 1982, I took up my new role with this new magazine. How my world was about to change; the poacher had turned gamekeeper.

That Strange Little Girl

I was now heading towards my final exams at college. I had always done enough to get by, but decided that a little more effort than usual was needed. I began to study properly. I didn't want to fail any of my exams at this late stage.

The exams were scattered over a few months from late March to the end of June, and I passed each one as it arrived. My final exam, podology theory, was probably a formality, and I passed it on 30th June 1982, as did Hazel. The summer was mine to do as I pleased, with climbing firmly on the agenda.

With the opportunity to travel far and wide, I put it to good effect. I'd already had a good new routing weekend with Neil and Bruce at Wintour's Leap earlier in the summer, but I still had further designs on the place. I was also about to challenge the ethical principles of the area.

I arranged another weekend with Marc Brown and had my eye on a few lines: most specifically on the North Walls, where an impressive tower of rock offered potential.

I'd already begun to test the resolve of a couple of areas with my bolting practices, so it wasn't a surprise that the bold looking nature of this piece of rock would fall to my bolt driver again. I wasn't really too concerned that bolts hadn't previously been placed for free climbing on the crag, as they had been used for aid on a few sections of the crag already.

So with this in mind, I placed the odd bolt to complement what I thought were two excellent multi-pitch climbs named *Strange Little Girl* and *Sweetheart Contract.* I wasn't concerned about the consequences. However, challenging the ethics of a climbing area where you don't even live generally incurs a degree of local outrage – something I've become used to over the years. I simply moved on to other things and let the dust settle.

Space Mountain

The scattergun effect I had of climbing over all parts of Britain to achieve my goal continued at Craig-y-Forwyn in North Wales, where my brother had spotted an impressive line. Over the preceding couple of years, Phil and I had been popping over to this crag, repeating many of its excellent routes and occasionally doing the odd new route. Having spotted an impressive pillar tucked away in the back of one of the bays, Phil had become somewhat obsessed by it. He was so concerned that local superstar Andy Pollitt was going to nick it off us that he arranged to 'throw a sicky' at work – Phil was a designer for Adams pottery at the time – and took a Monday off to climb the line.

We set off at our normal ungodly hour (Phil had always loved his early starts, from the days when he first started climbing) and arrived at the crag to do the requisite preparation of the route. A bit of ivy ripped off here, a couple of threads placed there, and a peg banged in just below the crux.

As I recall, we didn't need to put in too much effort to climb the route, and, as we drove home, the glow of satisfaction was pretty evident on our faces. Phil had chosen the name *Space Mountain* from a ride he had been on at Disneyland the previous year, and because he had found the line I was quite happy for him to name it.

However, when we got home, Phil found himself in deep doo doo. His manager had been round to our house to find out where he was. He must have had some important work that needed to be done and, of course, Phil wasn't there. It was left to Phil to explain his way out of that one, but I doubt he told him he'd been climbing. The Gibson brothers – still up to their old tricks, hey?

Gritstone calls again

These were important routes and important times for me. The prospect of a new job meant that I was determined to squeeze in as much climbing as I could before I became locked-in to a full-time working week; I had to return to Hen Cloud to pluck some of what I regarded as the last remaining big lines. I had 'tinkered' with a few of these the year before and managed to bag two good ones. However the arête to the left of *Rib Chimney* had spat me off when I tried it previously with Jon Walker, so I was back with Hazel for another go.

The problem was that I wasn't really sure how to go about protecting it. Paul Pepperday had done the lower part of the arête a year a two before, but the prize surely had to be its upper section? I brushed it clean and tried the moves and, to my surprise, they linked together quite well. All I had to do was to lead it; yet, the protection issue still nagged.

In the end, I decided to go with a runner in *Rib Crack* as high as I could place it without straying too far up. Then I went for it. Again, surprisingly, it all locked into place. It hadn't been so bad after all, and I moved onto another line that I'd seen on the same crag but way over to the left.

This little wall looked amazing. It had a thin crack running up its centre which, in fairness, was often prone to seepage. That day, with a lovely gentle breeze blowing across the face, it was dry. I gave it a brush and worked out the moves above a really good nut placement at half-height. I locked off my descendeur and just kept repeating the moves until I was confident I could do them easily. The problem was that I had no one to belay me. I asked a couple of blokes off to the side – who I think were about to do *Central Route* – but their unwillingness was palpable. I didn't know what to do.

The thought ran through my head that if I could solo up to the nut placement – moves I hadn't even tried – place the nut and attach an eight-foot sling from it into my harness, this would protect me for the moves I now knew like the back of my hand. It seemed plausible; that was until I tried the start, which was much harder than I'd expected. Up and off, up and off, it just didn't want to go, but then it all unlocked, and I managed to get the Rock 4 into the slot and attach the sling. But I hadn't realised just how much the start had taken out of me. Off I fell onto the nut. Fortunately it held. I unclipped and jumped off; I was knackered.

After a good rest, I was back at it and this time everything went just as I'd hoped. Unfortunately, after doing the crux, I was presented with another, much larger problem when I unclipped the nut and let the sling drop back down. I hadn't previously done the wide crack above the break, and I hadn't been sensible enough to even consider what an obstacle it would prove.

I decided the only thing I could do was to wriggle along the wide break, which ran across the face, and squirm out the other end. Today, with my bulk, I wouldn't be able to do it, but back then, a mere strip of a lad, it was a goer, and I came out the other end covered in green slime and 'spitting feathers' from the heather that I'd swallowed. I wrote the route up as *The Stone Loach* at E4 6b. Today it is usually done with bouldering pads, but all I had was a beer towel and hope.

Work–life beckons

In September 1982 I started my first ever full-time job, working as a chiropodist in North Staffordshire. I'd had other job offers in both Derbyshire and Gloucestershire; jobs were easy pickings in those days. However I chose to move back home, as Hazel had chosen a job in the same town as well as getting a flat just down the road from my mum and dad's.

I moved back in with my parents – a difficult decision after the freedom I had enjoyed at college. They welcomed me home with open arms, and I started my clinical work based in what I regarded as the capital, Burslem. My dad had a shop in the same town for around thirty years, so it was a relatively easy decision. It felt like home, and I loved it. Occasionally I would go for lunch and a chat with him or pop over to see Hazel, who was working in Hanley, a mile or so away.

To have money and the opportunity to go to work would provide me with what I needed in life. I had always been brought up to work hard, earn a living and pay my way in life, and this was perfect for me. I now had a good car, Hazel lived just a stone's throw away, and the world became my oyster.

The grand finale for the year was my *Peak District New Route* booklet. I had been working on this for a few months, and it was slowly coming together. With the support of Geoff Birtles, *Peak District New Route* was published in December 1982. It was my first publication, the first of many. Sure, the opportunity to publicise my own routes was a boost to my ego. But it was also the first in a long line of guidebooks that I've either written or been involved in since that day.

A whole new chapter in my life lay ahead ...

Confession

But before we get into that, there's something I need to tell you.

In the latter part of 1979, I did something which was really stupid. It wasn't planned and I never meant to hurt anyone. To this day,

I'm not quite sure why I did it. Was it was to do with my craving for fame or notoriety? Whatever the motivation, it was indefensible and inexcusable.

I'd spotted an unclimbed line at Tremadog. I abseiled down it and cleaned it. It was eminently climbable, but at a grade of E4 6b – harder than I could climb at the time. I named this route *Big Bug*, claimed the first ascent and sent the details to the climbing magazines of the day.

Six months later, I was sitting below the crag with John Redhead and Paul Williams. Paul rightly berated me for my lie. The week before, he'd tried *Big Bug* with John and Ron Fawcett but to no avail. 'How could someone like you climb that line, when both John and Ron have been running up routes much harder than this for the past two years?' he demanded. I tried to talk my way out of it but until now I have never admitted to the truth.

I cannot write this book without admitting what happened. It may shock people that it's taken me forty years to come clean. And there were other occasions when I was liberal with the truth. But, certainly for the last thirty years, I've been very honest, despite what I have been accused of.

I am, of course, not the first to cheat; nor sadly, will I be the last. Throughout climbing history, the truth has been distorted on many occasions. But cheating is always wrong and it's particularly wrong in climbing – an activity which demands scrupulous honesty. Let my example serve as a warning to those who would take short cuts in their pursuit of climbing fame, as I will have to live with my actions for the rest of my life.

Chapter 5

A Midnight Summer Dream

We all have a time in our lives, perhaps a year or a season, which stands out in our memory as our best or most productive. In my case, this is based on a variety of factors, the overriding ones tending to be challenges, experiences and consequent memories. 1983 was such a time. I felt that I had arrived on the new route scene, and it involved many specific events which today I look back on as being of importance in my life.

By 1983, I had established a number of key milestones in my climbing career. I also had a group of enthusiastic climbing partners, including Hazel and my brother Phil. But 1983 would bring new friends, new climbs and plenty of controversies, mostly of my own making. One would turn the climbing world upside down, others would be forgotten and one or two still come back to haunt me publicly or privately, even today.

One of the overriding things in the climbing world for me was that I was now the news editor for *High*. In my mind, this gave me an open ticket to present my new routes to the world, without restraint. Ironically, my reporting of new routes to the *Crags* news editor had now turned full circle; I was now the news editor of its reincarnation, *High*. My obsession could take me to whatever level I wanted.

The year started quietly and, as always, Wintour's Leap in the Wye valley was a good place to target over the winter months. The weather was less inclement in the south, and we could reach the crags easily in a day by car. Phil loved the place; it was where he'd done his first new route, the free ascent of *Kaiser Wall*, and, not least, there were plenty more 'spaces' to fill. What I wasn't expecting, though, was to tackle one of the 'last great problems' of the area.

After repeating some of the existing routes on the Great Overhanging (GO) Wall with Phil, I'd taken an interest in the line taken by the old aid route *Technician*. We'd already dealt a blow to one of the aid routes on the wall, so why not another? But the great barrier of overhangs that this route bludgeoned its way through was a far more intimidating prospect.

Me and Adam versus Technician

Throughout this time, although I had a number of climbing partners I could rely on, there was no one with the same enthusiasm for new lines as I had. I could go out for the odd day, here and there, but nobody would commit to a weekend or a few days away with me which was hardly surprising considering my previous encounters. I had been back to visit Jo Royle's where I worked previously, for my regular fix of pegs, threads and other ironmongery, and working there now was the super-enthusiastic all-round good guy, Adam Hudson.

Adam was up for anything, and when I told him of my new routing ambitions (which he'd probably already worked out from the stuff I was buying, as well as my name being in the magazines), he appeared almost as inspired as I was at the prospect and the adventures it might bring. There was also that twinkle in his eye which I had recognised in myself – that thirst for glory.

Adam was a great bloke to be around. He lived in a little two-up, two-down in Harding Street in Fenton, which he shared with a number of lads who were students at the local polytechnic. Andy Popp and James 'Barry' Barrett lived there, and Nick Dixon, who was on a course with Andy, would occasionally pop in, pardon the pun.

The youthfulness and exuberance of these guys (remember, at the ripe age of twenty-two, I was only a little older) was absolutely infectious. They were as keen as I was, and over the next few years they all added to my enjoyment of climbing and the camaraderie that went with it.

Adam was just the bloke I needed to help me tackle *Technician.* In a relatively short space of time, it turned us into very close friends. After we had been doing a bit of prospecting on the nearby Fly Wall, I persuaded him to help me investigate the barrier of overhangs pierced by the aid route. We traversed across, below the roof, and secured a good belay atop a pedestal, some thirty feet to the right of the alcove leading through the roof. After a bit of 'bang and dangle' and attempts at freeing the moves, it still didn't look possible. I tried this way and that and then, all of a sudden, managed to lock my knee in a position which allowed the prospect of free climbing to become a distinct probability. All we needed was to sort out what we would do above, if or when I succeeded.

We were both up for the battle and I couldn't wait to get back. Nothing else but that line was on my mind all through the following week before we vowed to return.

Sure enough, the following weekend we were back, and the first thing we had to do was sort out those upper pitches. On abseil, after a bit of cleaning and the placing of a few threads and a couple of pegs, we got stuck into the attempt from the belay we had taken the previous week.

Amazingly it all fitted into place quite quickly, and, after a couple of short airborne retreats and a good breather below, I unlocked the sequence through the roof to arrive at the belay perched above. Adam half-climbed, half-aided his way through, and, with a swift ascent of the walls above – which were nowhere near the difficulty of the roof section – the route was bagged. I'd already chosen the name of *Feline* as it seemed to fit in with the other names on the wall, and it was a Stranglers' track which made it even better. I publicised it in *High* with my customary arrogant stupidity.

Of course, that was never going to be the end of the escapade, as the local climbing fraternity came out in anger, claiming I hadn't freed the roof, I couldn't climb to that standard, etc., but Adam was a clear witness to the event and stood up for me whenever my ascent was challenged.

The Cat Gut experience

I'd climbed numerous routes on the GO Wall at Wintour's Leap with my brother in the early 1980s and had begun to search for new route opportunities whenever I could. One such was a line veering off to the right from *Kangaroo Wall.* I'd already press-ganged Adam into climbing on the wall when we did *Feline,* so another new route on it wasn't going to upset him a few weeks later. After doing the new first pitch, I rather fancied another pitch on the walls above. I'd already cleaned the line and decided it would be easier to abseil into the first main stance of *Kangaroo Wall* and continue from there.

The problem was that the stance of *Kangaroo Wall* lay below a series of large overhangs that prevented easy abseil access. I suggested to Adam that if I clipped into any in-situ gear on the way into the stance, I could get into the belay much more easily. When it was his turn, I suggested he unclip the gear and I could pull him into the stance from there. We could climb back out from there instead of doing the lower pitch again.

I left Adam with the climbing ropes, abseiled down the wall, clipping merrily into the old aid line of *Interstellar Overdrive,* arrived at the stance and shouted back up to him that it was his turn. He followed suit, unclipping the gear as he came down, and I duly pulled him into the stance. He let go of the abseil ropes and let them swing free into mid-air, some twenty feet out of reach.

I looked at Adam in shock. 'Where are the ropes?' I asked

'Oooh ... up at the top!' he replied, realising he'd forgotten them.

There we were, 150 feet above the ground, in the middle of nowhere, with no ropes and nobody around. The only means of escape was for me to solo boldly back up *Kangaroo Wall,* a route, that thankfully, I knew rather well.

Luckily, our new route posed considerably fewer problems; we'd had quite enough adventure for one day.

Into the Leap

Every Easter we would plan a regular family trip, which would include Phil and his wife Ruth, and Hazel and me. This time we had chosen Pembroke, following on from the previous year. We would set our sights more on just going climbing without the burden of new routing, but, if the opportunity arose, I knew Phil would be very supportive.

Pembroke had become a new route mecca around Easter time. Many travelled from all over the country to indulge in the delights of its numerous opportunities, and we were no exception: what more could a new route activist like me ask for?

We had good weather all week and our strong relationship, built on ten years of climbing together, reaped dividends. We climbed across the length and breadth of the coastline, from Mother Carey's to Mewsford, ticking a host of routes, mainly in the E1 to E4 category, and always keeping our eyes open for new lines. Ironically we only managed a single new route of real merit that week, but it was one which was to open our eyes to a whole new realm of possibilities on an otherwise neglected cliff.

The gash of Huntsman's Leap appeared from above to be distinctly unpleasant and inhospitable. But that had never stopped us before, and with our inquisitive nature it wasn't going to do so now. We ticked a couple of its four existing routes, and all we could hear from the people above was the chitter-chatter of unappreciative spectators. This wasn't in any way a criticism of our climbing style, but more of how they perceived the place to appear: dank and dismal like our initial impressions.

That couldn't have been further from the truth.

As we were climbing one of the routes, the slab to its right, which was relatively free of soil and vegetation and thereby requiring little in the way of cleaning, couldn't escape our attention.

After a bit of cleaning and a 'sprinkling of stardust' – which meant the placing of a peg and a couple of threads around natural 'bridges' in the rock – the route was dispatched with relatively little effort. Phil had already chosen its name: *Fitzcarraldo*, a film about pushing a boat up the Amazon. Considering the slightly bold nature of the upper section of the route, it seemed entirely appropriate.

Of course one route would never be enough for me. When we had been in The Zawn, we had made a good recce, and it was obvious that its walls were brimming with new route possibilities. My initial focus was the slabbier south side of The Zawn, as the north wall seemed devoid of features and was considerably more intimidating.

Sure enough, over a few weekends in late April and May, Adam and I were back, with Huntsman's being the main focus of attention. I had also collected a large number of pieces of thread and rope, kindly supplied to me by Troll, as offcuts from their factory, in readiness for our trip.

With a full quota of lines to go at, as well as our enthusiasm for cleaning, we bivouacked in St Govan's carpark while the weather stayed fine. Ironically, I only have one memory of that night's bad weather, and we thought the nearby St Govan's chapel would provide the perfect shelter we needed. How wrong could we have been? We threw our sleeping bags on the floor and didn't realise the muddy mess we had placed them on. Add to that, the doorway to the chapel acted more of a funnel than a barrier to the wind and you can imagine the picture, as rain and mist swept through the place. We might as well have stayed in the car park, as we emerged sodden to our underwear, cold and without having had any sleep whatsoever. Not a memory I will cherish!

First in the Leap was a wonderfully enticing line that I had seen at the tip of The Zawn emerging from the tidal boulder-bed onto an enticing face of black limestone. I had checked out the line with a relatively brief inspection (actually it needed fairly little cleaning) and discovered an old 'warhead' jammed into an alcove fifty feet above the floor of The Zawn.

That felt the right place to belay should the tide encroach too quickly.

When we set off, I soon realised that we needed to reach the belay fairly swiftly, as the tide began to race back in. As Adam joined me, a huge block in the water jutted out above the surface. Adam's almost philosophical view of the rock gave the route its name as he commented, 'That looks like some great *Mythical Monster*.'

The next day we were back, this time closer to the landward end and with less of a time constraint from the tide. I'd cleaned the line the night before and laden it with a number of threads, this time of a different colour to those on any of the other routes I'd done in The Zawn. *Quiet Waters* wandered around the wall, with a particularly tough start, but it seemed to capture all the things I wanted from the place at the time: wonderful technicalities, no particular line and an increasing abundance of in-situ gear.

In fact, the gear was helping me to develop an idea. If I could adorn each route with a different coloured thread, I could develop a sort of 'crag topo'. Although the thought simply tickled my imagination, it stimulated a degree of unrest in other climbers who enjoyed these cliffs. I was bringing my Peak District style of climbing – one that had been developed by others, but to which I had grown accustomed – to other areas of the country. This wasn't particularly liked by those who approached Pembroke climbing with a predominantly on-sight ethic. But my objective was to do what I had to do to gain my new route success. I didn't set out to divide local opinion, it just seemed the right thing to do.

The tide is high

Our return journeys home were always accompanied by the beat from Adam's cassette player, and, on this particular occasion, by the wonderful Heaven Seventeen track, *Fascist Groove Thang*; happy days! It wasn't all Punk Rock with Adam though. His eclectic musical taste brought something special to our friendship and the boom, boom, boom of the speakers made the journey home far more pleasurable.

Of course Adam and I weren't just in it for the new routes. Pembroke was still a relatively novel area to us both, and we did a significant number of the existing climbs as well. My primary intention was to use these to find new lines, but we weren't going to miss out on all the classics in the area.

We were also prone to a few mishaps, mostly of our own doing.

On one such occasion, we had decided to climb at Mewsford Point and had chosen the classic *Surprise Attack* as our first venture. I was going to climb the first pitch and Adam would lead through on the second.

We had driven down the night before, arriving in the carpark well past midnight. As usual, and much to Adam's annoyance, I was up at the crack of dawn fiddling around, looking for things to do. Adam eventually emerged from his sleeping bag, and we trudged off to Mewsford Point getting there around 9 a.m. We abbed down the line of *Surprise Attack* to reach the platform below the cliff.

It is worth noting, if you have never visited Mewsford Point, that the platform below tilts downwards towards the cliff, which means that from mid to high tide the sea cuts off any access. We had no idea what time high tide was, so we wandered around the rest of the cliff, looking up at the various routes and trying to spy out where they went. By the time we'd finished ambling around, the sun was just about glinting on the top of the platform, so we decided we'd have a sleep, to allow the bottom of the cliff to dry out. Unbeknown to us, we had come onto the platform at low tide and, as we slept, the tide rushed into the gap at the foot of the cliff. When we awoke, we couldn't reach either the route or our abseil rope. We simply had to wait for the tide to go back out again.

About six hours later, having moped around on the platform for far too long, we managed to get onto the rock and complete the route. We'd left our rucksacks by the abseil stake and, as I was hauling up the rope, a couple with two children came over to us and asked if we'd caught anything. I nearly fell off the crag trying to keep a straight face, while Adam burst out laughing. It made a fitting end to a bizarre day.

On another occasion, Adam came up with a brilliant suggestion of how to 'dodge' the orderly who manned the gate to the firing range when manoeuvres were ongoing. With a completely straight face and no hint of irony, he pointed out that if it was low tide we could walk around Chapel Point and back up into the range on the far side of Newton Head. If we did it this way, we could get into the range and go climbing without the orderly noticing.

He suggested I go first. I was to enter the range, then wave back to him from an appropriate point, and he would come round to join me.

What I great idea I thought. No sooner had he suggested it, than I was off. I walked under Chapel Point and scrambled up onto the headland of Newton Head. Just as I was coming up the slope, I noticed the orderly standing there with a look of complete disgust on his face. Adam was stood behind him, smirking. He'd tipped him off and I was quickly escorted off the range. Luckily I wasn't charged but I used the situation to my advantage by naming a route a few years after the escapade: *The Fascist and Me.*

One day, two new routes, two crags

There is something very strange about stories and how they can get muddled up in the mists of time and develop into something quite different to what actually happened. I had been looking at a new line on Craig Yr Ysfa with Hazel, after having had a pleasant day out climbing some of the easier routes on the crag. I had abseiled down it and cleaned it, but didn't have time to finish it off. I would have to come back the following week; but I just couldn't wait. It seemed obvious to ask Adam if he fancied doing it with me the following Tuesday.

As ever, Adam said yes, and I arranged to pick him up early that day. I would have to ring in sick, but that wouldn't present a problem if I did it the day before.

The following Tuesday I arrived at Adam's to find that he had cried off the idea. Luckily, Andy Popp was around, and he agreed to come along instead.

What I hadn't realised was that Andy had just hitched home from Wales and had arrived back at the house in the early hours of the morning, having walked the last fifteen miles or so.

We set off around 7 a.m. In those days, the roads were relatively quiet and a brisk two-hour journey landed us at the parking place before the walk up to the crag, which normally took about an hour.

With the walk completed and a quick look at the line by abseil, we managed to climb this wonderfully atmospheric pitch, which I had already named *The Haunted*, and then wandered back down to the car.

But that wasn't enough – is it ever? We had time to kill, and, as I had seen a line on Dinas Mot in a guidebook the night before, I suggested to Andy that we do this as well.

Of course it needed a bit of cleaning, but the route didn't take too much effort and we even had a bit of spare time to do *The Windmill* as well; we were lucky enough to be home before it went dark.

Since that time, it's amazing how my story has been embellished by other people to the point where I have been accused of claiming a new route in Pembroke and a new route in North Wales on the same day. It is true that I have driven for over four hours to do one route that I thought someone else might grab but I have never been stupid enough to suggest that I could do two new routes in completely different parts of the country in the same day.

'*Apparently, too good a day for some to accept, and that is where the myth comes in. Gradually, this regular day out, on which we did two new routes on separate mountain crags in Snowdonia, has become twisted and transformed so that legend has it that Gary dashed from Crag yr Ysfa to Pembroke or even Lundy to add his second new route of the day. Preposterous! But somehow also believed. The reality may have been more prosaic but it was no less telling of the man. Yes, there was a drive there, but it was fuelled by above all else – before all else – by a simple passion for the climbing. I know; I was there.*' Andy Popp

The Pen Trwyn era begins

Throughout my early days of new routing, I met some fabulous climbing buddies at the Roaches, such as Gary Cooper, and the brothers Fred and Ken Crook. These two certainly weren't in their teens; they had only started to climb late in life.

Whenever I used to pop up to the Roaches, you could rest assured that they would all be hanging about below *The Sloth*, doing a bit of bouldering or a route here and there. They knew the place almost as well as I did.

I had many a competitive soloing time with Gary, in a rush to outdo one other. I used to solo up *Ruby Tuesday* and down *The Sloth*, and then up *Humdinger* and down *Saul's Crack*. It even got to the point where I would solo *Elegy* on a regular basis and even committed to soloing *The Swan*, *Ascent of Man* and *Hunky Dory* – pure madness!

On a few of these visits to the Roaches, Fred entertained me with his stories about his mid-week new routing with Bill Wayman, who worked at Plas y Brenin. He talked endlessly and engagingly about a new crag they were developing on the Great Orme, with easy access and miles of new rock to go at. But he wouldn't let slip exactly where it was.

Then one day it all came out. I thought I knew the North Wales limestone area quite well, having climbed loads of stuff in the Craig y Forwyn area with Phil. But I knew relatively little about the Ormes. Fred finally told me about Craig Pen Trwyn, above the Marine Drive. 'It's an "endless" escarpment of limestone, with loads of new routes to do,' he said.

The blue touch paper was lit; Phil and I were off there the following weekend.

When we turned up, we didn't really know what to expect. We had probably driven below the crags with our parents when we were toddlers, but that hadn't left any lasting memories for two kids who were probably more interested in sandcastles and swimming. Back then, climbing certainly wasn't on the agenda, except perhaps for trees and the outside buttresses of my local school.

Once we had found the parking place, we wandered along the road below the cliff looking at where to climb, until we arrived at the striking crack of *Plum Line*. As we scrambled up to it, we were surprised to find a number of other climbers on the platform around the base of the cliff.

Andy Pollitt and Paul Williams were about to embark on the second ascent of *Gold Rush*, just to the left of *Plum Line*. I'd never really met Andy before, despite having eulogised about his new routes in the magazines and exchanged a few letters with him and Paul; and, well, Paul was Paul. It was great to meet them both.

Phil led me up *Plum Line*, and we wandered back down to the beginning of the cliff to have a look at a new route that I fancied. Phil, supportive as ever, belayed below the line I'd chosen on Mayfair Buttress as I proceeded to dismantle the crag, before climbing *Violator*. In hindsight, it was a terrible route, one that has been almost written out of the modern guidebooks, but for me it was the beginning of an affinity I was to have with the place over the next few months.

The great thing about my return trips to Pen Trwyn, whether with Hazel or my other mates, was the delightful sense of live development it had about it. A vast array of superstars had chosen to congregate at the cliff: Jerry Moffatt, Andy Pollitt, Paul Williams, Tim Freeman, Chris and Dave Lyon and, of course, Ron Fawcett. The place had a carnival atmosphere. New routes were being put up across the entire length of the cliff, from relatively straightforward ones in the lower extremes, to those at the cutting-edge of difficulty for the time. No sooner had they been climbed but most were repeated almost instantly by the waiting hordes. And, in between, everyone would nip off to the now famous Parisella's café for ice cream and coffee. It was wonderful.

Interestingly, one of the most noticeable things about the development of Pen Trwyn at the time was the rather open-minded attitude towards fixed gear, particularly bolts. There were already a number of old aid bolts on Mayfair Buttress and the attitude was that if a route was felt to need a bolt, it might as well get one. Bolts weren't being placed everywhere, just 'minimally'. Of course I'd placed a handful of bolts previously, but this began to open my eyes more to the idea.

There was also a problem with the top of the cliff. Many of the routes disappeared into vegetation or even large rubble bands. With the close proximity of the road below, that presented something of a problem. One of the routes we repeated early on our visits was *Solid Gold* and I remember topping out and pulling off numerous fragments of rock before I reached the belay. Similarly, a number of the cliffs which had yet to be developed sprung directly from the road at the far end of the crag and ended at a horrendous band of rubble.

We thought long and hard about how to solve the problem, and I came up with the idea of placing bolts at the top of the cliff, as a sort of easier method of belaying or getting back down to the ground. This would negate the problems of loose rock and vegetation. I may not have been the first to place such lower-offs, but, certainly to me, they seemed a perfect solution.

Usually we would abseil in to clean and place any in-situ gear. On one occasion, I decided to climb up the gully to the left of my prospective line, ease across to the top of the route and place a bolt. It didn't turn out to be that straightforward; when I got to the top of the gully, I realised that the space to get to the top of the route was quite narrow. I crawled across the break on hands and knees to get to the top of the route and then hand-drilled the bolts. It was a relief to get back down to the road.

Downward Bound ...

After a relatively mellow trip to Lundy in July 1983, I returned to the Peak with a fresh initiative in mind. I'd added a couple of new routes to Pen Trwyn, but now my main focus was a line I had seen at Chee Tor, slap bang up the middle of the bald-looking face to the left of *Sergeyenna.* With a number of good hard routes under my belt from the week's trip to Lundy, I was confident of being able to do it.

I spent a while cleaning the line and fixed a couple of my trademark threads above the crux. I reckoned that, once I'd reached them, the route would be in the bag. The only problem I had was with the hard section, after leaving the sanctuary of a thin crack halfway up the route. It had a worryingly smooth appearance. While the climbing didn't look particularly hard, it did seem extremely bold for my somewhat nervous disposition. What pushed me on was Adam's confidence in my ability. I wasn't quite so sure.

When I reached the top of the crack, I placed two or three of what I thought were bomber wires and prepared myself for the short, technical crux. I stepped left and committed to the sequence without hesitation. Once I got through it, however, I realised that I'd led myself into a blind alley. I was just to the right of a good hold, from which I'd be able to clip the first thread. As much as I tried to reach the hold, the further away it felt. I quickly began to tire and decided that I had one last chance to do it. With one final lurch, I reached the hold and, just as I pulled the rope up to clip the thread, my foot slipped and down I went. With one fell swoop, I hurtled head-first to finish about three feet off the ground. I was mortified by the fall and turned into a blithering wreck. I wasn't going back up to do that again!

After retrieving my gear via a neighbouring route, we walked along the dale, chatting nervously about my fall. I wasn't happy about going on it again and needed something to give me confidence to have a more positive attempt.

Suddenly it came to me later that night, like a flash of light from above – *A Midnight Summer Dream*? The year before, I had witnessed Ron Fawcett climb his route *Tequila Mockingbird*, which lay within a stone's throw of my line. His route was, without doubt, at the cutting-edge of the British grading system at the time, a remarkable E6 7a. Ron, however, had chosen to place two protection bolts on the previously impregnable wall. I'd always envisaged Chee Tor as being a bolt-free zone, but my hero had taken this unusual step. I thought that this would be the resolution to the problem of the bold section of the route that I'd just fallen off, even if it was at a 'normal' grade.

Two days later, we were back to lay the ghost. I placed the bolt, everything went tickety-boo and the route was complete. It seemed remarkably easier through the placement of one bolt; although I'd challenged the boundaries of ethics before with a number of bolt placements, this one was on a whole new level. In my own mind, I felt the tide had turned, and that bolts were the future. Such an action would open up a whole new range of possibilities for my new routing.

As we walked down the dale, overjoyed with our achievement, we stopped and gazed up at the Cornice. Such an extensive section of cliff had little in the way of existing routes. Of course there were a few aid routes but very little else. We looked up in awe at a section of cliff that nobody had even bothered to aid but which seemed perfect for free routes at a grade that I could achieve.

'Perhaps we should just put a line of bolts up it and climb it ourselves,' I commented. Adam just smiled back at me in his inimitable fashion, and we walked out together. I knew exactly what he was thinking.

Clarion Call and all that

There is nothing predictable about anything in my climbing life. I had always been on a mission to achieve fame and fortune and had certainly gone against the establishment's principles (ethics) along the way. The criticism I was getting almost always washed over me: either that or I was so stubborn that I didn't care back then. I was driven; I reckoned that my fame meant that I could get away with anything.

I had slowly been persuaded by my own thinking that bolts were becoming the norm – or at least a mainstay in British climbing. I had been party to a significant movement on the North Wales coast, including the use of bolt belays. *A Midnight Summer Dream* had tipped me over the edge in deciding that the line I had spotted on the Cornice in Chee Dale was the logical next progression. I felt it was just 'the right time' to do it, even though I had little if any knowledge of what went on in other countries.

Having seen that prospective line on the Cornice, where only a smattering of free climbs existed, the placing of the five bolt runners and a lower-off felt the next logical step. I abseiled the line to thoroughly clean the dust and muck that coated the face, and it was ready to be climbed. I returned the following evening to climb it, having already chosen the name: *Clarion Call* was intended as a call to battle.

At E4 6a, this route was significantly below the cutting edge of the climbing grades of the time, but to me that was the whole point of the exercise. I'd seen the superstars placing bolts on the hardest routes of the day and didn't understand why bolts couldn't be used at any other grade. Why not on an HVS or an E2 if it made the route more enjoyable – a real anathema to British climbing? Or why not just construct a whole route with bolt protection? It was being done, via the old aid routes, so why not on a new line?

I decided to take the issue to the next level and see what such a litmus test of British climbing ethics would achieve. I had rarely cut corners; I'd rather just go direct to the heart of the matter.

My drive, my passion and my insatiable desire for new routes took me beyond the previous norms. It all just seemed the right thing to do at the time.

Once people knew about *Clarion Call*, it became popular immediately, with numerous ascents over the following weeks. Even before the news hit the climbing press, it was being talked about all over the Peak District and beyond. But the gossip wasn't about the user-friendly nature of the route, it wasn't about the quality of the route and it most certainly wasn't about me developing something that could become popular with climbers. No, it was about the sheer audacity of a young, disreputable climber placing five bolt runners on a piece of rock that could probably be climbed without. For me, the criticisms did, and still do, completely miss the point.

Before *Clarion Call* had gained general acceptance, two well known Sheffield climbers, Paul Mitchell and Andy Barker, decided that enough was enough. Within a month of the first ascent, they took it upon themselves to remove the six bolt hangers from the route.

I was duly informed that the route had been stripped. On my next visit to Stoney Café the following weekend, I discovered that the hangers had been left for me behind the counter with an accompanying note from Paul and Andy, explaining their actions.

I wrote back to Paul, whose address was on the letter, explaining that while I appreciated the hangers being returned, what about the expense of the bolts in the rock? The outcome was amusing, in that Paul returned the cost of half of the bolts – the princely sum of £3 – but affirmed that, as Andy had been party to their removal, he owed me the money for the rest. I still chuckle now when I read Paul's letter.

Looking back today over the events surrounding *Clarion Call*, it makes me think about the positive effect it ultimately had. It was undoubtedly the first intentional sport climb in Britain. The following year, Nick Dixon climbed the route without the bolt runners but with a handful of pegs as protection. And now the route is back to its original form, with one less bolt. It is generally recognised as one of the warm-ups on a crag that is today littered with high-class sport climbs – one of the most important venues of its type in the country.

I suppose the latter point suggests that my thought processes were significantly more advanced than most people's on the issue of bolt protection. Or was it just a pure case of greed? Sport climbing has since become accepted in this country and many other countries. I'd like to think that *Clarion Call* was pivotal to such development in the UK.

Chapter 6

To Bolt or Not to Bolt

MY PERSONAL LIFE was never 'put on hold' despite all the climbing that I did. I now had a full-time job and worked voluntarily for my lifelong football team (which meant going to as many matches as possible), and the Stranglers filled my life with music. Most important of all, I had a wedding coming up.

Hazel and I had known each other for around four years when we decided to get married. Whether it was me proposing to Hazel or vice versa, it just seemed the right thing to do. Hazel had been my 'one and only' girlfriend. In the autumn of 1983, we bought a house halfway between our places of work. Hazel had been renting near Hanley Park, and it felt like 'dead money'. She moved into the new house, and I continued living with my parents.

We picked the date of 17th March and planned a simple wedding with just a few lunchtime guests and a home-made evening do, inviting everybody we could think of. Hazel's parents had given us £1,000 to do with as we saw fit. We thought it prudent to spend some on furnishing the house, hence our not splashing out too much on the wedding.

The arrangements were easy to make. My mum and Betty, my future mother-in-law, had sorted out the food for the evening. In the meantime, there was climbing to be done. We'd heard on the grapevine of a climbing area near Llangollen, and, after a bit of detective work, discovered a line of excellent limestone crags with loads of potential.

There was no guidebook to the area as yet; however, in the early part of 1984, Stuart Cathcart, who had been developing the area somewhat in isolation, published his own guidebook. We – that is the Stoke team, Adam Hudson, Andy Popp, Nick Dixon, James 'Barry' Barrett and me – needed little more enticement.

But we weren't the only ones aiming to tap the area's potential. John Codling, someone I knew relatively well, and John Moulding, were also very active there. I thought of them as Punch and Judy, due to the tiffs that they always appeared to be having. In terms of cleaning and climbing, a couple of months of hide and seek ensued, and, in the depths of a cold and frosty winter, we managed to climb a number of excellent routes. The relatively competitive environment enhanced it still further.

However, as March came around, our wedding became our sole focus of attention. Hazel is an extremely adept seamstress and made her own dress, while I bought my first-ever suit. Nowadays, when I try it on, I've put on so much bulk that I can't even get my arm inside the trouser leg.

We were getting married at noon, and my dad had decided to go to work on the morning of our wedding. A friend had lent us a white car. By 11.45 a.m. my dad still wasn't home. It was a ten-minute drive to the registry office. At 11.50 a.m. he waltzed in, said, 'I don't know what you're worrying about,' got himself ready and off we went. I think my mum was on the verge of a nervous breakdown.

As we met at the altar, Hazel looked radiant in her jade-coloured suit. She was the love of my life and she still is, and I will never forget that wonderful moment. We had a lovely, private lunchtime gathering with all our close family celebrating alongside us.

The evening do was at the local community centre near to my mum and dad's house, and we even invited Geoff and Jackie Birtles, and Ron and Gill Fawcett. Unfortunately Ron couldn't come but we were graced with the presence of everybody else. My abiding memory is of our climbing mates dancing with Hazel's auntie Sadie and other relatives. It's an evening that Hazel and I will cherish for the rest of our lives.

However, by the next morning you'd have thought I'd completely forgotten all about it, such was our (my!) chosen honeymoon destination. By 8 a.m., we were sitting in Strensham services on the M5, having raced down the motorway, heading for Wintour's Leap. We planned to go on holiday to Tenby, followed by a trip up to Llandudno. We had very little money back then, and Hazel seemed quite happy to follow my lead in terms of spending time in these areas, despite my ulterior motives.

I had already arranged a climbing day with Matt Ward on the Sunday, and then we would go off to Tenby. We hadn't booked any accommodation, deciding just to wing it. I'd read about my hero Ron Fawcett and his wife Gill doing new routes on their honeymoon – so why not us? In fact, they had named one of them *Honeymoon Blues,* which encouraged me still further.

We arrived at the crag quite early and Matt, who lived nearby, was waiting to meet us. I already had three routes cleaned and, after a bit of tinkering, we ticked them off comparatively quickly. In similar fashion to Ron and Gill, I had to go and call one of them *We've Got the Honeymoon Blues Two.* Next stop: Pembroke.

The Beast from the Undergrowth

Prior to my wedding, I had spent a stag weekend with my mates in Pembroke. While there, we had been looking at a few new lines in Huntsman's Leap. These were mainly on the South Wall, due to the North Wall suffering seepage after the winter. One of the routes I wanted to do would need a big cleaning effort and the other would need a big climbing effort. I decided that my honeymoon week would be the ideal opportunity to do them.

One of the lines was a 'field of grass', but that had never deterred me before. When cleaning new routes, there is no greater joy than when grass peels off easily in big chunks. You could hear the clods landing in the sea and turning it muddy brown as it receded with the tide. I jumared out, feeling pretty chuffed with myself. As I reappeared over the cliff edge, Hazel took one glance at me and said, 'You look like the beast from the undergrowth.' So there was its name, even before we set foot on the line.

The next day we were back for the blank wall to its right. I had chosen to clean it the previous evening, testing out the moves as well; we just had to wait for the tide to go out, and *The Pulsebeat*, as I called it, was finished. While we were there, I decided to have a look at a diagonal line on the wall directly opposite. There appeared to be a series of good holds and scoops that connected it all together. I gave it three separate abseil inspections and cleared off a fair amount of loose rock, as well as scraping the mud out of cracks for nut placements and placing a couple of threads. However it was still a little wet in places, and so I decided to wait until I was back with my brother over the Easter weekend.

The remainder of our honeymoon was a much more tranquil affair. We did some more climbing on the Ormes, but the main focus was just spending time together, going to the local cinema and just having a good time.

In Llandudno we went for a meal at a Chinese restaurant towards the top of Mostyn Street. To be honest, I'm not the greatest fan of Chinese food, but it was a nice meal all the same. After the main course, Hazel had a look at the dessert menu and decided to have apple pie. 'With cream?' the waiter asked. 'But of course,' Hazel replied. When it arrived, we both fell about laughing. It was a Mr Kipling's apple pie, still in its tinfoil wrapper. I don't think Hazel has ordered apple pie at a restaurant since.

The last two nights of our honeymoon were to be spent in Buxton, as I had been invited to the BMC Conference, to take part in a panel debate on bolting. Fellow panellists were Jill Lawrence (anti-bolt), Paul Nunn (anti-bolt) and Don Whillans (couldn't give a damn) and it was being chaired by Ken Wilson. For a bit of fun, I decided to dress up for the event as a member of the 'ACME Bolting Company' with bits of in-situ gear hanging off my boiler suit. Ken wasn't too impressed and berated me for it, until Don Whillans stepped in and told him to shut up.

Looking back, I can't remember much of the discussion, save that they lambasted me for the placing of bolts in Chee Dale and elsewhere, but I can stand up for myself when I have to and the discussion just fizzled out.

During that weekend, Phil and I got into a discussion with Pat Littlejohn about some of the lines in Huntsman's Leap which I had cleaned and prepared, most specifically the diagonal line across the North Wall which Phil and I were planning to do over the Easter weekend. As a courtesy, I asked Pat to leave it for us until we had a chance to try it. Without any hesitation, he said he would.

Shortly afterwards, despite our discussion, he went ahead and did the line. I was so livid that Phil and I repeated it over the Easter weekend and, in sheer stupidity backdated our ascent. I had chosen the name *The Badlands*, which now seems sadly ironic (moronic?), as opposed to Littlejohn's *Witch Hunt*.

Letter after letter ensued: the magazines berating me for my appalling ethical stance on the matter; even the Climbers Club became involved. They told me that this was counter to the traditions of British climbing. In a spirit of peacekeeping, they agreed to leave matters there unless any further instances occurred. Of course they were right to berate me for what I had done but they were unaware of the discussions which had preceded the event, not that this justifies any of my actions over it.

'*Gary had spent a considerable amount of time cleaning a new route in Huntsman's Leap, only for it to be "picked off" by Pat Littlejohn the following weekend and subsequently named* Witch Hunt. *The arguments that followed are history now but the way he rounded on Gary with a letter he sent about him "tinkering" with the route and littering it with coloured threads seemed hypocritical and arrogant. This was particularly so, given that Littlejohn, in describing his first ascent of* Darkinbad the Brightdayler *at Pentire Head, in* Mountain *magazine, had admitted to abseiling the route and pre-placing gear.*' Phil Gibson

Shorncliffe

In between visits to Pembroke, we had heard a rumour that in the Wye Valley there was an impressive crag that had yet to be developed. Matt and I had only a vague idea of where it might be. Apparently it overlooked Tintern Abbey and was below a well known obelisk of rock nicknamed Pulpit Rock. We had a good look around the forest below Pulpit Rock, but, after three or four efforts thrashing around in the undergrowth, began to believe that the rumour had no substance to it and was just that, a rumour.

One night, about three weeks after our last failed attempt, I received a phone call from Matt. Now Matt, lovable person that he was, is quite reticent but on this occasion, I couldn't believe the tone of his voice when he proclaimed that he'd found it.

Unfortunately Hazel and I were off to Pembroke for the week but arranged to meet Matt on our way home to go and have a look at the place. Matt had tagged the path to the crag with some climber's tape, and, after a bit of a bushwack through the vegetation, we arrived at the foot of this almost pristine, eighty-foot limestone slab. We just couldn't believe it – pure gold!

We had found Shorncliffe: a wonderful crag with a wealth of relatively easy-grade opportunities along its length. Although I returned on just a few more occasions, for Matt it provided the honeypot he needed to get his new routing tally up to a significant level. Unbeknown to us, the crag had been climbed on before by Roy Thomas and his mates, but had fallen into disrepair, and the ever encroaching ivy had engulfed it. I'm really glad to have been part of its rediscovery.

My Armistice Day

Having had my wrists slapped because of my bolting on the Cornice in Chee Dale, I had begun to rethink my strategy over the new routes I was going to climb there. I remained absolutely convinced that this had been the right approach for the development of the cliff; however, due to the weight of opposition (resentment) to my actions, I didn't want to incur the same hostility again so soon. I may be stubborn in my approach to things, but I could only take so much abuse in a given period of time.

I was still prepared to add the odd bolt here and there because other climbers had done the same, but I wasn't prepared to go full bore until the tide had begun to turn; if it was ever going to. Instead, I went more minimalist with some of my lines, perhaps the most pertinent being *Armistice Day* immediately to the right of *Clarion Call*. Here was a line that I peppered with a ragbag bunch of in-situ gear, including one bolt, two pegs, a hammered-in nail from the railway track and a RURP (Realised Ultimate Reality Piton). It was effectively a sport route but it didn't have a plethora of bolts. There was no criticism in the magazines.

Of course nowadays *Armistice Day* is a fully bolted sport route, one of many on that cliff.

The great Ken Wilson

Throughout the spring and summer, a regular event on Tuesday nights in the Peak District was a meeting of Manchester area climbers, nicknamed the Altrincham All-Stars. Among these were such people as Martin Boysen, Ian Dunn and Ken Wilson. They would choose the crag they were going to meet at and follow it with a beer or two in a pub closest to the cliff they had climbed on. Occasionally I would bump into them and enjoy their company and banter.

A line I had been looking at on the Cornice in Chee Dale was, more often than not, seeping, due to a stream that emanated from the cliff above it. By chance, in the middle of July, it had completely dried out, and I decided to have a look to see if it could be climbed. After a lot of cleaning and the placement of some fixed gear, including a couple of bolts and a peg, I was very pleased to realise that it would go. Unfortunately I was on my own and had no one to belay me; unlike today, the Cornice was a relatively neglected crag, with very few routes.

I wondered what to do and decided to see if there was anybody climbing on Chee Tor, which was a little way downstream. There on the other side, to my surprise, were the Altrincham All-Stars. I paddled across to see if I knew anyone. Among the throng of climbers at the foot of the cliff was Ken Wilson, who I knew slightly. Rather cheekily, I asked Ken if he would hold my ropes on the new line I'd just cleaned, and he replied he would be only too happy to do so. I told him where to find me, and he joined me around twenty minutes later.

I loved Ken for what he was, what he brought to British rock climbing and what his opinions were, despite the fact that they conflicted completely with mine over in-situ gear, most specifically bolts. Without a dissenting murmur, he held my ropes on *Up the River Without a Paddle.* He will always have my deepest respect for that.

South Wales climbing, here I come!

I have always been enthusiastic about visiting other climbing areas across England and Wales, and after bumping into Tony Penning at Wintour's Leap, it wasn't long before we were visiting South Wales at his invitation. This was an area I knew relatively little about, save for what I had read in the magazines which, to be honest, wasn't much. Tony was particularly enthusiastic about a superb, untouched and somewhat protectionless section of wall that he felt should by now have been climbed. He thought I might be the person to do it, although he didn't elucidate any further until we got down there.

Tony and his wife, Lynn, lived in the relatively tranquil village of Blackwood in the South Wales valleys. He was working at the local Curry's store as a sales manager – and what a sales manager he was! He had certainly sold this virgin piece of rock to me, save for the fact that he felt, with its unprotected nature, it might need a bolt. My reputation had clearly spread by the autumn of 1984.

Not being from the local area, I knew very little of local climbing ethics. Yet, to be honest, if I felt a bolt would give me a better chance of doing a new route with less chance of getting hurt, I would certainly consider placing one. The challenge was on, even though I hadn't yet seen the line.

Morlais Quarry was a fairly bleak place, with relatively little protection from the elements. It was a pleasant enough day, and as I abseiled down the line, I realised very quickly that it was completely devoid of protection. Tony was certainly right about that.

One line, which had been done on the right-hand side of the wall had a bunch of pegs in it for protection. I therefore decided to place a bolt in the new line to protect its crux. I have always regarded pegs as unnatural protection, in that you have to bang them in with a hammer. At the time, I saw little difference between that and a bolt, and I always perceived their origins to be from aid climbing anyway. Making a distinction seemed a bit pointless to me.

That evening at Tony's house, there was at knock on the door; Tony had invited around John Harwood round, a friend of his. John had seconded Andy Sharp on the first ascent of the other route on the wall. He certainly wasn't too happy about the fact that I had challenged local ethics by placing a bolt and told me so in no uncertain terms. He felt it should have been left as a last great problem until someone with enough courage could climb the line without such an 'offensive' piece of ironmongery.

It was obvious that Tony had well and truly set me up for this; however, for my part I thought I had done the right thing. I was shocked to find that someone could decide the ethics of climbing in this way and dictate to others how it should be.

Naturally the discussion which ensued was, at best, conflicted. John was appalled that I'd brought my ethical style to his neck of the woods. For my part, I was having none of it. At the end of the evening, we agreed to disagree over my ethical stance on the aforesaid new route. It felt appropriate that I had named it *Rogues Gallery*.

Lundy calling ... again

Interestingly, by 1984, Hazel still hadn't been to Lundy, nor had a number of my mates. To resolve this, I booked 'East and West' for the last week in July. Hazel probably had an image of some grandiose building on the edge of the island, alongside the Old Lighthouse.

As we arrived at our abode for the week, I can still remember the look of disappointment on Hazel's face. That she had injured her ankle a few weeks earlier and wasn't in climbing mode must have dampened the experience even further. We had only been married for a few months, and I had brought her to this.

My frantic drive for new routes went straight into action as soon as we landed on the island.

I had it mapped out from previous visits, and the fact that I had been invited by the Royal Navy and Royal Marines Mountaineering Club (RN&RMMC) to write the next guidebook provided me with even more ammunition to get going. They must have assumed that I would go to the island and check out all the existing routes. Obviously they didn't know me too well.

Between swimming, a little bit of sunbathing and fooling around, I had spied this wonderful face of green sea grass, beneath which I thought I could spy a thin crack running the full height of the wall. As is the case with most Lundy situations, you are never quite sure what you are going to get until you start brushing the thing clean. So, the next day, armed with the usual array of cleaning paraphernalia, including a flat toilet-brush I had brought from home, the wall revealed what I had thought from the very outset: a wonderful crackline leading to a perfect headwall finish. It provided one of the best routes of its grade on the island; *The Indy 500* took more work to clean than it did to climb.

I had always wanted to do a new route alongside one of Pat Littlejohn's iconic test pieces on the island. I'd read so much about them in the magazines and guidebooks. The year before, I had seen this wonderful strip of wall at the back of Deep Zawn which was crossed and recrossed by *The Stone Tape*: I wondered if it could be climbed direct. With a bit of cleaning, it provided a route of which, even today, I am particularly proud. We gained it by a long abseil into a stance, well above sea-level, thus avoiding the inconveniences of a tidal access.

This was the complete ethical opposite to most new routes done previously on the island. Generally people had climbed on sight or with a limited amount of cleaning, where necessitated by the vegetation and line. But I was prepared to tackle the issues in a way that I thought best for me, and that I had used everywhere else.

I took a similar view of in-situ gear. For sure, pegs had been used previously on the island, and I came with plenty of those, but I also brought along my bolt driver. Others had similar intentions on sea cliffs in other areas of Britain, examples being Rowland Edwards in Cornwall and Ron Fawcett's *The Cad* on Gogarth. I had read about these and thought it perfectly acceptable that I should do the same on Lundy.

I placed a bolt apiece on a couple of routes, one on the Diamond and one on Flying Buttress. I was pretty chuffed with my efforts, which meant I could write them up in the new guide and think little of the long-term consequences of my actions.

Paradoxically, the final route of our week was to prove the complete antithesis of my exploits with the bolt driver. On a visit to the Parthenos, I had seen a wonderful line weaving in-between the overhangs from atop a thin, inviting flake. I had given it a cursory clean, but it looked a little too bold for my liking. I chose instead to take a sojourn to the Marisco Tavern with Matt for some beer-fuelled encouragement. An hour later, my boldness increased by a couple of pints, I managed to summon up the courage to lead the line and name it *Cithaeron*.

Maybe I could have climbed the other routes without the bolts, but I chose not to. I'm still not sure whether this was due to the pressure of external factors, such as the influence of other climbers using bolts, or my complete ignorance, or even disrespect, for local ethics and styles. My view, looking back, is probably that external factors were influencing my actions, but in future years it was certainly I who was the driving force.

In the spring of 1985, my first-ever full guidebook was published by the RN&RMMC. Although I had contributed to a number of other guidebooks, as well as writing a 'Recent Developments' pamphlet to the Peak District, this was the first fully-fledged guidebook with my name on it. I had relied on work done by a number of other writers, but this was a landmark achievement for me.

I had, where possible, tried to develop my literary skills, as well as doing the groundwork on the existing routes on the island. However, in retrospect, it was a vehicle to publicise my routes in print, so much so that photos of my routes were on both front and rear covers. No one, other than me, could know them better or have a more inflated view of them.

On the back of this, we were invited to the annual dinner of the club at Tyn-y-Coed in Capel Curig. We had been offered a free evening meal and accommodation for the night, in return for a short talk on the island's climbing,

What we hadn't realised before we arrived was that this was a proper bib-and-tucker do with the appropriate dress code of suit, shirt and bow tie. And to cap it all, the president of the club was none other than the Admiral of the Fleet.

After the opening formalities, we were introduced to the club members, some of whom I knew by name, but not by face, through correspondence. The Admiral himself was an extremely interesting and engaging man. We had a long and informative chat about many things including the Royal Navy, and my interest in climbing. As we finally got around to eating, I noticed something odd. I hadn't realised that there was a certain form at the dinner table. Both Hazel and I had started eating, but nobody else in the room had. Nor had the Admiral.

Then it became clear. The Admiral was engrossed in discussion with me and with every move he made to start eating, you could see everybody else about to start too. Then the Admiral would put down his knife and fork, and the sigh of disappointment from the club members was almost audible. This went on for about five or ten minutes until, at last, the Admiral really did start eating, and everybody else in the room started their food as well. This was the form of which we were completely unaware; they must have thought us particularly impertinent.

The Diamond beckons

The main focus of my interest a year later was the Diamond, the left-hand side of the face having not yet been climbed. We had arrived with the intention of putting that to rest, as well as putting the guidebook out of date. With Matt and Simon Whalley, we certainly had the manpower and ability. All we needed was the time to clean the routes and the right conditions to climb them.

The journey to the island presented more of a problem than usual; the winds were particularly strong and it wasn't until we reached the jetty on the lee side of the island that we were finally away from the gale. I have never been a good sea traveller, and I'd been sick a couple of times en route; however I wasn't alone in that respect, as the boat's cook had been sick at least twice in the galley as well.

Luckily for us, certain sections of the most southerly part of the island were sheltered from the breeze, which gave us a good start to the week, but we still made a few journeys to get stuck into the cleaning efforts on the Diamond itself. For this, fortune was certainly on our side. One of the assets of the wind was that when you cleaned away the sea grass, it blew back up the face, not back down onto it, meaning that there was less effort involved – even if our faces were covered in the remnants of the stuff by the end of the day.

After a number of trips up and down the island, cleaning our 'stripes' in the face – I had cleaned one, Matt one and Simon one – and trying to get onto our lines, the wind abated on the Thursday, and we could get onto mine.

I had chosen the most central feature of the cliff, a superb line of delicate and intricate face-climbing, culminating in a 'butch' sequence of moves to finish the thing off. I had placed three bolt-runners – one on the first pitch and two on the second – to protect the line, as well as an in-situ nut; it just made the whole thing feel balanced. I hadn't got enough micro-wires for the placements on the route anyway.

I was so chuffed with the thing. It was just the type of climbing that I enjoyed: technical and intricate in the extreme, sustained but not on the strenuous side. You just needed strong calf muscles. I also loved the rock, so pure and clean – well, save for the indiscretions of my three bolts and the in-situ nut, of course. All we had to do was finish off the other two lines, the next day.

I had already decided on the name of the route and writing it up in the Marisco Tavern logbook had become common practice. *Watching the Ocean*, a lyric from one of my favourite Stranglers' tracks, remains, even today, one of my all-time favourite climbs, perhaps enhanced by events that were to happen four years later.

Sadly for us, the following day was extremely windy: Mark 7 on the Beaufort scale. As we walked up the island, forcing ourselves into the headwind, we knew only too well that we couldn't get onto the face and would have to settle for other routes in a more secluded bay on the island. I vowed to return in the autumn for the lines.

Unfortunately Steve Boydon and Paul Harrison had also been on the island while we'd been trying to grab all of the available rock on the Diamond. They'd had the same intentions, but since we had got there first (they'd had an even worse journey than ours) they decided to leave us to it. However the wind played into their hands. After we left, they finished off the remaining lines on our behalf, including a superb diagonal traverse of the face, which we hadn't even considered.

Paul and I have known each other for years, certainly long enough to tease each other mercilessly. When Steve had climbed one of 'our' lines on the face, they toyed with the idea of naming it '*Too Goey for Gary*' as a jibe at my use of bolt protection. Steve eventually named it *Wild Heart*.

I was so frustrated that I just had to come back in the autumn for revenge. We couldn't get to the island by its normal route from Bideford;

instead we sailed on a small dory from Clovelly. By chance, we were accompanied on the boat by two other island regulars: Chris 'Boris' Gilbert and Doug Kerr.

Like a pair of kids, Doug and I sat in the back of the little dory on the way over to the island. It didn't take long for us to realise our error. Neither of us was very good at travelling on a boat, and it wasn't long before we were heaving up. Solid ground couldn't come soon enough.

It was one of the best weeks of new routing I ever had on the island. I was climbing very strongly and was hyper-motivated by having lost out to Steve with the routes on the Diamond. Of course my bolt driver was still at hand for one or two routes, but the week's prime focus was an attempt at a line Steve had been trying without success himself: a crackline underneath the arch of Flying Buttress. I was so surprised to climb it without drama; it must have been due to all those years of crack-climbing education I'd received from Phil. I also had an apposite name as a riposte to Steve's efforts on the Diamond: *Brinkman's Ship.*

Frozen solid

I love the winter months; they always seem to give you a break from the routine of the summer and allow you to focus on a little bit of training at a local climbing wall. By now, these were slowly developing across the country, and we had starting using one in Altrincham. A bunch of us would travel up there twice a week, honing our strength on the problems and doing a few 'reps' on a pull-up bar. I'd met a few enthusiastic lads from Biddulph, and that transposed in the winter months, as soon as the weather was dry and frosty, to trips outdoors, with my focus usually on somewhere quick-drying, such as Pen Trwyn.

With a carload of mates and a bellyful of enthusiasm, we spent a number of days over the winter months developing sections of the cliff, hitherto relatively untouched. The only problem was that the only dry section of crag was also very, very cold. Now that has never bothered me before but for Hazel and my mates, it was a bit of a trauma, and for our dog, Dill, it was even more concerning. The water in his bowl froze over in about ten minutes.

The other issue was that I couldn't test whether my new fitness levels had improved with the training, as the routes we were doing were only up to about E4, as well as being rather bouldery and short. The fitness test would have to wait until it got a little warmer. A fortnight's trip to Pembroke was planned.

In the spring, Pembroke had become the prime target of our attentions. I'd become a member of the Climbers Club (the old adage of: 'I wouldn't be a member of a club that would have me as a member' didn't ring true!), which gave us the opportunity to use their hut facilities within shouting distance of St Govan's Head. We'd booked a two-week holiday, blocked out our clinical work and booked into the Climbers Club 'hotel' for the fortnight. As chance would have it, the army firing-range was open for the entire fortnight, the weather was dry and settled, and the place was empty.

En route to the hut, I wanted to lay to rest the ghost of a route I'd been trying at Pen Trwyn over the past year. It seemed logical to try it on the Saturday as we travelled down to Pembroke, and, to my surprise, I managed it first go. I was shocked; the training had certainly had the effect that I hoped it would, and our trip to Pembroke provided the avalanche of new routes that I had intended: I was particularly proud of one that I named *Orange Robe Burning.*

In the meantime, we'd heard all about a venue in the South Wales valleys by the name of Dinas Rock. It had been mentioned in the magazines, and we thought we may as well pop in, as it was only a short detour from the start of the 'Heads of the Valleys Road', on our return home from Pembroke.

I was taken aback by the amount of unclimbed rock there. Shallow grooves, overlaps, hanging slabs, roofs and line after line after line – the only problem being what looked like a dearth of protection, probably the main reason for its being so virgin. Since I had already trampled on the ethics of the area with my 'bolted' ascent of *Rogues Gallery,* I decided on a reconnaissance of a line on the right-hand side of the main wall that appeared to have some good protection opportunities. Sure enough, after a brief jumar ascent, I was relieved that the line had a number of threads and small wire placements for it to be climbed without too much controversy.

While this route, *Spain*, as I called it, tackled such a blatant feature, I had enough time to have a look at the shallow snaking groove in the centre of the cliff. From below, it looked possible but had no obvious gear placements, and from abseil it was just so. I couldn't get any pegs in above the low roof, so, while I was at it, I placed two bolts which could just about protect the route, but without over-protecting it; they would suffice. I wasn't against boldness on routes – I never have been – but you analyse things in your mind's eye and make a decision. In this instance, a classic line furnished with just the right amount of fixed gear seemed the right way forward.

With *Berlin*, I again took my personal stand on a climbing ethic in an area where perhaps I had no right to do so. Rather than follow local custom, I was happy to climb the routes in a way that I saw fit, firmly believing that the practice of in-situ gear was here to stay. Some chose to try and do my routes without the bolts. They chose to top-rope them first, before trying to lead them, but my view was that this was simply another way of bringing the route down to your level, as I had done with the bolts.

I wasn't the greatest climber of the day, but why shouldn't I, just like the next man, enjoy a great piece of climbing on a wonderful piece of rock? Elitism, to me, seemed to make climbing inaccessible to the common man, which I just couldn't understand. I didn't believe that the elite of the climbing world, or those who dictated ethics, should have the right to tell me how I should climb my new routes. I believed all along that the climbing establishment needed shaking up, and I had every intention of doing so.

Too Jugless ...

Throughout the winter months, Hazel and I would often walk through the dales with our dog, Dill. Apart from it being refreshing exercise, we had the chance to see some of the cliffs more clearly, with the foliage less prevalent than in summer and autumn.

On one such occasion, when walking through Chee Dale, I saw two friends, Paul Harrison and Doug Kerr, cleaning sections of rock on the right-hand side of the Cornice. I had planned to do these lines myself and felt a little disappointed that they had beaten me to it. Generally, I won't pinch lines that other people have cleaned. Nevertheless, this was to be an exception.

Towards the end of April, I was back in the dale and realised that Doug hadn't returned to his line, which by now had completely dried out. Then, all of a sudden, I had a cheeky idea. The following day I was back. I banged in a peg, placed a thread and Hazel and I climbed the line. The story doesn't end there. A couple of days later I was in Stoney café and, as usual, I wrote the route up in the new route book, waiting for Doug and his team to see my success at his expense.

I'm told that when Doug came across the route name, he didn't get the irony nor did he appreciate my stealing the line from him. However his mates were vastly amused. I'd named the route *Too Jugless for Dougless* and from then on they referred to him as Jug, rather than Doug.

Bolts and boldness

By the mid-1980s my attitude to bolts was fairly well established, albeit to a lesser degree than today's fully bolted sport routes. However the tide of public opinion was still against my idea of how routes should be developed. With the odd bolt or two here and there, I once again cast my net across Chee Dale, wishing that I could just bolt the routes from top to bottom, while at the same time, questioning what reaction that might bring. *Cosmopolitan*, so-named to identify the international attitude towards bolts, *Case Adjourned* and *Open Gate* were all meant to be provocative statements about my position. With the latter, the name had an added meaning to it; I had placed one bolt on the headwall, which was committing to clip as well as to leave. Just as I finished the route, I looked down to see that the gate on the karabiner had indeed opened, and my rope had become unclipped from it. Could there have been a ghost in the machine?

These routes were on relatively unfrequented sections of the dale but I was determined to add more routes to Chee Tor. I took something of a contradictory stance to my previous route *A Midnight Summer Dream* by not placing any more bolts there. I had chosen a relatively short wall on the right-hand side of the crag. After cleaning it, I realised there was no one around to hold my ropes, so I decided to try and solo it instead – the complete antitheses of my well-protected, bolted ascents. As I remember, it was cold and my fingers were numb, but I was still confident I could do it. As I got towards the top, a small flake hold broke, and I tumbled backwards, landing on my feet with a thud in the muddy bank below. Give up? No chance! I dusted myself down and just went back up and did it, calling it, somewhat appropriately, *Hot Aches.*

This was the new routing game I was playing and it perhaps illustrates the variety of ways I sought to achieve my goal. I wasn't driven to bolt and peg up everything, as I was quite happy, when the mood suited me, to climb bold routes. Ultimately it was about achieving my goal. The fervour for new routes had well and truly become my driving force in climbing. Looking back, some of the lunacy I indulged in was bizarre.

One such example was during a weekend we spent in Pembroke. My brother had been commissioned to produce a number of crag drawings for the forthcoming guidebook. As his expenses were being paid, Hazel and I took the opportunity to grab a free lift with him.

I'd seen a really good-looking line on Trevallen Cliff, which seemed a little bold for my usual tastes. Walking back along the crag while Phil sat behind a boulder drawing the cliff, I decided to test my boldness by soloing up *Sunlover,* a route I knew quite well from a previous ascent. I don't know what Phil must have thought as I appeared above the line of boulders, wandering up the wall without a rope.

It set the tone for the weekend. I managed the new route, which ironically included a big fall, hence *Abandon Ship.* While I was at it, I thought I'd retrieve a jammed nut from just below the crux of *Barbarella.* I assumed that, once I'd removed it, it would be easy to reverse back down to the ground. How wrong I was! I got to the nut, only to find I was totally committed. Phil and Hazel were within shouting distance but had no rope or gear with them. My only solution was to solo the rest of the route – a rather sobering conclusion to the day, even though I got a new nut as a reward.

The Emerald Isle

Until then I hadn't really travelled abroad, except when my brother had us going to the Dolomites. However John Codling invited us on a week-long summer trip to Ireland. John had previously visited Ireland on a handful of occasions, sampling the delights of the new route potential, as well as making friends with one or two of the locals. He spoke passionately about the cliffs of Fair Head and the Mournes and their potential.

He had chosen the Burren in County Clare as our first port of call, but before that we would rendezvous with Martin Manson, a friend of John's, who lived just to the south of Belfast. By now, the legendary tales of an 'Ulster fry' had percolated to my taste buds and, sure enough, after a long and tiring journey via Stranraer, we were rewarded the following morning with just such a breakfast – the rumours were in fact true. Next stop the Burren.

When we arrived, we found a wonderfully disparate caravan site where we could stay for the few nights we were there. Better still, there was a pub, McDonagh's, close at hand. This was just what I thought Ireland was about. Wonderful people, a quiet and barren (not Burren) landscape and a pub with all the charm of the Irish – in the corner sat a trio of squeeze-box, penny whistle and violin. And the Guinness was the best I have ever tasted.

As for the climbing, I couldn't believe my eyes! The Burren's main attraction was the legendary Mirror Wall, almost a 100-yard expanse of clean, darkened limestone, plunging straight into the sea. And it only had two routes on it. Added to that, the cliffs bordering its edges had numerous lines calling out to be climbed. A few months earlier I'd seen a photo in a magazine of a route which had an impressive arête to its right. The route in the magazine was named *Wall of Fossils*, and I had already named the arête *Fall of Wossils* as it came 'out of' that route.

We were like kids in a toyshop. The sea-washed lines needed hardly any cleaning and were all to my liking: technical wall climbing not covered in jugs but a face climber's dream. The only problem was that the Mirror Wall was tidal, which would limit us to a five-hour window. That didn't stop us, though, as we managed to bag four routes.

The only problem was that the one line I had cleaned was only possible at dead low tide, and the next day we were about to head north for Fair Head. I had a simple solution. Get up at 5 a.m. and climb the route, something I have done on a number of occasions over the years. Hence, in line with the theme of the wall, I named it *Prism Sentence*, which was exactly what it had been for Hazel.

Our next stop was to be Fair Head. John knew it well, understood the layout of the crag and had our itinerary planned. He had also chosen where to stay. After an evening in a local pub, we were whisked off by John to our abode for the night. Little did we know why we had been to the pub before it went dark! It was drizzling heavily, and the mist was rolling around the fields as we drove down country lanes and along a very muddy track. Finally we arrived at our accommodation.

We found ourselves in the upstairs section of a cowshed – that's really what it was, I'm not being cynical. Downstairs were the living quarters for two cows, which were happily steaming away as we slept above them. It was an awful night's sleep. Rats scurried around the damp confines of our 'bedroom'. The next morning, the ladies informed John in no uncertain terms that we were going to stay at a bed and breakfast in Ballycastle from then on. He couldn't say no.

Ballycastle was a lovely but odd little place. In the centre of town was a set of traffic lights with a chip shop on one corner and the Rendezvous restaurant on the other. Debbie and Hazel didn't fancy fish and chips, so the Rendezvous it was to be.

As I recall, John did choose fish and chips, and the rest of us ordered chicken and chips. When the food arrived, John's appeared to be steaming hot but mine looked half-cold, and it was. None of the three chicken portions were properly cooked: they looked raw in the middle. The waiter, who also worked in the chip shop across the road at the same time (!), apologised and took the food away to be cooked properly. When it came back, the chicken was perfect. But when I popped a piece of cucumber into my mouth, it too was piping hot. Sure enough, they'd put the whole lot in the microwave, chicken, chips and salad. I've never eaten hot cucumber since.

I was completely blown away by the magnitude of Fair Head, its distinctive columnar shape and its vast swathes of untouched rock. As we surveyed the Grey Man's Path area, John pointed out a route here and a route there. In between, though, was an incredible, slim groove-line piercing the entire height of the cliff.

In one or two sections, the groove appeared completely devoid of protection, and so I hammered in a couple of pegs, which was against the traditions of the area. I was even more challenged by the lack of an appropriate belay at the end of the second pitch. Sure, there was a huge expanding flake that I could get a Friend 3 behind, but there was no way I intended to rely on that alone. Without any thought of the consequences, I felt that a bolt belay would be the logical solution.

At the time, I was very pleased with my route, *North Winds Blowing.* The line and climbing were fantastic, and, to my mind, the bolt was entirely justified in view of the dearth of natural protection. It remained to be seen whether my antics would be accepted by the locals. We were to find out when we returned the following year.

One thousand and counting

Towards the end of 1984, I was getting very close to a personal goal – completing my thousandth new route. I was also getting a bit of sponsorship from Troll and Berghaus. Troll would provide me with their new prototype harnesses to test, as well as the offcuts of their webbing, which I could use for in-situ threads. Berghaus gave me boots from Scarpa. For their part, when Troll heard of my thousandth new route, they wanted to film it as a product promotion. This seemed a strange idea to me, but as I had seen my hero Ron Fawcett on Rock Athlete, I thought of the glory it would bring.

I had spied a relatively insignificant line on High Tor. Nevertheless, as it was on such an iconic crag and the *Crags'* front-cover photo of Ron on *Supersonic* had inspired me to do new routes in the first place, it seemed the perfect opportunity to stamp my name on the cliff. I'd also enlisted Geraldine Taylor, the best female climber in Britain, to climb the route with me.

The cameraman settled himself in the correct position from the perch that we abseiled into and filmed as we climbed, to arrive in triumph at the top of the cliff. Ironically, just like Ron on *Lord of the Flies*, the cameraman ran out of film during the ascent and we had to do it all again. How life for us ordinary people mimics life for our heroes!

This was all followed by an interview at the top of the cliff about what I thought of Troll and its equipment. I have never seen the video, but if memory serves, I think I made a complete fool of myself, telling people all about my thousandth new route, as well as what I thought of their gear. A mate, John Smith, has seen the video and never fails to remind me of my folly when I see him. But isn't that what mates are for?

G.O. Wall calling

During the winter of 1985, I decided on impulse to go back and sort out a new first pitch to *Feline* on the G.O. Wall. I had been really proud of my efforts on the route a couple of years before but felt that the wall below offered a good new entry, which would improve the upper pitches and thus the route as a whole still further. Relatively speaking, it was a trifling effort, but something I wanted to do to finish the route off properly.

As ever, I was reliant on Matt and, after traversing below the great canopy of overhangs and doing a bit of cleaning, we managed to complete the pitch in a relatively short time and abseil back down to the ground. As we wandered around the foot of the cliff, to my absolute amazement, we noticed quite a bit of potential between the existing routes. Before this, I had assumed the place to be worked out, but once again it seemed that we had stumbled across another treasure trove of possibilities.

Unfortunately it seemed we were back to our old problem of how to clean the things. I could tie two ropes together and pass the knot, but the stretch on two normal 9 mm climbing ropes would be awful, rather like pinging around on a bungee rope. To combat the problem, I used the 100 metre static rope I had bought for Lundy. This solved all the hassle of the knot and the stretch, in one fell swoop.

To prevent the rope from sliding through my descendeur when I was cleaning, I used to wrap it around my leg. However, as this would become painful over time, I devised a system where I would have a jumar above my descendeur, which I would lock off as required, and hence I could do the cleaning in comfort. I could unlock it easily, descend to the next section, and lock it off again, and so on.

But there is a problem when you tie off a static rope, as they tend to slip a little and, can in theory, pull back through the knot. As a precaution, before I abseil, I have always left a long tail of rope, around an extra ten feet, so that I know the rope can't pull through.

In December, I would set off from home at around 5.30 a.m., arriving at the top of the cliff around 8 a.m. My intention was to make the most of what daylight there was available. Together with my cleaning gear, I sorted out the rope and tied it round a large sycamore tree, leaving the tail of rope as described. I attached the descendeur to the rope, with the jumar just above, leaned back and started my descent.

As I eased carefully down the rope, I felt the descendeur come loose. I had tied onto the tail of rope! The end of the rope had gone through the descendeur and, with barely six inches to spare, the jumar had locked. I was 250 feet up, swinging free, purely on the jumar. I scurried back up the rope, trembling in shock. I couldn't believe how lucky I'd been. It was as though another one of my nine lives had just been used up. How many did I have I left?

Despite this almost fatal error, I wasn't going to be put off, and, through the ensuing weeks, the cleaning continued unabated. The crashing of blocks and the removal of ivy and vegetation would be accompanied by the occasional howl of delight as the lines became cleaner, and, by the middle of January, the routes were ready to be climbed.

During the preparation, we had embraced the ethics of fixed protection, as the wall had been home to numerous partially aided ascents that had started to be eliminated.

Whether this meant pegs, bolts or threads was immaterial to me, although placing bolts was a time-consuming affair as I still hadn't purchased my first drill. I was beginning to wonder whether, in certain circumstances, fixed gear was the way forward – perhaps already anticipating the advent of sport climbing. Whatever the area, this was about to preoccupy me for the next few years.

Chapter 7

A Fork in the Road

'*THROUGHOUT THE PEMBROKE development years, Gary kept Dougie and me fed with a stream of fantastic new routes. At times, we travelled down there every other weekend to find another batch of E4s, E5s and E6s that, quite often, were well protected and decorated with thin threads – Gary's signature at the time. So, from my perspective, I and a lot of climbers owe Gary a great deal.*' Ian Carr, 2018

The mid to late 1980s presented me with a dilemma. I had placed the odd bolt here and there across the inland crags, as well as the occasional bolt on Lundy, but it now presented me with something of a fork in the road. I had become obsessed with climbing in Pembroke over the winter and spring months and was in a dilemma over what to do about the in-situ gear ethos I had taken to other areas.

At the end of February 1985, I chose which fork to take and it was most definitely correct for me at the time. The bird restrictions on Mowing Word and Stackpole hadn't yet come into effect, and, over a lovely calm weekend in February, I wanted to have a closer look at a couple of blank-looking walls I had seen on a previous visit. There weren't going to be any lower pitches, which made access relatively straightforward. In fact, cleaning the lines wasn't a problem, save for brushing a little bit of lichen off one or two holds. The problem was boldness, neither line having much in the way of natural protection.

I had considered the solution to this problem in relation to the corrosive nature of the sea-cliff environment and by then had acquired a handful of stainless-steel hangers and bolts. I chose to test the water and committed to placing the first bolts on the South Pembrokeshire cliffs (some had already been placed on the North Pembrokeshire coast). I placed one bolt runner on each route, before offering the provocative names of *If I Ruled the World* and *Dawn Chorus.*

There was no shock reaction to my decision, not in the climbing press nor in the May Cottage logbook. Having taken such a step, placed the bolts and not received any censure, it seemed psychologically easier to continue placing bolts in the area, if I deemed them appropriate.

The use of pegs, though, presented something of a different problem. Until that time, I hadn't found a source of stainless-steel pegs, being happy to use the soft-steel variety instead. However, in 1987, I discovered a company (Peck) that provided them by mail order. That discovery, together with the later purchase of a drill, would accelerate things even more towards the end of the decade.

For now, though, I was happy with the stainless-steel bolts and pegs that I had in my collection. Over the next few months, I added bolts to just a handful of routes. I focussed on placing them where they would be least affected by the corrosive nature of the sea and chose Stennis Ford and Huntsman's Leap. It seemed logical, as these hugely impressive walls were relatively sheltered from the sea and the wind. There were five routes, with eight bolts in total.

This doesn't mean that everything I did had a bolt in it. On the contrary, I had done a number of other routes that required boldness and commitment, taking major lines on important cliffs, but it was the drilled gear that was to tarnish for good my reputation in the area.

Looking back, maybe my obsession and lust for fame determined my somewhat ruthless approach to new routing. I had a fixation that fixed gear was OK wherever I climbed. We would always stay at May Cottage, and many were the times that I'd get up as dawn broke and go off to clean some routes, leaving everybody else in bed. As soon as I had finished, I would return to the hut, have breakfast and get back out to climb them.

There was nobody around that I knew who had the same attitude. Nevertheless, there were others staying at the hut who would reap the benefit of my efforts, Dougie Hall and Ian Carr being two. Many were the times they'd be following me around, in search of the next second ascent or early repeat. They knew that if I was there, there would be a whole list of new lines for them to do.

'*The morning after was a slow start in the busy hut. After all, the tide was on its way out, so there was no rush. To our shock, and perhaps dismay, as we were leaving the hut, Gary was just returning. He was boasting about three big new routes in the Leap, having been on the crag since 6 a.m. Most people just don't get the dedication and the hard work that Gary was putting into his climbing, especially the new routes. Throughout these times, he could always count on an enormous amount of patience and support from Hazel.*' Ian Carr, 2018

Unfortunately there were one or two unsavoury incidents regarding my climbing in Pembroke. One such incident was when Pat Littlejohn and Steve Monks came down to do a new line on St Govan's Head, one which I also had my eye on. After they had done it, there was an appalling series of allegations aimed at me in the May Cottage logbook. They accused me of chipping the line, and their accusations were accompanied by a tirade of abuse, aimed specifically at me. Hazel and I were horrified by their accusations; in fact I have never seen such a pile of sanctimonious nonsense in all my life, so much so that it was tantamount to libel.

What next transpired also astonished me. The logbook went missing, and Littlejohn accused me of stealing it. Why would I nick it (and I most certainly did not!) when it was full of such unproven allegations? I found such defamation of my character entirely unacceptable. As you can probably tell, it still rankles, even today.

As an aside, back in the Peak, I had again started to lean towards the more fully bolt-protected routes. I'd had my fingers burnt in 1983 over *Clarion Call*, but I was still prepared to push the envelope a little further on the Embankment in Chee Dale. As the crag dried out, I set about cleaning a handful of lines, with spaced bolts for protection, to test the reaction. The routes became popular almost instantly, and the bolts stayed in. In the Peak, it seemed, the tide was starting to turn.

Another Ireland challenge

We had certainly made our presence felt in Ireland the year before, so, without any hesitation, we planned another trip with John Codling once again at the helm. My knowledge about the miles of available rock at Fair Head, together with the other cliffs we had visited, compelled us to return. I had a particularly impressive piece of rock on Fair Head that I fancied having a go at, and John had similar intentions on a line he had seen to its left. Furthermore, we weren't going to ignore the Burren either.

After a preliminary visit to Martin and Barbara in Newtonards and the compulsory Ulster fry, we drove up to Ballycastle the following day to sort out our B&B – we knew by now we had little choice – and then drove over to Fair Head.

My initial intentions were to give the line I had seen a good clean and suss out whether it needed any fixed gear. At first, I had no intention of placing any bolts. I banged a few pegs into the upper wall and a single one on the first pitch: this section was going to be very bold, but I felt I had the ability to do it with just the one peg for protection. The problem was where to place a belay on this 200-foot wall.

Fortunately there was a ledge running horizontally across the wall at half-height, but there was no substantial belay. I couldn't get any pegs in, and there were no nut placements to be found anywhere nearby. As John had placed a couple of bolts on his line to the left, I committed to placing two for the belay. I could have traversed rightwards into an adjacent corner but I felt that would ruin the continuity of the route. As we left, the boldness of the lower wall was, however, still playing on my mind.

While we were cleaning, a few heads kept popping over the top of the cliff to see what we were up to. When we finally got back to the top, in the grey and rather misty weather, a few guys came over to say hello. We had a long and engaging chat, mentioning to them that we were heading off to the Burren for a few days but would be back at the end of the week to climb our prospective lines. We thought nothing more of it.

Our visit to the Burren was highly enjoyable. We stayed at the same caravan site as the previous year, but the price of the place was even better. It had decreased, yet our caravan was an improvement. Irish inflation, we thought!

Unfortunately, compared to the year before, the weather wasn't so kind. The sea was rough and, consequently, access to the Mirror Wall wasn't so simple. Luckily, the line I had chosen, which was a thin crack splitting the lower half of the wall, took barely any cleaning. This was hardly surprising considering the fact that the full height of the wall is regularly wave-washed during the winter months and high seas.

With a window in the weather, we returned the following day to climb the routes. They posed comparatively little problem and all we had to do was name them. I had been reading a story about Jerry Moffatt doing the first on-sight flash ascent of a route in Yosemite named *Phoenix*, and so *Phoenix in the Mirror* it had to be. John chose *Focal Point* for his route.

Not only did we enjoy the climbing, but we indulged ourselves in the social side of the area with a few visits to some hostelries, complete with folk music, before returning to Ballycastle for the lines we had cleaned at Fair Head. The weather had changed to clear blue skies and a gentle breeze, perfect for climbing conditions at the crag.

As I returned to my line, I was still having doubts about my ability to get up the lower, almost protectionless, wall without falling off. I had worked out all the moves, but its boldness still nagged at me. As John had committed to placing a few bolt runners on his line to the left, I chose to place a couple on mine. You'll have to accept my word when I say it wasn't an easy decision to make, but I made it nevertheless.

After we had finished our cleaning, we jumared back up to the top of the wall to find that a crowd had started to gather; the chaps from our previous visit must have informed the entire climbing community of Ireland about our antics.

Both ascents went relatively smoothly although, once I'd done my first pitch, I chose to abseil off and wander back round for a cup of tea and a sandwich before abbing back in and finishing off the top pitch. John did his route in one push, with a mid-height belay on two bolts, and we left Ireland pretty chuffed with our efforts.

We were blissfully unaware of the fallout of our actions. Two 'foreigners' had arrived in Ireland, cleaned off one of the most impressive walls at their most iconic crag, added a few bolts and left what they thought to be glittering prizes. It would never be as simple as that, though. Our actions were completely outside the prevailing ethical code and were dismissed outright. The view was that they should have been left for someone better to climb in a purer style and not 'stolen' by lowering the ethical standards of the crag.

Today, looking back, this might seem strange, since my line has been soloed on-sight. I had forced the issue about in-situ gear, an issue that would have further reverberations throughout the climbing community in the years to come. Whether I could have risen to the challenge of the line as it is today is neither here nor there. I made the decision to place the gear at a particular time. I didn't think about the repercussions, nor did I think about leaving it for someone bolder or better. My obsessed mind dictated that I *must* climb the line, come what may, and I even gave it a contentious name as well: *1066*.

'*We had a brilliant trip. World-class climbing and lovely people. In retrospect, we shouldn't have bolted our two routes on Fair Head, probably the best crag in the British Isles.*' John Codling

A personal perspective

Perhaps at this point, it might be useful to summarise what my intentions were in relation to new routes and, more specifically, in-situ gear. I had decided that placing pegs or bolts was acceptable on any cliffs I chose to climb, save for gritstone, where the ethical stance was already very well defined.

In other areas, such as Lundy, Pembroke and even Peak limestone, I felt that the lines of acceptability as to how an ascent was achieved were more blurred. Many who had gone before me had cleaned routes top-down, had placed in-situ gear and had even been quite liberal with the truth about their styles of ascent. Not everybody climbed on-sight, as they claimed.

However, by the mid-1980s, I was climbing at a relatively high grade. I worked hard at my climbing yet remained obsessed by the new routing bug and, by the end of 1986, I had even developed my own method of drilling a hole to take a peg and disguise the fact that I was using 'manufactured' gear placements. I believed that in-situ gear was the future of British climbing, and I hadn't even travelled abroad yet.

Other people encouraged me along this path, and others used in-situ gear in the same mode as I did in Pembroke and on Lundy. Even some, who would later turn against the increasing tide of pegs, bolts and threads, were enjoying the freedom of climbing without danger. I repeated existing routes, yes, but they led me to the gaps which my new route mania craved.

Roy Thomas

'*Generally speaking our days at the crag were filled with laughter and banter. Finding and developing crags, we were like excited kids with a jar of sweets, picking out the lines and getting stuck in. Gary had a more methodical approach, a set system, a fixed routine for each job; a dropped nozzle, a misplaced drill bit, a rope coiled differently, the "wrong quickdraw" on a borrowed hammer, could produce a storm in a teacup. Five minutes later all was forgotten, business as usual as we beavered away happily.*' Roy Thomas

There's something very special about friendships, and I've developed many over the years. Yes, some have withered, due to unfortunate circumstances, such as people moving out of the area or giving up climbing, but some friendships last forever, such as that with the incorrigible Roy Thomas. His sense of humour, his like-minded attitude to life, his similar obsession with new routing and his willingness to climb on the unthinkable have made him an endearing and enduring friend. Likewise, in terms of injuries we have both been through it. More importantly, I think we share a common view on climbing. Get out there, climb for fun and bugger everything else. I've spent many happy hours climbing and drinking with Roy, sometimes trying to demolish a bottle of whisky over an evening, on a trip to France, or just supping in two of our favourite pubs, the Prince of Wales in Kinvig and the Plough and Harrow at Nash Point, on our way home from a day's climbing.

One of our memorable weekends was the last weekend in February 1987. Before he retired, Roy was a teacher and, if we could grab a long weekend at half-term, we would. This time we chose Pembroke.

The weather was great: cobalt-blue skies, a heavy frost at night and no wind. A few days out on Mowing Word and Stackpole were the perfect antidote to the winter blues. I'd taken a Friday off work, and we'd chosen to stay in a deserted May Cottage. As usual, I was up with the lark, pounding around May Cottage, waiting for Roy to appear – this is standard practice whenever we climb together.

We wandered out from Broadhaven, past Raming Hole to reach the distant cliffs of Mowing Word. The rest of the day will live forever in my memory. We did a good new route on the *Widowmaker Wall* and then set about cleaning prospective lines for the following day. In February, it goes dark at around 5 p.m. at the latest, yet we were still there come 7 p.m., cleaning our lines with head-torches. I remember sitting at the top, freezing my proverbial nuts off, as I could see Roy's head-torch bobbing around, almost at sea level, as he finished off cleaning his line for the following day.

This obsession, which we share, has led us to continue these activities, even to this day. Cold, almost Baltic conditions, wet gear and rotting rags for clothing are all part of the game for us.

Jersey Royal

Over the Easter weekend in 1987 we were invited on a trip to Jersey by our good friend, Ian Smith. Ian had visited the island for climbing on a number of occasions and enticed us with tales of new route opportunities on the golden granite of the north-west coast.

It was (is) a lovely place to visit and climb, having a very calming influence on my excitable nature. The speed limit is 40 m.p.h. and our local companions for the trip, particularly our guide, Kevin Ellery, were fantastic.

Lines were so plentiful that most of the time I chose to climb on-sight; a VS here, an HVS there and an E2 nearby, but there were some impressive harder lines that needed just a bit of a cleaning before an ascent: *Dreamtime, Walkabout, Totem Taboo* and *Perry Coma* were all wonderful pitches. Surprisingly for me, I barely placed a piece of ironmongery on the island all week, save for a couple of pegs on an E6 that we climbed.

While we were on the island, we came across a few characters, one of whom had been nicknamed Mr Mad; once I'd met him I could certainly understand why. He fitted the bill perfectly. The locals nicknamed me the Grolsch Monster, based on the amount of lager I drank (not a great badge of honour really). In commemoration of the event, I just had to name a route *Mr Mad Meets the Grolsch Monster,* a description of our rather bizarre first encounter.

Always the Sun

Roy and I had already tapped into the potential of Raming Hole, and before too long I was back with the extremely enthusiastic Paul Donnithorne (now rightly regarded as Mr Pembroke), who had moved up to the area from Devon and was also intent on grabbing some new routes. Route after route fell along the seaward wall of Raming Hole. In-situ gear was plentiful, none of which was drilled, but it wasn't until mid-May that I placed my one and only bolt there on *The CIA*.

Of course it wasn't just about one crag, although my obsessive eye tends to mean that I pick one crag and almost completely work it out before I move on. In this instance, I was continuing my trend, with the odd bit of drilled gear on things like *Boat to Naxos* in Huntsman's Leap. Although I wasn't the only person using drilled gear at the time, I seem to have been the only one blamed for it.

Over one long weekend in May, I had set my sights on two particularly impressive lines: one in Huntsman's Leap (*Boat to Naxos*) that fell without incident and one on the Space Face at Mother (S)Carey's Kitchen, which proved a little more problematic.

I'd seen this towering groove high in the centre of the face, and, having cleaned it, realised just how frightening it was going to be: safe but bold and well away from gear. So to get myself psyched up and mentally tuned for the line, I decided to solo *Zeppelin* at high tide. I've no idea why, but I knew it would well and truly set me up for the ascent.

Back on my new line, once the tide went out, Hazel could get a belay on the boulder beach without the potential of getting the ropes wet. I got up to below the hanging groove and suddenly, as I pulled into it, panic struck. I'd forgotten a crucial wire placement, which was now just below my feet. I knew that if I fell off, I would drag Hazel up the cliff, and I would be in for a really long fall. As fortune would have it, I just about managed to keep myself together and finish off *Fireball XL5*.

But my luck (the more I climb the luckier I get?), was about to change. Hazel wanted me to take her up the route I'd soloed earlier. We belayed below the line, and, for some reason, I decided to place a clutch of bomber wires below the roof, when normally I would only have placed one. I lurched out from the back of the roof, grabbed the large flake at its lip and cut loose – in more ways than one. Just as my feet came free, I heard this cracking sound, and the whole thing came off, taking me with it. This was the flake from which I'd hung while soloing, only four hours earlier. The wires held, as Hazel was pulled upwards. Thank goodness I'd placed them!

A few weeks later, while climbing at Stoney Middleton, I badly tore my right biceps and had to take six weeks off to recuperate. Now injuries and me are not good buddies, and the frustration I felt whilst wanting to climb was indescribable. I went fishing, took long walks, did whatever I could to relieve the boredom, but, by mid-June, I was back with a vengeance.

Before my injury, I had looked at two routes: one in Stennis Ford and one in Huntsman's Leap. They were plum lines, on which I had already done a bit of preparation before my injury. *Internationale* in Stennis Ford fell cleanly at E6, yet the line in Huntsman's (*Black Lagoon*) was to offer a little more resistance.

I had placed a number of pegs and threads on it and after a 'slick' start, managed to get almost to the end of the difficulties when my foot slipped off. I couldn't hold the crimp that I was clinging onto, and off I came. I lowered back to the ground. Martin Crocker, who was climbing a new line just to my left, couldn't understand why I did this, because when he fell off, he chose to get back on and continue. I was a little more precious about my line than that and felt I had to do it from the bottom, in one push.

On publishing the two routes in *High*, I made a fatal error of judgement, as I also alluded to the fact that Stackpole Head still had a number of impressive unclimbed lines on it.

I just couldn't believe what a foolhardy mistake I had made, because, after the bird restriction had eased, we decided to have a holiday in the area to try and climb some of the lines I'd alluded to. I never thought that others would read my column and see the opportunity I'd offered to them.

Sure enough, come the bank-holiday weekend, while climbing with Roy and Hazel, we were joined by Martin Crocker, Matt Ward and Pete Oxley for a frenetic few days of developments. The atmosphere was friendly yet competitive, as everyone chose their line or section of cliff to exploit.

My main aim was the hugely impressive arête sitting centre-stage in the middle of the crag. I'd certainly had a good look at it, adding a couple of pegs, as well as playing around on some of the moves, just to see whether I could do them or not – and I could. I'd even tried the thing the weekend before with Hazel, but taken a tumble, just before the difficulties were over. This time I was back for revenge.

First though, Roy and I picked off a handful of other excellent routes, perhaps the best of which was the arête, which formed the very headland itself: *The Mighty White*. This though was just a prelude to the main event: the arête. Roy and I abseiled in, and, with Hazel set for the photographs and Pete and Martin watching nearby, I wandered up to the half-height ledge for a good rest. Then I went for it. I had good gear in the break and, using a small crimp/layaway around the corner, managed to scamper my feet up to catch a small ledge on the left. I missed and hurtled backwards onto the gear. I was certain the next go would be more successful. And it was. The whole sequence flowed perfectly, and, before I knew it, I was stepping right into a short finishing crack and the top.

Roy followed in good style, and we sat at the top, somewhat overwhelmed by the event and the quality of *Always the Sun*. The photos Hazel had taken emphasised its class and boldness, and they were later used on the front cover of the guidebooks to the area.

'1987, it was nearing the end of my long summer holiday when Gary called, saying he was keen to have another crack at a stunning new line on Stackpole Head. We met up at the top of Neptune, close to low tide, then abseiled in onto the still damp and slippery boulders. After a thorough drying and squeaking of boots, he set off. The first part seemed to pass steadily, then progress slowed, a slight pause as boots were checked, ropes clipped, and he launched out onto the arête proper. More and more rope went out, and I began to brace myself for what could be a monster whipper. My apprehension eased as he asked for rope and gear was clipped, then off

he set again, pausing only for a couple of shots by Hazel.

My turn came and all went well until the crux section on the arête; after more than a couple of sags and tugs, I topped out. There was quite a throng gathered at the crag that weekend including Martin Crocker, Pete Oxley etc.

"Got a name for it, Gary?" I asked. "Always the Sun, *youth," he replied.'*
Roy Thomas

Hilti power

At the beginning of 1988, I decided to invest in a rotary hammer drill. I'd already trialled a Makita version, but it wasn't up to much, only drilling a few bolt holes in a session; my Hilti TE10A had two batteries and proved to be much more productive. Until then, I had accepted that hand-drilling bolts was the way forward. I had even found a mechanism for drilling holes for pegs to be inserted, but this was a laborious and time-consuming task. My quest for new sport routes, which had clearly become my intention on the inland limestone crags, would be better served by a drill.

It also gave me an outlet for drilling 16 mm holes, into which you could bash one of the stainless pegs. I thought these would be much longer lasting than the softer steel stuff I was using and could help fill the gaps on the protectionless parts of climbs I was unsettled by.

As was common practice with the limestone crags in the Peak still seeping from the autumn and winter downpours, we kept concentrating on the Pembrokeshire sea-cliffs. We tapped the potential of the area across a range of cliffs, such as Trevallen – where we added *The Fascist and Me* – Gun Cliff, Bosherston Head and Raming Hole. I didn't find the need for any drilled gear, although I did place a few in-situ pegs and threads.

Another Moatside Attraction

The early part of 1988 was an unusual one for Water-cum-Jolly. Over the previous winter, the water levels below Rubicon Wall had tested the weir to its maximum. The old gate had been raised to reduce the pressure on its walls which were starting to crumble away, and it became jammed. This meant that the huge silted-up pond had dropped to a level that made the aptly named Moat Buttress more easily accessible. When the moat was at its normal level, you couldn't walk below the buttress, but now, with the water levels down by well over a metre, the whole face was easy to reach. This made it fair game to the new routing fraternity and come the spring, once the face had dried out, it was open season.

I had already been looking about the place in the latter part of 1987 and, in the early part of the following year, ticked off a couple of minor offerings on the right-hand side of the face. When Keith Sharples climbed a new line on its left-hand side, my attention shifted. I had seen a line to its right, which I'd already decided to name *Another Moatside Attraction.* I dumped my gear under the cliff. There was a convenient tree at the top of the cliff from which to clean it and which would also provide a suitable lower-off. I'd placed a few bolts and a couple of pegs and then jumared back up to the top with the intention of walking back down to collect my rucksack.

Once at the top of the cliff, however, my adventurous spirit gave me the idea that I might be able to find an easy way down over to my right, and so I walked across and peered over the edge to see if I could either scramble down or abseil down more easily. As I leaned over the edge, some fifty feet or so up, the piece of ivy I was holding for support snapped, and I tumbled head first down the cliff.

I landed with an almighty thud and rolled down the hillside, to be conveniently stopped by an old sawn-off telegraph pole – evidently left there to stop me ending up in the muddy silt! I stood up, thinking no more of it and glanced across the pond to see three people gazing at me in utter astonishment. They shook their heads in stunned silence and wandered off, either in amazement at my casual attitude or, more likely, at my sheer stupidity and good fortune to still be alive.

The problem was that I was now back at the foot of the crag, where my rucksack was stashed, but I still had to retrieve my rope from the top. I gathered my thoughts, dusted myself down and retrieved the rope. As I started to walk back towards the car and across the bridge, I bumped into Geraldine Taylor. She looked at me in horror. 'Gary, are you alright?' she exclaimed, 'You look like a ghost.' I told her what had happened and she kindly asked if I was in a fit enough state to get home. I said I'd be OK and set off back to my car.

I drove back through Sheldon into Monyash and, as I reached the top of the hill on the single-track road, off the A6, I came over all sickly and faint. So I thought the best course of action would be to have a lie-down on the grassy verge alongside the road. As I lay there, the farmer who passed by in his tractor must have had the shock of his life.

My belayer's suffering

During all of this, I feel I have to mention the suffering my wife has to endure as my belayer. Not only the cold, wet, boring experience of holding my ropes while I try to climb another route, but the consequences of a rather large weight imbalance between us.

If you know us, you will realise that I am twice the size of my wife, which presents a significant problem should I fall off, or even just weight the rope. One such problem occurred while I was trying the second ascent of *Subversive Body Pumping* at Dinas Rock. Surprisingly, I managed to climb the low bouldery crux on my first attempt and was continuing up the impressive crackline above, which was laden with a number of Roy Thomas 'specials' – homemade pegs from water bar or something similar.

As I approached the lower-off, I shouted cockily down to Hazel, who was belaying me, with Roy in hearing distance, that I hoped these bits of ironmongery were strong enough to hold my weight. Suddenly, a hold broke, and I went hurtling through the air. Hazel was wrenched skywards with a very strong jolt, and we met at the first bolt, as the belay device and rope jammed in it. Hazel had been propelled fifteen feet into the air, and I had fallen about thirty feet. Lesson learnt?

Project Lundy

Having had the joy of face climbing on the Diamond, as well as bagging half its lines, it was time to shift emphasis to another section of crag when I returned the following year. Black Crag had only one route, which ventured onto its main face, and I was certain there was scope for more. I had packed my bolt driver and once again Matt again was up for the challenge. No sooner had the boat touched the shore, than we were off in a race to abseil down the face and clean our lines as quickly as we could get to them.

The weather was fair, and a gentle breeze blew across the face as we cleaned our respective lines. Matt was to the right of me. My usual trick when I'd finished cleaning was to switch over to jumars and then go back up the rope, checking everything. This time, when I got about halfway up, it suddenly jerked to the left. I looked up, to see a microwave-sized block hurtling towards me. I dodged to the right, as it shot past, giving me an idea for relevant route names.

Over the next six days, we managed a total of five new routes, three of which sported bolt runners. Two of these, *Emergency Ward Ten* and *Mayan Skies*, were particularly impressive and as good as anything I'd done on the island.

It was inevitable that we'd be back for more the following year. There were unfilled gaps on Black Crag, as well as other wonderful lines scattered across the island.

Obviously we went to Lundy to climb; nevertheless life wasn't just about climbing. On our next trip, we were joined in Bramble Villas by a group of friends who had come along to sample the other wonders of the island, as well as the crags. We were also up for any fun we could get. The island's volleyball team had yet to be beaten that year, and we were challenged to a game. Now, when it comes to competitive spirit, we weren't prepared to be outdone, as was obvious by our attitude during the game. It was edgy stuff, but we left with our pride intact and the island's volleyball team no longer had an unbeaten record.

As for the climbing, Hazel, as ever, was happy to play a supporting role and hold my ropes. I had specific designs on two routes on Black Crag. With an odd bolt here and there, I managed to tick off two E6s, *Intensive Care* and *Mexico Speaks.* But Black Crag wasn't the sole purpose of the visit.

Incidentally – it probably seems utterly irrelevant now – I'd also worked out how to protect the bolts from seawater. I'd brought a mastic gun, along with a tube of sealant to the island, which once it had been squeezed out around the bolt, provided an appropriate seal. The brown sludge camouflaged the bolts, though I wasn't trying to hide them, merely protect them from corrosion.

I'd also prepared a handful of new routes to do with Matt. He was no less productive in his pursuit of quality, coming up with the superb *Mal de Mer* and *Sea of Tranquillity.* In turn, I captured the striking crackline of *Too Precious* on the Parthenon. We did many other good routes without the attendant ironmongery of those on Black Crag and the Diamond.

However the culmination to the week was once again on Black Crag. I'd looked at the diagonal break crossing the wall and conjured up the idea of climbing it, to create a kind of girdle traverse. After having a good look at it from other routes, we discussed it in the Marisco Tavern on the penultimate evening of our trip. Initially Matt staunchly declined to follow the pitch. Of course he would happily hold my ropes, but that wasn't my idea of fun. As we plied him with more and more alcohol (and a little gentle persuasion) his attitude mellowed, and, by the end of the evening, he was up for it as well.

I prepared the route the following day and Matt, Hazel and I abbed in to do it. After trying to connect a series of holds, which didn't lead me into the line at the start, I sorted it out, finished off the rest of the pitch and reached the belay. At first, Matt was fine about things, until he got to a small ledge about halfway across the wall. At this point, things started to go awry; he began to feel intimidated and wanted to go no further, offering instead to abseil the line to retrieve the gear.

But I wasn't having any of that. I bullied, more than encouraged him, reminding him of his duties(!) and, as he moved out and unclipped a crucial piece of gear above him, I took in the rope; now he couldn't go back. After much encouragement from me, we completed the pitch and *The Colour of Life* was complete. Perhaps I should have just reversed it, as Mike Owen did on the second ascent.

Taking the next step

In relation to the fixed gear issue, 1988 was the year that broke the camel's back. I'd come armed with my drill and a bag of stainless-steel bolts ready for use. I had seen a number of lines and firmly believed that this was the way forward for the future development of climbing on the island. But, while I had been indulging myself in these activities over the previous few years, others had begun to register their disapproval of my antics. Clearly I wasn't listening.

I bagged a whole host of quality lines, the drill helping me equip them far more quickly than previously, which meant that I was also more likely to add more bolts: *Roy of the Rovers, the Pyramid of Success, Out Come the Freaks, That Semi-Detached Feeling* and, the most poignantly named, *The Demons of Hilti.* I barely stopped to consider the ethics of continuing my pursuit of new routes with fixed gear. My final route of the trip – perhaps the final nail in the coffin of my bolting activities on Lundy – came on Black Crag with *Hey Gringo*: a great route, but in retrospect tainted by the five bolts that I placed on it.

I was somewhat naively pleased with my efforts and continued to applaud my achievements in the magazines. However, there was a growing tide of animosity towards my erosion of climbing ethics on the island. It hadn't become personal – nobody had actually said anything to my face – but a major part of the climbing community in the south west had had enough of my exploits.

This may seem like a history lesson, but it isn't intended to be. It is more an attempt to put my attitude into context towards my activities. By now, I was the only one still placing bolts, though a few had placed bolts on the island before. Certainly I had been supported without challenge by those who climbed with me, but I wouldn't have surrounded myself with people who were antagonistic towards my direction of travel anyway. That just couldn't have worked.

The final straw?

We had booked a week off at the end of May and decided on yet another trip to Pembroke to have a look at a few of the lines I'd spied over the preceding months. I had already decided that some would need the accompaniment of drilled pegs to satisfy my lust for reasonable protection. With my new drill, I could drill about six or seven holes big enough for pegs in one go, so things couldn't have been easier.

Where there was an area of rock which I regarded as lacking in protection, I would add one or two drilled pegs. I was prepared to mix it though, depending on the environment and my inclination – but this was to be the straw that broke the camel's back.

Two weeks prior to our main trip, I'd had a good long look at the big wall on the right-hand side of Stennis Ford and an impeccable wall at Forbidden Head. My first port of call was Stennis Ford. I chose to drill three peg runners on what I regarded as the most challenging section. Roy was on hand to climb it with me, and Hazel was well positioned to photograph what came to be known as *Ghost Train*.

Over the next couple of days, we added the even harder *From a Distance* in the centre of the wall, and *Everything* to the right of *Ghost Train*, a route on which I had to use just that, both in terms of strength and fixed gear. Despite the fact that not everything we did had fixed gear in it, the true focus really was about pushing the drilled-peg agenda, so much so that we moved over to Forbidden Head to add three more routes with some drilled gear: *Baroque, Vladimir and Serge,* and *Not for all the Tea in China,* which I had been drawn to by a route with drilled gear by Martin Crocker.

Looking back, it's really difficult to convey my thoughts on these routes at the time, but, for sure, I was very proud of my efforts. I was also confident that the ethics I'd brought to the area were the right ones, as others were indulging in similar practices alongside me. At the time, my feeling was that this was the best way forward for the area in the long run. I had never sat in other camps, and perhaps my opinions were seen through my own rose-tinted glasses; however, for now, the routes had been done and I moved onto other things in other areas.

Chapter 8

A Kind of Death

'*It's only been four months, but development of the Escarpment at Ban-y-Gor is nearing completion and Matt and I now feel it safe (ha!) to let Gary in on all the fun. We go through the woods and begin to show him around. Gary drops his sack, gets geared up and promptly disappears with rope in hand, despite not having had a proper look at the place. This was the moment, I realised later, that new routing was more than just climbing new stuff – but rather a state of mind.*' Gordon Jenkin

Somebody once asked me that if you were to choose two or three 'Kodak moments' in your life, what would they be? Well I suppose, apart from meeting Hazel and experiencing the death of my parents, an incident that happened at Ban-y-Gor in 1988 will always be one of those moments.

It was after a relatively intense period of development by Matt Ward, Gordon Jerkin, Martin Crocker and a handful of others, that I was introduced to Ban-y-Gor. It had been an awful summer, and they chose to keep the crag a well-guarded secret, so that people like me wouldn't come along and upset their intentions. Sure, I had heard of another 'undisclosed' crag in the area, but I hadn't been let into the mystery by Matt, until most development had taken place.

Once I had been introduced to the place, I was stunned to find a 300-metre length of virgin cliff now accompanied by a large number of new routes. Although I managed some repeats and a couple of minor new routes, what I hadn't accounted for was that the main cliff, somewhere off in the distance to the north of the developed section of crag, had still been left untouched. Sure, it had been climbed on in the past, but there was a major problem in that the top of the cliff ended in people's gardens, and the first ascensionists of those routes weren't invited in for a cup of tea when they topped out! I had to take a look.

At the end of one of our climbing sessions, I wandered along, broke through the vegetation just beyond Ladder Gully at the far end of the escarpment and descended to the main crag proper. I couldn't believe its size: around 200 feet of cliff piercing through the undergrowth but providing one more major problem – the ivy and other vegetation that hung down like the Hanging Gardens of Babylon.

The crag was composed of four tiers, the bottom two of which seemed to merge together. Taking a good long look at its potential, I came up with the idea that if I placed belays at the top of the second tier, I could lower off and not have the problem of the gardens above. Sure, it was a big cleaning effort, but as that hadn't stopped me before, I vowed to return.

On a dry but misty November morning, Hazel and I, along with a good friend of ours, John Holdcroft, set off to test that theory. If I was right about my assertions, I could foresee a long and fruitful winter of cleaning and development. We arrived in the parking place at our normal ungodly hour and wandered along the base of the escarpment, past Ladder Gully, to find a suitably comfortable spot to place our rucksacks before I started work. It would also provide a suitable viewing spot for Hazel and John while I beavered away on the crag about sixty feet away.

After putting on all my cleaning gear, complete with drill and rope, I soloed up a crackline at the right-hand side of the face and manoeuvred my way along the terrace to set up a useful abseil spot from a convenient tree. After I'd cleaned a couple of routes, and before I re-joined Hazel and John, I decided to have a look at just one more line. I remember quite vividly abseiling in through the overhangs and placing a couple of bolts to pull me back in, in order to clean the section of crag before putting my jumars onto the rope to get back to the belay. And that is where my memory ends.

We think, and this still remains the logical theory, that a large chunk of rock perched in the ivy above me was dislodged and struck me on the head, instantly fracturing my skull. The rock then severed the rope and I fell through the trees to the ground, some seventy feet below. I was already unconscious when I hit the ground. This perhaps saved me from further injury. It may have also saved my life.

Out of the corner of her eye, Hazel had seen me fall to the ground. Her immediate reaction was to scramble down to see what the damage was. I was lying prostrate on the ground, with a gaping hole in the front of my skull. Clearly I was badly injured, perhaps fatally so. It must have been a horrifying sight.

It was lucky that there were three of us and, instinctively, John clambered up via Ladder Gully to the houses skirting the top of the cliff. Apparently he asked permission to use the telephone, which, amazingly, was refused. He simply took no notice and used the phone to summon the Severn Area Rescue Association (SARA) and RAF helicopter anyway. He knew that I was in such a bad state that carrying me out from this extremely inaccessible place could adversely affect my chances of survival.

It was clearly a freak accident, but that is where my bad luck ended. When SARA arrived at the scene, I believe Hazel was heard to say, 'He's down there; I think he's dead.' However, that wasn't going to be the case. The rescue team took care of me to the best of their ability, but, luckily, the RAF was on exercise nearby, and my accident also happened to be close to the only access point through the forest canopy. Within about thirty minutes of the call being put out, the RAF medic was tending to me on the ground.

They eventually airlifted me to Frenchay Hospital in Bristol, where I was immediately taken into the major trauma centre. Hazel and John travelled by road to be with me. When they arrived, they were led to the bereavement room as I wasn't expected to live until the next morning.

What I love about climbing is its close sense of community. A huge amount of support was given to my wife and family over an extremely traumatic time. Differences of view were left just where they should be left – removed from personal tragedy. Hazel had the most wonderful support from some of my best friends, including Matt Ward, Gordon Jenkin, Tony Penning and Martin Crocker. I have the deepest and most enduring respect for them.

As for me, it was a different matter. I was completely dependent on the surgeons and nurses to get me through the trauma, as my injuries were truly life-threatening. I had suffered a major fracture to the front of my skull; I had fractured both orbits and fractured my jaw. I was placed in an induced coma for five days, during which I had two major haemorrhages, for which I had two metal clips, and a craniotomy to release the pressure to my brain. I also lost around half a centimetre of the frontal lobe. All of this damage would have to settle down before any repair work could be undertaken.

Even now, thirty years later, Hazel is still distressed by the whole event and finds it very difficult to talk about. Without her and John, I wouldn't be here. I owe my life to them, the SARA, the RAF medic, the surgeons, the nurses and a number of very close and supportive friends.

The following weeks were a slow process of rehabilitation. I remember very little of my time in hospital. It seemed as though I was in a state of fugue. The ward certainly wasn't a very pleasant place for my family to visit. I vaguely remember one man, who was suffering from a particularly severe tumour to the brain, shouting out orders at around 5 a.m. He was obviously from a military background. Then there was another man who was admitted, after a horrific car accident. Sadly, neither of them survived.

Towards the end of my stay in hospital, I underwent a twelve-hour operation to repair my facial damage, repair my jaw and put me back together, as best as possible. It was a difficult job, considering the jigsaw pieces that now made up my skull, the displacement of my orbits and the damage to my misplaced jaw; yet the surgeons did an incredible job.

As I was about to be discharged, my consultant, the wonderful Mr Cokeham, sat me down to have a long chat. I'd been in the middle of writing and editing two guidebooks and just couldn't wait to get back to climbing – such was my foolhardiness. He told me to ease off and not put any strain onto my traumatised brain. It was a well meant piece of advice, but there was absolutely no way that I was going to take any notice. I was determined to prove to myself that nothing in my life had changed. I didn't stop to consider the emotional damage it had done to Hazel and the rest of my friends and family.

I was discharged from hospital exactly one month to the day of the accident. I'd lost well over two stone in weight, I was desperately sore and felt completely and wholeheartedly demoralised. I'd upset Hazel, my parents and my close friends – but at least I was alive and thankful for the fortune that had been given to me. I don't believe in God, but I could well believe that I had a guardian angel somewhere. It was just not my time to be called.

The next few weeks of rehab were awful, and I remained very, very weak. Hazel and I went for a walk down to the local country park, where they had erected one of those 'training' courses. I tried to do a pull-up but couldn't, and I broke down in tears at the thought of my weakness. Hazel though was fantastic. Always encouraging, always supportive and never trying to prevent me from going back to the sport that I loved so much.

Over the ensuing weeks, I was determined to finish the books that I had started writing and editing – *Staffordshire Gritstone* and *New Climbs 1988* – and single-mindedly get back to climbing as soon as I could. I was just under eleven stone, but, by the turn of the year, I felt strong enough to summon up the courage to go climbing again. For some reason I chose Pen Trwyn and managed to climb *Plum Line*, E3, and (ridiculously) *Scary Canary*, a bold E5 as my second route, just to prove a point to myself.

But however traumatic it would be, I knew I had to return to the scene of my accident. The routes were still there, waiting to be climbed. Ban-y-Gor had almost, but not quite, killed me off. I was seeking revenge.

'*Gary had become one of the most controversial climbers around in the 1980s, yet his popularity remained undiminished. This became evident during the dark days of November 1988, when a rock became dislodged and hit him during a cleaning session and, as a result, he lay unconscious in intensive care for over a week, his life hanging barely by a thread. My telephone never stopped ringing for days from well-wishers and climbing friends.*' Phil Gibson

'*I always find hospitals unsettling. Wandering through the myriad corridors of Frenchay, I wasn't sure what to expect. The news of Gary's accident was grim. Finally, getting to the correct ward, I became confused as I walked back and forth scanning the faces around me. I couldn't find him anywhere until suddenly I spotted Hazel and realized that the occupant of the bed now in front of me was Gary. I felt deeply shocked – he was unrecognisable from the person I knew. It was a disorientating moment of meeting mortality: realizing that none of us is as invincible as we'd like to think.*' Gordon Jenkin

Chapter 9

Rehabilitation and Redemption

THE WEEKS FOLLOWING my accident were a phase of major rehabilitation, both mentally and physically. While I am not a believer in revenge of any type – an eye for an eye makes the whole world blind – I had one act of reprisal that I needed to carry out. It may seem bizarre that I would want to return to the scene of my accident, but I felt I had to climb the route that had almost proved to be my downfall. I was also prepared to take any measure to achieve it.

I had already returned to the crag with Roy to add a few bits on the right-hand side of the crag but, understandably, Matt and Gordon were loath to return. Instead, I had to drag Hazel back to the chilling scene for an attempt at the fated line. She didn't complain, perhaps understanding me better than anyone.

After a short recce, which in itself was traumatising, I could see that I would be unable to get past the overhang from where, five months previously, I had plummeted to the ground. Others may be able to get past it, but not me. I tinkered here and there, and finally came up with a simple solution to how to climb the damn thing: glue a hold on. Did I care? Not a jot. That area of rock had nearly got me, now it was my turn to repay the gesture.

After (quite literally) a few throws at it, I finally latched onto the hold and wrestled my way around the overhang to success. In my mind, I had defeated the undefeatable, and the route had become real. I had to name it something suitably ironic. I thought long and hard and eventually came up with *Head Tennis*, a footballing term which seemed highly appropriate. This initiated a macabre trend of route naming. Other routes nearby fell, over the following months, with similarly themed names: *Sea-King Me, Chin-Hooks, Almost Me, Hummin' Bird, Head on the Line* and the wonderfully morbid *Stitch That!* I just couldn't resist.

My involvement with Ban-y-Gor, whilst essential to my mental rehabilitation, was playing on my mind. Returning there with such an obsessive vendetta was weighing heavily on the others with whom I climbed, most importantly, Hazel. Therefore I had to find a more neutral venue, which would avoid further mental turmoil and physical drain. My body was still trying to put itself back together; however the long-term trauma would come back to haunt Hazel and me again, over the following years.

Luckily, while walking on the Offa's Dyke path in Shropshire along the Welsh border, we happened across a big brooding cliff near the village of Llanymynech. Well, when I say new, it wasn't that new to me, as I'd visited the place with Phil back in the mid-1970s.

To see a crag littered with huge, relatively unclimbed walls was just what I needed. Some were over 150 feet high, patterned with wonderful hues of pink, grey, black and white. Sure, there were routes already there, yet, as we wandered back and forth, its vast potential couldn't be ignored by someone like me.

The great relief of finding such a place so early on after my accident, proved that the obsession hadn't left me. How could it? Nevertheless, did I have the drive to develop the crag?

I spent hour after wonderful hour visiting the place on my own. My power drill was still out of action; in the Ban-y-Gor fall, it had suffered even more damage than I had. All the same, I was used to hand-drilling. Being medically signed off from work, I certainly had time on my side.

For some routes, mainly on the protectable main wall, which was seamed with horizontal breaks and limited features, I chose a trad approach, save for the odd peg or bolt here and there. For another wall, a great pink edifice, I chose a minimalist, sport-climbing approach due to the restraints of drilling the damn bolts. Anyway, this was generally the approach in 1989, a far cry from your modern-day sport route.

It was just what the doctor ordered; well, it wasn't what he ordered at all, but, for my psyche, it fitted the bill perfectly. I would spend a whole day cleaning, and when the weekend came around I would be back with Hazel to climb the routes. John Holdcroft would also come along to offer his support and photographic skills. It was like a reunion of the Three Musketeers but without d'Artagnan. The only other companion I had was John Codling, and, generally speaking, we had the place to ourselves.

Pembroke retaliation

While I was in a coma, issues in Pembroke had come to a head. A significant number of climbers weren't too enamoured of my approach to new routing in the area – particularly regarding the drilled gear, whether pegs or bolts. Before I had climbed there, the local ethic was to climb on-sight with little or no preparation, or fixed gear. However, I, and others, had tipped that ethic on its head, and once the battery-operated drill came into effect, it was the proverbial straw that broke the camel's back.

After designing a piece of equipment to extract drilled pegs, they removed as much of the drilled gear as they could. This action heralded a statement of intent that the original area ethic should remain, i.e., where possible, new routes should be climbed with no fixed gear at all. Coincidentally, the fateful decision was taken on the same weekend that I'd had my accident.

It was inevitable that I would be disappointed by such a discovery. Quite a few climbers had encouraged me on my new routing activities and many had supported my attitude towards in-situ gear. Yet it was clear, in the eyes of the majority, that this was not the way forward and, by removing my fixed gear, a line was drawn in the sand. I had been quoted in the climbing magazines as being 'really upset' by these events. However, in reality, for about four months I was completely unaware of them, given that I had been in hospital and then undergoing a steep rehabilitation programme during which further upset and stress were to be avoided.

Sadly, another occurrence happened in St Govan's carpark that complicated the matter even further. Just before my accident, we had bought a Volkswagen camper van, intending to travel to climbing areas without the encumbrance of camping fees, etc. One day when we had been out climbing in Huntsman's Leap, we returned to find that, to our horror, someone had crawled under the van and smashed our exhaust pipe to pieces with a hammer. We can only assume it was someone taking out revenge on me because of my approach to new routing. We just couldn't believe that someone could be so vindictive.

With debolting, although I'd really felt that my (and others') new ethic would be the way forward, I surprised even myself by accepting the debolting actions without animosity or conflict. What else could I do? I had been as close to death as I ever could be and fighting against the debolting movement would have been futile. To accept the consensus of opinion was the right thing to do.

Many would ask why I hadn't acted that way in the first place; but that is a hard question to answer. I had perhaps been the victim of my own circumstances: believing what I was doing was right while things continued to move on without being challenged. And, as others joined in, my obsessive nature took me beyond what was acceptable at the time. It wasn't belligerence or rebellion; I was just driven to do what I did. We all choose a path, and sometimes that path leads you to the wrong place; the drill made it even easier. I had clearly chosen the wrong fork.

Looking back, you may well say that what I did wasn't right. Many have vilified me for it, and some still do. I was prepared to challenge the boundaries of ethics, and always will be, although in this instance, the battle was lost. I simply had to live with that. There was nothing I could do about the new (old?) order, other than to climb within the newly defined boundaries in Pembroke or not climb there at all. The latter was something that I was not prepared to contemplate.

Over the next few years, I set about ensuring that I would no longer use drilled gear on the Pembrokeshire cliffs. I sought to put right some of the wrongs I had undertaken

The number of routes I climbed without the drilled gear may have been small – only five – but they included some very bold undertakings. Perhaps my best effort was *The Subterranean* in Huntsman's Leap. For me, this route was already a challenge with the two bolts that I had initially placed. To climb it without them seemed way beyond the bounds of possibility. Yet I was determined to have a go as I loved the route so much.

I had a good look at it, tried a few of the moves on an abseil rope and committed to leading it. The irony was that a certain exponent of the anti-Gary brigade, one Mark Hopkins, a big lad if ever I saw one, chose to try and intimidate me on my ascent by climbing the route next to me. But I wasn't having any of it; in fact, it drove me on even further.

I then undertook to try another prize possession of mine without the two bolts, *Boat to Naxos*. This one, though, got the better of me. After a good sixty- to seventy-foot plummet, including winching Hazel off the ground to a height above where I finished, I decided to call a halt to my campaign and leave the bold climbing to someone better than me.

Out come the bolts

Lundy, though, was a completely different kettle of fish. I had added significantly more bolts to routes which suited my style: off-vertical, technical wall climbing. We planned a trip back there in the summer of 1989. My consultant had warned me not to climb steep walls where, if I fell, I might swing into the rock and smash my head again. The more slabby faces of Lundy would be ideal, even if falling off the routes without bolts might mean I'd hit the ground. Clearly I had a strange view of the world.

When I came out of hospital, the debolting which had taken place in Pembroke hadn't yet happened on Lundy; probably due to the difficulty of getting there, the winter season and the bird restriction. Nonetheless, I still dreamed of doing a few new routes on hitherto untouched pieces of rock that I had seen. I just couldn't wait to get back.

Then, in the June editions of the climbing magazines, I read about a visit to Lundy made by Pat Littlejohn and Nick White. Their intention was to make a similar statement against the plethora of bolts that had appeared on the island. As well as doing a few new routes, they also managed to climb a few of my routes without the bolts. They made clear statements, both in the magazines and the island logbook, about what they viewed as the damage to the island's climbing ethos by my use of hammer and drill.

The Cullinan, and my beloved *Watching the Ocean* and *Charles Mattless* – which ironically I had already soloed – all received the bolt-free treatment in contrast to my previous ascents. Although what happened on *Watching the Ocean* riled me a little, not against Pat Littlejohn but more about pure style; the bolt hangers had been left in place during their ascent, which gave me the opportunity to improve things even further. This was not to say that Littlejohn would have clipped them though, in my view, it reduced the psyche of the ascent somewhat. I decided to improve on it, even if only minimally.

During the seven days we spent on the island, Roy and I managed to climb *Chase the Ace, Smear, no Fear, Smear or Disappear* and, of course, *Watching the Ocean* without the previously placed bolts, all of which were removed before the re-ascents.

Yet this was still not enough for me. The Diamond, probably my favourite piece of rock, had become something of a symbol of the bolt wars. Nevertheless I had to move on to Black Crag to finish the job off, good and proper. I spent a long evening removing the bolts from three of its routes, as well as trying out some of the moves, in particular on *Mayan Skies*. This was going to be the most serious lead I had ever contemplated.

The next day I was back with Hazel, and both the aptly named *My Life in My Hands* and *Emergency Ward Ten* fell without too many problems. The new pegs I placed on the latter route served much the same purpose as the two bolts I'd placed previously. But it was to be *Mayan Skies* that remains, even today, my finest ever lead.

I can remember it all so vividly, smoothly climbing the vague rugosity streak up the centre of the crag to a point within ten feet of a jutting peg. This I knew to be the end of the difficulties, but before it lay the crux 6b move. I had it wired in my mind and, with the comfort of protection, I wouldn't have hesitated. However this was no place for failure, for I have no doubt that it would have resulted in a ground-fall from some ninety feet. I paused for just a moment. I knew it wouldn't be a good idea to consider the situation for too long, and with little more than a stutter and a gentle rock-over onto a small edge, I was at the peg. The route was in the bag.

There was no euphoria after the ascent, just a few moments of quiet satisfaction and contemplation. I'd achieved my goal of proving that I could push myself to the limit without the security of in-situ gear. It wasn't something that I wanted to pursue for the rest of my life, of that I was certain; however, for now, I felt fulfilled by my achievements. In the long run, I would inevitably go back to the need for sound in-situ gear, but, for the time being, I sat wistfully watching the ocean, satisfied by my success.

Time to be a 'slate-head'

Throughout the spring and summer months of 1989, I had been steadily improving, by climbing on an amazing variety of rock types, mostly on the slabbier faces that were available. New routes were always the focus, although the joy of climbing is what really matters, established route or not.

We really got into the slate-climbing boom around Llanberis. John Redhead and friends had been developing a significant number of routes across two of its most impressively steep slabs. One was named the Rainbow because of a peculiar 'wave' of rock that stretched across the face.

For most people, slate climbing initially feels quite peculiar. Thankfully, around the edges of the slate quarries, a number of well-protected (i.e. bolt) routes had been established. This was a particularly useful development for getting your head into climbing on the stuff before venturing onto the more committing pitches created by Redhead and co. John had decided at the outset that he was going for a Joe Brown-type philosophy (Brown had famously limited himself to a maximum of two pegs per pitch). On slate, the outcome was inevitable: some very bold and lonely leads.

I got into slate climbing, firstly with Hazel and then with John Codling (John led some of the bolder pitches too). With them both in support, I did what was regarded as the introduction to bold slate – *Poetry Pink*. In his Llanberis guidebook, Paul Williams had described this route as requiring a sprinter to prevent a ground-fall from an unnerving mantelshelf at seventy feet. As it happened, that was more hyperbole than fact; but hey, never let the truth get in the way of a good story!

The route certainly had a reputation at the time for scaring a number of very competent climbers. For me to find it relatively straightforward, what many would term 'a path', was a great boost to my confidence. It was also the first rung on the ladder of success on this type of rock. Slate isn't for everybody but back then I couldn't get enough of the stuff.

The progression was inevitable. I was so consumed by slate that I had to tick everything I could in between my new-routing sessions elsewhere though, surprisingly, I have yet to do a new route on slate itself. I thoroughly enjoyed *Cystitis by Proxy, Splitstream, Naked Before the Beast* and, finally, the wonderfully bizarre and perfectly named *The Rainbow of Recalcitrance.* There remained, in my eyes at least, one more route to do on the slab: the incredibly bold and highly regarded *Raped by Affection.* I had scant idea of how many people had climbed it and in what style, so I decided that a good abseil session was the best way to approach it.

I spent about an hour and a half working out all the moves up the most unprotected section of slab and having a good long look at the crux, knowing exactly what I had to do should I get to that point.

With Hazel and John in support, I found it all fairly reasonable, save of course for the unnerving lack of protection, until I managed to clip the bolt with a big sigh of relief. The crux move was perfect for my long span and, while desperate, it seemed to pass in a blur. Other than my first ascents, this remains the best lead I have ever managed, and it signified a breakthrough in my personal climbing career. The memory of the ascent is still vivid in my mind, even today.

Other routes on the slate followed, although none of them matched the magnitude of climbing *Raped by Affection.* Consequently, it wasn't long before my interest in slate waned, and I haven't been back since – a pity really.

Back to Ireland ... again!

By now, we had been to Ireland on two occasions. On reflection, I felt I had unfinished business to take care of on the Burren. Now that we had our camper van, it was much easier to plan a trip and tootle off somewhere – in this case, back to the Emerald Isle in July 1989. John Holdcroft came with us. We found wonderful Guinness, wonderful people and wonderful landscape with little, if any, tourism.

Our van may have been relatively basic, but it had all the requirements we needed. The only concern was the amount of petrol the tank would hold. We had planned an overnight journey, catching the ferry from Stranraer to Larne and then driving through the night, down to the Burren. The question was whether there would be enough petrol stations open. I doubted it very much, so concocted the idea of getting a large plastic barrel, filling it with petrol and carrying it in the back of the van.

I was right. There was nothing open on our route. We poured our

Sept. 1988

Cliff fall man improves

Gary Gibson: Still serious

A well known North Staffordshire climber injured in a freak abseiling accident is winning his fight for life.

Gary Gibson plummeted 70ft down a cliff face when a flying rock sheared through his abseiling rope and smashed into his head.

Mr Gibson, 28, a chiropodist of Rothesay Avenue, Sneyd Green, was rushed to Bristol's Frenchay Hospital following the accident in the Forest of Dean.

His wife Hazel, who was also on the climb, watched helplessly as her husband was sent tumbling down the rock face.

Surgeons have operated to remove a blood clot from his head, and today Mr Gibsoin was taken off the critical list.

"He has shown an improvement since yesterday but his condition is still serious," said a hospital spokeswoman.

Mr Gibson, who writes for a number of mountaineering journals and is well known nationally among climbers, had to be airlifted to safety

Mountain rescue team member, Jim Hewitt, said ot the accident: "I've never come across a case like this before. He was the victim of a million to one chance."

Climber may have to quit after fall

ROCK climber Gary Gibson (left) fears he may have to quit the sport because of a freak accident which sent him plummeting 70ft down a cliff face.

A flying boulder seered through a rope holding Mr Gibson and smashed into his head when he was abseiling in the Forest of Dean last month.

Mr Gibson, 28, a chiropodist, of Rothesay Avenue, Sneyd Green, finally left hospital after a desperate fight for life.

But he says some of the injuries he suffered in his horrific

By Edward Verity

plunge may stop him returning to the rocks for the rest of his life.

"I would love to take up the sport tomorrow if I could because it is in my blood," he said.

Waking

"But my sight has been poor since the fall and I don't know if it will ever improve enough for me to start climbing again.

"And I would certainly never go back if I wasn't full fit."

Mr Gibson's accident happened when he was "cleaning" a rock face — preparing it for three other climbers in his party — at the picturesque Ban-y-Gor rocks at Kidenham.

He says he still can't remember anything about his ordeal except waking up in hospital in Bristol.

Doctors have told Mr Gibson he should stay away from work for at least another six weeks.

He said: "I just hope my wife Hazel can put up with me being in the house for that long — so far she has been wonderful."

Climber in 150ft. fall

JAN. 1977

A YOUNG CLIMBER escaped with only cuts and bruises yesterday after falling 150 feet down a North Wales rock face when a rope snapped after a slab of rock weighing about half a ton became dislodged.

The rock hit the man's climbing companion, but he, too, escaped serious injury.

The accident happened on a crag close to Tremadog School.

Police named the men as Philip Gibson, 21, and Tony Ross-Gower, 19, both students, of Stoke-on-Trent.

The two were roped together but as the rock fell, Mr Ross-Gower was able to hang on to a tree despite being hit by the rock. Mr Gibson was dislodged from the rock face and fell when the rope snapped.

A rescue team from Aberglaslyn Hall Mountain Centre took both climbers to an ambulance waiting on the main road about 100 yards away from the crag.

Both men, who visit the Tremadog Rocks regularly, were taken to Madog Hospital, Porthmadog, where they were detained overnight.

Top two headlines following my near fatal accident. Some memories still haunt Hazel and me.
The third 'extract' is of Phil having a very big fall after a block cut his rope on a route at Tremadog.

Left: The first ascent of *Watching the Ocean* on Lundy. Three bolts yes but I did climb it later without.
Photo Hazel Gibson.

Left: Cabbage Disease in Chee Dale.
From left to right: Andy Popp, Ian Riddington, Graham Hoey, Nick Dixon, me and Ian 'hotshot' Johnson.
Photo Hazel Gibson.

Ooh, that water is cold. Lyons, Colorado.
Photo Hazel Gibson.

The incorrigible Roy Thomas.
Photo Carl Ryan.

My lovely wife at The Queen's Garden Party in 2015.

Photo Gary Gibson.

The ride of our life?

Photo Andy Birtwistle.

Outside Number 10 Downing Street with Leo Houlding and Sir Chris Bonington in 2008.

Photo Gibson collection.

Receiving a national award for services to my profession.

Photo: College of Podiatry.

Come on Matt, you can do it. And your reward is… The first ascent of *The Colour of Life*, Lundy.

Photo: Hazel Gibson with thanks to High Magazine.

Space Mountain, Craig Y Forwyn.

Photo taken for a lecture series by Allen Williams.

The first ascent of *Always the Sun* in Pembroke. Another seminal moment for me.

Photo Hazel Gibson.

Matt Ward seconding the first ascent of *The Indy 500* on Lundy. I knew there was a crack under that sea grass!

I was recovering from a serious head injury so stuck to bold slabs! *Splitstream,* Llanberis slate quarries.

Photo John Holdcroft.

The first ascent of *Slapstick* Craig Pen Trwyn.

Photo Hazel Gibson.

The first ascent of my 4000th new route, Stoney Middleton.

Photo Mick Ryan.

The first ascent of *Le Mans,* Lundy.

Photo Hazel Gibson.

The first ascent of *On Reflection* at the Burren, Ireland.

Photo Hazel Gibson.

Allen Williams' photograph brilliantly captures *Quiet Waters* in Pembroke.

The first ascent of *Zorba the Greek*, Lundy.

Photo Hazel Gibson.

Having fun on a roof over the road in Majorca.

Photo Hazel Gibson.

The first ascent of *Ghost Train,* Stennis Ford, Pembroke that sparked a series of events to reconfirm the ethics of the area.

Photo Hazel Gibson.

White Wand at Stanage. I can be bold when I want to be.

Photo Martin Kocsis.

A heady mixture of clothing? The first ascent of *Was it You,* Avon Gorge. Yes it was me!

Photo Hazel Gibson.

'I love dark miserable quarries'. The first ascent of *Exo6* in Masson Lees, the Peak District.

Photo Hazel Gibson.

petrol into the tank as and when we needed it. The only problem, I am told, was the smell of the damn stuff in the back of the van. As a result of my accident I had lost all sense of smell so the petrol smell was never going to bother me, but for Hazel and John it must have been dreadful, and we didn't even consider the hazard it posed.

We raced across Ireland, stopping only for toilet breaks and perhaps a cup of coffee or two. Now when I say raced, the van would do nothing of the sort, as it could only just reach about 60 mph going downhill with a tail wind. It was a relatively peaceful journey, save of course when we crossed the border between the two countries.

At the crossing point, we were confronted by an unmanned gatepost, although close by was a patrol station, complete with armed personnel. A red beam of light shone across the road. Apparently we were only meant to pass when it turned green. Of course we were completely unaware of this. We stopped, looked at the light and then just carried on. Having since spoken to other people who have crossed that border, we learnt that we were rather lucky not to have had our lights shot out.

We arrived at the Burren at around 7 a.m. You'd have expected us all to just want to go to sleep. Not me! I had a bite to eat and was straight into checking out some new routes for the next few days. By now, I had relinquished my ideology of bolt-protected routes in Ireland and stuck to the task of climbing the routes with as little in-situ gear as possible. I did place the odd peg, but I was quite comfortable with that idea and didn't think it would run against the ethical attitude of the climbing community.

Pushing myself to the absolute limit was the order of the day, and I couldn't believe what we achieved in the six days we were there: a wonderful new finish, on-sight, of a route to which I'd previously done the start in 1986, a batch of superb pitches on the Point Blank Wall and a really impressive pitch (at E7, I am sure) on the left-hand side of the Mirror Wall, which I named *Mirror Signal Manoeuvre.*

I wrote all these routes up, as is my wont, identifying the lines, the dates, the seconds and the names of all the routes. I then sent them off to the Irish Mountaineering Club. Unfortunately, I received no response. A little later, the guidebook to the area came out, the authors appeared to have completely ignored all of my routes. In fact, some of the lines had been credited to others after the dates of my ascent and given different names, while others remained supposedly unclimbed.

Perhaps now, in the cold light of day and considering my past indiscretions of adding bolts to the premier crag of Fair Head, I can fully understand the reasoning behind not giving me coverage and awarding the routes to someone else – something which, in retrospect, I had brought upon myself.

On our way back through Northern Ireland, we visited the Mourne Mountains, an area we'd heard so much about. Our mate, John Codling, had done a number of first ascents there and, having looked at a photo of some of his routes, I saw an obvious gap on the crag where they were.

We booked ourselves into a bed and breakfast in Newcastle and decided to have a look around town. We drove into the centre and parked up, leaving our dog, Dill, in the van while we wandered about. To be honest, it was a town like any other. However, when we returned, we noticed a sign by the side of the road where our van was parked, stating that any cars presenting a safety concern might be removed or blown up. Lucky old us – and lucky old Dill!

That night we went for a meal in one of the Chinese restaurants on the high street. It was a fairly basic affair, but, considering we'd been eating out of the back of our van, we thought it would make a welcome change.

We picked a table and, a short while later, a group of Irish lads came in and sat at the table next to us, with another mate arriving about ten minutes afterwards. No problem, we didn't think anything of it at all. We just ate our food and had a drink or two.

All of a sudden, there was a kerfuffle in the restaurant. The group of lads, apart from one of them, had left without paying. The restaurant staff were trying to get the remaining lad to pay for everything, but he wasn't having any of it, stating he wasn't with them, when he clearly was.

About two minutes later, in marched the Royal Ulster Constabulary, brandishing their rifles. It was a frightening experience as they frog-marched this chap out of the restaurant with a gun poking him in the side.

The turn of the bolt

The irony of my attempts to reduce the in-situ gear on some of my bolted routes on Lundy and in Pembroke, as well doing some of the bolder trad routes around at the time, was that in other inland areas, such as the Peak and Yorkshire (and even North Wales), sport climbing was just about starting to take off. A number of other climbers had realised that some of the crags in these areas were fair game for this new style of climbing.

I had seen the opportunity for such a development in 1983 with *Clarion Call*, but until 1988, few other climbers had been bold enough to take the same step beyond the 'establishment rules', to convey what they thought right for the sport. In 1988 the tide finally began to turn. Bolted routes, still mainly in the higher grades but not at the cutting edge of the sport (although they were beginning to creep down), began to be added across a number of selected areas. It may have taken another decade, probably until the late 1990s, for sport climbing to become fully accepted, yet it was clear that attitudes were beginning to change.

Titanium man

Almost twelve months after the date of my accident, I had to go back under the surgeon's knife. My accident had left me with a few side effects, including the occasional severe migraine and the loss of my sense of smell. However, the remaining damage to the front of my skull – an indentation of about 5 cm by 1 cm, with a depth of well over half a centimetre – meant that my skull provided virtually no protection to the frontal lobe of my brain.

This was a worryingly serious issue for me. Consequently, after a number of appointments with the consultants, it was agreed that the best solution would be to have a large titanium plate made for my forehead in order to protect my frontal lobe region.

The plate was made and, following a six-hour operation performed by Peter Leopard – which involved stripping back the skin across my forehead, fixing the plate with a series of screws, replacing the layer of skin and finally carrying out a jaw realignment, named 'Le Fort Osteotomy' – I was good to go.

Well, not quite; I had a large drain inserted to draw off excess fluid from the area, followed by what seemed like a very long week of convalescence in hospital.

One abiding memory, apart from friends visiting and referring to me as Frankenstein (amongst other things!), was the removal of this drain, which formed a complete loop around my forehead with the vent popping out of the side of my head.

The Senior House Officer came round to remove the drain (shunt). He decided that he could just pull the whole thing out. Now I knew it was a complete loop, with no end to it; so, as he pulled, the whole thing started to drag across my forehead. He said it wasn't, but I knew it was. Now I ain't squeamish, but this thing was extremely painful. You could feel the skin tear underneath and serous fluid squelching away as it went. I asked him to stop, but he wouldn't. After about ten minutes of me wriggling around, he came to the conclusion that I might be right. So he snipped the drain at one end and, hey presto, out it came. All was well again in the world.

The irony is that when I am finally cremated, with this titanium plate in my head, they will certainly know the ashes are mine. I might ultimately be worth something in monetary value!

My friends also derived a new name for me: by shortening the word 'titanium' and adding 'head'.

The scene of the crime ... again!

Once again, my rehabilitation took me back to Ban-y-Gor. This time, I was much stronger and quicker in recovery. Over the winter period, both Doug Kerr and I took to cleaning up the rest of the crag; I had to sort this place out, once and for all. Every Sunday, over the winter months, I would set off at about 6 a.m. and pick Doug up in Birmingham, to arrive at the crag as early as possible. We had each chosen a section of crag to clean; in fact, they were probably the most vegetated sections of cliff that had yet to be developed. We challenged each other to see if one of us could push a block off, in the hope that it would roll all the way down, into the river. Ironically, on each section of crag there was a large pinnacle, and you could probably hear the whoops and hollers from miles around as we egged each other on. I think Doug got there first with one of his efforts, although I doubt I was far behind.

At first, bolts were placed at a relative premium, due largely to expense, though, of course, it was always my intention to develop the crag solely for sport climbing. With the relatively long trek to access the crag and with all the vegetation, it seemed logical that this was the only way of keeping the place popular and clean (although this wouldn't happen fully until about 2008).

When we finally got around to climbing the lines, through the winter of 1989 and into the spring of 1990, it was a great relief for me to finally lay to rest the ghost of Ban-y-Gor, which had haunted me for more than twelve months. Closure was immensely satisfying.

Chapter 10

Completing the Circle

'*YOU ARE MAD...*' Dr Ken Barrett

The mid-1990s were to see three significant changes concerning my private life, my work and my climbing. All these changes were to take my life in new directions.

Following on from my accident, both Hazel and I were suffering from the unavoidable mental trauma of such an event. For me, returning to climbing, whether on a permanent or temporary basis, was inevitable, as psychologically I wasn't going to let the accident keep me from my passion. But my drive to 'get back on the horse' had consequences that I could never have envisaged.

My determination to lay to rest the ghost of Ban-y-Gor and my almost tunnel-vision narrow-mindedness meant that I never even considered the effect that my accident had had on Hazel. Add to that, the fact I was beginning to show signs of serious post-traumatic depression, and you can imagine the consequences.

The repercussions were probably inevitable. Hazel and I began to drift apart, and we had some real concerns about the future of our relationship. I could have understood if she had packed her bags and walked away from me. She had been my aide, my confidante and, most importantly, my best friend for more than a decade. It would have been devastating.

Instead, we chose to uproot and move away from where we had lived in Stoke-on-Trent for almost ten years. Hazel scoured the estate agents and found a lovely house, a renovated old chapel in a little village near Alton Towers. When we went to look at it, we immediately fell in love with the place. It was, without doubt, the right thing for us, and we moved in on 12th February 1993. It wasn't going to be the panacea for all of our problems, but it was a start.

I also had to take stock and consider how I was damaging our relationship. My GP, who had been so supportive of us both following my accident, referred me to a psychiatrist who, ironically, I worked alongside at my local hospital.

He gave me a full medical assessment, leading to the conclusion that I was suffering from post-traumatic depression. After a course of treatment, including cognitive therapy and medication, I began to recover enough for my and Hazel's relationship to improve. It was a defining time in our marriage. How could I have allowed this to happen? I realised that I had to change my attitude to life and sort myself out.

A union man

'*You won't get me, I'm part of the union.*' Joanna Brown, former CEO of the Society of Chiropodists and Podiatrist

The second life-changing event occurred at work. In every NHS organisation, a group of staff is entitled to have a staff representative to represent their concerns. Such a position requires a knowledgeable, determined and confident individual who is prepared to stand up for the rights of his or her colleagues. Our representative was about to stand down from the role, and a new one would have to be appointed. My colleagues decided that I should be that person.

Naturally I was flattered by their trust in me, and I took the role. I knew little about unions, save for hearing about people like Arthur Scargill and the consequences of the strikes in the late 1970s and early

1980s. I really had no idea what I'd let myself in for. Imagine me, Gary Gibson, trade union rep? Perhaps now you can – but certainly not then.

I turned up at my first union meeting, where the three main representatives of the two largest unions, namely UNISON and the RCN, were present. It was a small room, and they were re-appointing the collective union officers amongst themselves. There was no voting as such, but just a discussion about who would take which post. John Underwood had been there for so long that it was fairly obvious he would once again be re-appointed as the chairman. However, they also wanted a secretary, yet no one appeared to want the post.

Before I realised it, they had offered it to me. It was like a whirlwind, and I was so flattered that I just accepted the post, there and then. What I didn't realise was that the secretary was the main focus for the unions. The secretary organised the meetings, sorted out the record-keeping, such as the minutes etc., and was the contact point for the joint unions. Without realising what I'd got into, I was suddenly in it, up to my waist.

Over the next few months, I attended various meetings in my local work area, before going to a regional meeting of reps for our professional body. They were held on a quarterly basis and chaired by our then Director of Employment Relations, Eddie Saville.

It was a quiet little affair. Eddie's modus operandi was to set up a network of regional coordinators who would liaise directly with our national committee at our headquarters in London. I had already met Eddie on a few occasions and felt he had a lot of faith in me, so I accepted the role for the Midlands region. It offered me the opportunity to broaden my knowledge and further my future opportunities as a union rep, vis-à-vis a practitioner. It would also lead to a more active role in the future direction of my professional body.

Looking back, I most certainly made the right decision.

My final calling card

The third event was the move towards the rationalisation of where bolting should and shouldn't take place in British climbing. For almost all my climbing life, I had challenged the boundaries of what was and wasn't acceptable in relation to the ethos of numerous areas in the country. Although I had lost those battles in Pembroke and on Lundy, it seemed that sport climbing was moving towards a degree of acceptance in British climbing.

I still hadn't given up on the traditional areas, as I had my eyes on a number of lines in both Pembroke and Lundy; however, in all honesty, my commitment to both these areas was beginning to wane.

For two of those lines in Pembroke, I enlisted Roy as my climbing companion and Hazel as my photographer. To follow this climbing trip, Hazel and I planned to set off to Ireland with a bunch of friends for a cycling holiday.

It may seem strange that I should choose to single out these two climbs. However, today I regard them as perhaps my final 'calling card' to the area: *Lemon Crushed* on Stackpole East not only fitted in with the names of the surrounding routes but indicated the fact that I had to push myself to the limit to get up it; *Falling Towards England*, on the Green Bridge, and named after a Clive James memoir, on the other hand epitomised another style of climbing that I loved – steep, juggy, sustained and well protected – despite my normal preference for technical face climbs. I couldn't wish for two better routes with which to sign off.

Yet Lundy was a completely different kettle of fish. Sure, I'd fallen in love with Pembroke, but Lundy meant even more to me than that. Having spent so many wonderful holidays on the island, for which I have so many fantastic memories of friendship, fun and climbing, Lundy felt like home. I'd been involved with it since writing my first full guidebook to the island in 1983, and in 1992 I was once again invited to write the next chapter in its history, this time by the Climbers' Club.

Guidebook work may have been the main reason for going there, but

I also had a number of loose ends I wanted to tidy up. Roy would join us in our second week, and so, given my usual work ethic, I started to write up the guidebook manuscript for the island, while doing some route checking and tackling a few of the new lines that I'd previously overlooked. One of these I named, somewhat appropriately, *Blood, Sweat and Smears.*

The final chapter ended with an event which, for me, was to outdo all my activities during my involvement with Lundy Island for over a fifteen-year period, and it had to be Roy who provided it.

Roy's indulgence with cleaning activities outshines even mine, which really is saying something. He'd chosen a line up the back of Pathfinder Zawn, which was nothing more than a vertical field. At the end of each day, off he would go to clean a section of the 'allotment' of rock that he aspired to climb. Every day he would return, festooned in sea grass and vegetation, and in the need of a good shower.

However, Roy's extraordinary gardening effort had left one rather difficult obstacle to overcome. He hadn't finished cleaning his route until the Friday night, and we were supposed to be catching the ferry the following day. 'We'll do it in the morning,' he proclaimed. We prayed it would stay dry.

Thank goodness it did. Early the next morning we dashed across the island, climbed the route (*Bathfinder*) and arrived back, just in time, to catch the ferry. What a wonderful memory for my last day on this fantastic island! Sadly, I've not been back since.

New cliffs, new areas

The South East Wales climbing area was one about which I had limited knowledge, save for reading about the exploits of Pat Littlejohn and, more recently, climbers such as Andy Sharp and Martin Crocker. Here, in the sandstone quarries and inland limestone crags, the emphasis had shifted towards minimalist sport routes. How ironic that this should be the case, some ten years after my early exploits at Morlais Quarry!

Although I had climbed on a few of the crags in the area, somewhat sporadically over the preceding years, my first proper introduction was at Witches Point at the eastern end of the infamous 'little big crag', Ogmore. Martin Crocker had done a handful of routes there, ironically naming one *The World vs Gibson*, but the remaining gaps were plentiful. All the same, we still had the problem concerning the sustainability of the in-situ gear – it was a sea cliff, and we had little access to cheap stainless-steel equipment at the time.

Luckily for us, Pete Oxley had developed a method of forming marine-grade stainless-steel bars into U-shaped bolts, known as staples. After drilling two holes, a staple could be glued into the rock with an epoxy resin. This method at the time proved to be one of the best solutions to the problem of fixed-gear corrosion. Placing them was a little more time-consuming than placing normal bolts, but the end product was far more effective and long-lasting.

Pete had been using this process to good effect at Portland from about 1992, and, by way of making some extra funds, was selling them to those who were interested. It was perfect for us. We had our eyes on Witches Point and we were also looking for a solution to the problems of re-gearing other routes for the benefit of future generations.

It was the ideal testing ground for our new-found bolts. We spent two good summers climbing a number of quality lines as well as re-equipping – this was in 1993/94 – the handful of other routes on the cliff.

A screw loose?

Towards the end of 1992, I had to visit my consultant for another operation. While training for the London Marathon, I had been running through the local streets when I felt an unusual trickle of moisture run down my face. I say 'unusual', as the temperature was about two degrees at the time. I put my hand against my forehead, and, when I looked down at my palm, it was covered in blood. I then looked at my white T-shirt, and it too was covered in blood. Clearly I had a serious problem.

When I got home, I cleaned my head with water and had a good look in the mirror, to see what had happened. What I saw astonished me. Part of the titanium plate that covered my forehead (beneath the skin) was now protruding through the old scar on the bridge of my nose. It was a shocking and awful sight.

The next day and after examination, my consultant discovered that not only did I have a piece of the titanium plate sticking out above the bridge of my nose, but that one of the small screws, inserted to secure the plate to my shattered, jigsaw-like skull, was moving around in my forehead. So, I really did have a 'screw loose'! Both this and the piece of protruding metal would have to come out.

A few weeks later, I was back under the surgeon's knife. They were doing well out of me and, courtesy of our wonderful NHS, I was doing well out of them. The offending pieces were removed; in fact, they removed two screws that were floating around the front of my skull. Now, all that needed to happen was for the scars to heal.

Generator one ...

'*Eventually he re-appeared wading back along the flooded track, soaked, teeth chattering and looking distinctly blue and disorientated. It took some persuasion to get him into the spare dry clothes and drink a hot coffee, but he eventually warmed up. The rain stopped and round two commenced - just another wetter day than usual in the life of an obsessive*'. Roy Thomas

Within a few weeks, Roy and I were assessing the potential of the crags in South Wales, where we visited a number of venues. However, on our return to Dinas Rock and, following on from a period of activity by Martin Crocker and Andy Sharp, we were very surprised to find a significant number of possibilities. Ironically, Martin and Andy had chosen to utilise fixed gear where necessary, which further emphasised my feelings about what was most suitable for the crag. The fire was once again alight, and this time I had a drill, stainless-steel staples and Roy, the perfect partner in crime.

We each picked a couple of lines, and I was lucky enough to come up with two routes which I regarded as future classics; *Still Life* and *The Sharp Cereal Professor* – the latter name reflecting my ability to take the piss out of another climbing hero of mine.

It was a good opportunity for a significant number of quality new routes. Nevertheless, we also wanted to take the opportunity of re-gearing the existing routes and to move away from their mix-and-match protection. We concluded that if we re-equipped these alongside the new routes, the crag would become more popular. However there was still a large amount of cleaning to be done as the crag was swathed in ivy and other vegetation. There was a small-scale re-gearing programme underway on other cliffs in the area, but the extent to which we were looking to re-gear this crag was on a whole new level.

The trouble was that my battery-operated drill only had the capacity to place twenty or so through-bolts or around a dozen staples. We needed a solution.

On the drive home, I had an idea. If I could get hold of a 12-volt drill and a 12-volt industrial generator and lug these up to the crag, we would have our solution. In addition, we needed an autumn weekend when the cliff was dry and we could do everything in one go. Roy was very much up for the idea, if I could sort out all of the necessary equipment. A friend of mine, Mark Elwell, was happy to lend us his Kango drill, and all I had to do was hire a generator from a local hire shop, at £50 for the weekend.

We chose a suitable weekend, and I set off for South Wales at around 6 a.m. on the Saturday, arriving at the crag at around 8.30 a.m. As time was at a premium and I knew Roy would be there soon – he lived about forty minutes drive away – I thought I'd take matters into my own hands and haul the generator and drill up to the cliff. I parked at the end of the track and realised that I would have to pull the thing along a narrow catwalk above the Kennelgarth Wall to reach our objective. This was about thirty feet high and about three feet wide, at its narrowest point.

I got the generator up to the narrow passageway, and then, as Roy arrived, without dwelling too much on the thirty-foot wall below, we dragged it across, down the step and along to the huge roof that guarded the left-hand side of the main cliff. Unfortunately the river was in swell after heavy rain which had been falling over the previous evening, but luckily the cliff remained dry.

All we had to do was get the drilling kit, our cleaning gear and the bolts and glue across to the terraced wall on the opposite side of the flooded crag base. Roy wasn't too keen on the idea but having spent money on hiring the generator, as well as dragging it all across to the cliff, I didn't hesitate. I stripped down to my undies, and together we struggled across to the other side, managing to keep everything dry.

By this time, I was completely soaked and had become bitterly cold. I was absolutely freezing; my teeth were chattering, and I was beginning to show signs of hypothermia. But that wasn't going to stop us, as we managed to re-gear something in the region of fifteen to twenty routes, as well as equipping and cleaning a significant number of new lines. The ivy and vegetation were removed, and the whole crag began to look much better as a result of our efforts.

When I look back twenty years later, I'm staggered at the lengths to which I've gone, just for the sake of a bunch of new routes and cleaning up a load of existing ones. It was perhaps this event, more than any other, which got me into the cycle of re-gearing routes for the benefit of future generations.

Generator two ...

'The glue was of a high spec used in the construction of the new Severn Bridge and had been "acquired", so I'm told, in a deal involving a bathtub and a sink. Offset against its cheap price were our headaches and sore hands trying to force it out of the applicator. When darkness and low tide arrived,

we were only too glad to hide the generator in the undergrowth and scramble down to the beach.' Roy Thomas

The winter of 1994/5 was memorable for Roy's discovery of another new crag on the Gower. He rang me one night to tell me about the place, and I just couldn't shut him up. This is unusual, as Roy is quite reticent when it comes to such things. His enthusiasm was incredible. 'You should see the place. It's about 400 yards long and has corners here and there, arêtes, walls, it's just incredible. You'll have to come down and take a look.'

I needed little encouragement. My first visit to Oxwich with Roy gave me the same impression. Loads of new routes to do, the perfect sport-climbing venue, requiring little in the way of cleaning.

Following on from Dinas Rock, the solution to our problems of bolting the crag seemed only too obvious: the generator and drill. I procured the drill again from Mark and hired the generator. Roy had found a source of free glue: a friend of his had traded a bath tub for a number of tubes of glue from a mate of his who had been working on the new Severn Bridge project. Problem solved.

The only trouble was that when we arrived the tide was in, and we would have to haul the generator along the top of the crag and then lower it down to its base. Of course, at the end of the following day the tide would be out, and we could lug it back across the beach to my car.

We dragged and pulled the drilling equipment, including ropes, bolts, glue, harnesses and brushes, across the top of the crag. We found a good place from which to lower it in, and then we set to with the drilling. I always wonder what people must have thought as we carried the stuff past them.

After we had drilled enough routes – and got through a whole host of old drill bits – we set to the task of gluing in the bolts. If we had enough holes drilled, it would save on the amount of glue nozzles we'd need.

Now this was a really cold January day, and although we were quite warm from our drilling efforts, it was a completely different matter once we started gluing. The temperature was around two degrees at best, and, as the glue in the tube just wasn't fluid enough, it wouldn't flow properly at all. It was an extremely time-consuming and smelly exercise. Nevertheless, over the two days, we managed to bolt around twenty-five routes, which just left us with the task of getting the drill, generator and gear back. We heaved a major sigh when we finally returned in one piece without breaking any bones.

We never used the generator idea again, instead investing in a better drill with capacity to drill more holes. I also left some of my cleaning clothes there. The infamous rugby top I chose for the photo shoot on *Quiet Waters* still lies beneath a boulder at the foot of the crag.

Although, most of the crag is no more as it slid into the sea during the winter of 2018-19, perhaps due to the weight of the equipment we had placed in the crag?

Sid, Sid the Karachi Kid

'*I really started to get to know Gary after Smalldale. As a psychologist, I found Gary very interesting. He turned out to be NOT NORMAL, but not disturbed either, but wait, possible OCD — Obsessive Climbing Disorder. A friendly, driven guy, who has been misinterpreted, misrepresented and misunderstood, and often insulted by the climbing world. I personally know what it is like to be an outsider and different.*' Nadim Siddiqui

In the summer of 1995, Nadim Siddiqui ('Big Sid' to his mates) had written an article about a new crag that he had developed in the Peak District, which he'd christened Crag X. I thumbed through the article in the local climbing shop and heard, by chance, that the owner of the shop, Richard Pickford, was going there that night. He allowed me to tag along.

We managed to do a few of the routes, but, as always, my eyes were drawn more to the lines that hadn't been climbed than those that had – an opportunity I wasn't prepared to let pass me by. After a mid-week cleaning session, I climbed three new routes and planned another visit to finish the place off. Ironically, on my next visit, I bumped into Big Sid himself.

I had met Sid previously while knocking around in Stoney café and at the YHA on Deansgate in Manchester in the late 1970s. It was so good to see him again, although I'm not sure how he felt about my intruding on his patch. After an engaging evening, we decided to join forces, and together we finished off the development of the crag over the next few days.

Sid was really enthusiastic about some more new routes he had looked at on another crag that he felt still had potential: Smalldale. As I hadn't been there for a number of years, I agreed to meet him at the crag, together with another friend of his, Jim Burton, a week or so later.

I couldn't believe my luck. In between its existing lines, there was a mass of potential on the main wall, as well as the right-hand crag. I could see the possibility of adding something in the region of another forty new routes to my ever-growing list.

Sid and Jim each chose a line, but I don't think they realised just how fast I worked. Every evening after work and every weekend, I was there cleaning and climbing. I just wanted to blitz the place as quickly as I could before winter set in. We focussed on the main crag, but I spread across to the side walls, however small they were.

Over the ensuing few weeks, I managed twelve new routes of my own, whilst Jim bagged his and, finally, Sid completed his. It was ironic that Sid was the last to climb his route, after all of mine were completed.

I don't think they quite realised what a whirlwind had hit them. I knew Jim had warned Sid about the consequences of letting me into their little secret. Anyway, it was the beginning of a great friendship with two terrific guys.

Topo time

It was around this time that I got an idea about how to publicise these new routes and the development of the crags. The guidebooks were well and truly out of date. Even if a guidebook came out on a Monday, with my rate of new routing, I'd probably have put it out of date by Friday. The magazines were no place to update things; they were just news related and, by then, my routes were hardly important news, and I wasn't there to write about them.

I pondered over how to go about it and came up with two ideas: a website that could be continually updated and a series of topos that I could promote and sell through the local climbing shops.

My first website was named *Climb High Productions,* a name that I poached from a Stuart Cathcart route on Clwyd limestone. It later became *sportsclimbs.co.uk,* which seems much more appropriate nowadays.

In the case of the topos, I was lucky enough to know enough people who ran climbing shops and who would support my intentions. I began by selling the topos across the Peak District and later getting them into shops in London, Bristol, Cardiff, Birmingham and Manchester. It proved a success, and the proceeds helped to financially support my bolting – an early example of a bolt fund, I suppose.

Completing the circle

There was, however, one burning issue in the Peak District that needed to be resolved: the issue of bolting. Many of the older climbing fraternity were still dead against the ideology of sport climbing, and in many ways the champion of this group was the wonderfully direct and ardent anti-bolter, Ken Wilson.

Ken was particularly vocal in his attitude against my actions on a number of cliffs in the Peak. In his view, they were weakening the ethos of British climbing to the point where it would be unrecognisable as the sport he once knew. This was despite the fact that he'd held my rope on a new sport route in Chee Dale, in 1984.

An atmosphere of distrust towards me permeated every BMC Peak area meeting I attended. Although I was big enough to take the flak, it really had to be sorted out, once and for all. I respected Ken's opinions, but I didn't agree with some of them. I always felt we needed to come to an agreement at some point as to where we should and shouldn't place bolts.

In 1994, Sid and Bill Birch had developed a number of new routes at the esoteric and somewhat forgotten Harpur Hill quarry. While there were some old and relatively neglected trad routes there, they felt that adding a number of sport routes across the grading spectrum would bring the place back into the public arena. They created some excellent long sport climbs, the pick of which was a superb F7a on the lower tier, named *Cairn.* But Ken, Colin Ford and a few of their friends didn't like what Sid and Bill had done. They decided to remove all the bolt hangers from the routes and climb a few of them, with conventional protection.

The true bolt wars had begun, and such a stand-off was inevitably going to spark a flood of abuse from both sides. You have to admire Ken and his friends for taking such a stance, despite the animosity it created. But the bolt wars had to be settled, one way or another.

A short while after all this had happened, I decided to keep an eye on the cliff to see if people were indeed climbing the routes without the bolts. Of course they weren't, and the crag once again fell into disrepair.

In 1998, I decided to take things into my own hands, firstly re-equipping the majority of Sid and Bill's routes and then moving onto the other areas of the quarry. My intention, though, was to spark some form of reaction which would lead to a local area meeting, focussed solely on where bolts should and shouldn't be placed. There was certainly an increasing acceptance that bolts were here to stay. But the message from the anti-bolt brigade – that it would lead to all Peak limestone being bolted and then eventually spread to places such as Stanage – was, to my mind, preposterous.

The BMC eventually came to realise that this debate was coming to a head and arranged a meeting in Sheffield at the Foundry climbing wall one Friday night. Many of the main participants who had a vested interest in the debate were invited, and Derek Walker had the dubious honour of chairing the event. It reminded me of the panel I had sat on, at the BMC Conference, back in 1984.

Ken was given the opportunity to articulate his feelings about bolting in the Peak District and the danger it might cause to the future of British climbing. He was entitled to his personally-held views, but, as was usual with Ken, it all felt a bit too dramatised for my liking. Many others chose to pitch in with their viewpoints, either counter to Ken's stance or in support of it, but I kept my counsel.

Eventually, Derek turned to me. I explained, as firmly and honestly as I could, that it was never my intention to bolt all of Peak limestone. In fact, I had never been asked what my view of the situation was in the first place. I explained that I did not support the principle of bolting up every crag in the Peak District, and crags such as High Tor and Chee Tor should mostly remain bolt-free, except for a few isolated instances. I also explained that, in my view, there was a place for bolted routes and that sport climbing and trad climbing could co-exist, side by side. This was greeted by stunned silence.

What came out of the meeting was an agreement on where bolts were and were not allowed. It seemed that the cycle of events, following on from the *Clarion Call* episode some fifteen years previously, was almost complete. It was an historic line in the sand and the culmination to so much controversy. I never thought Ken would subscribe to it, but he did. I would love to go back and ask him what he thought of the whole episode, but sadly he passed away a couple of years ago.

Who could have imagined that through an incredible series of events, from the early 1980s into the twentieth century, the bolting issue would finally be resolved? From that meeting onwards, my vision of sport climbing through the grades, from lowly 4s, right through to 9s, would be accepted as part and parcel of British climbing. Finally I felt we had achieved something of lasting value.

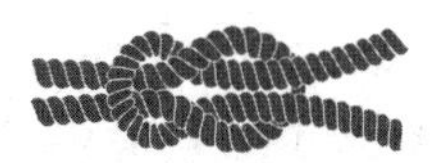

Podiatry

When I spoke to a friend about writing my autobiography, he queried why I would include anything about my working life. He said that I had to consider the nature of my audience and what they might be expecting to read. He suggested that my working life simply wasn't an area which would interest people.

I respectfully beg to differ. My work has played such an integral part in my life that I don't think I can leave it out. It highlights my commitment to other interests besides climbing. Some climbers may never have held down a full-time job while striving for climbing success. Conversely, my commitment to my work, following my graduation from college, lasted almost thirty-five years. It's been a big part of my life.

I've already mentioned how I chose podiatry and, how, over the years, my career and professional status steadily progressed. In 2009, I was voted by the membership of my profession into the position of a council member on the board of my professional body. This made me a director of the Society of Chiropodists and Podiatrists, giving me responsibilities way beyond my primary role as an NHS practitioner and my secondary role as a trade-union representative.

Specifically, it gave me the opportunity to represent the members at all levels, via national meetings, local representation groups and government bodies. Perhaps, even more importantly, it allowed me to be of some help and have input into shaping the future of my profession which eventually became the College of Podiatry.

This didn't always go to plan. It's fair to say that, at times, other members of the council had sharply differing ideas to me. Many were the times when, after attending meetings, I'd go home in frustration. But that's how democracy works. You don't always get your own way in life.

I had to travel down to central London on a regular basis, sometimes more than twice a month. Luckily, I was able to make my own travel arrangements, and I regularly ended up in first-class on a Virgin train more cheaply than I could have gone in second-class.

Sometimes I would sit in the carriage on my journey home, accompanied by the glitterati of the television and sporting world. I had the pleasure of encountering such people as Sandi Toksvig of television fame, Trevor Francis the first one-million pound footballer, Tony Pulis the football manager, and the wonderfully inebriated Shaun Ryder of the Happy Mondays, one of the most likeable people you could ever wish to meet. In fact they were all likeable people. I trust that when I pick up their biographies, they will likewise comment that they were lucky enough to meet Gary Gibson!

Despite the travelling and commitment, there were a few rewards for being a council member/director. One of these was the opportunity to be invited to meet Camilla Parker Bowles, Duchess of Cornwall and the patron of our professional body, at one of our centenary events in 2012. The meeting was at her residence, Clarence House, a mere stone's throw from Buckingham Palace. Although I am in no way a royalist, I couldn't help feeling that this was quite an honour.

I caught the train down to London and walked into the reception area with a number of other guests and colleagues. Being a 'Burslem Boy', I just couldn't resist picking up some of the crockery to see where it was made. I found myself holding a choice piece of Minton. Suddenly the heavy hand of a member of the Clarence House staff tapped me on the shoulder and asked me to put it down. 'That's a rather expensive piece of china,' he loftily informed me. Oops!

We filed into the room, waiting for Her Royal Highness to arrive. Everyone in turn would get to meet her. I was next to last in line. By the time I was introduced, I'd consumed rather a lot of champagne. I had also been informed to address her as ma'am (which rhymes with ham) and, in a fit of nervousness, I tried not to call her ham. With all that champagne, I could have flunked it.

She asked me where I came from. 'Stoke-on-Trent, a little village close to Alton Towers,' I replied. 'Oh, I've been to Alton Towers with my family,' she said. A thought crossed my mind: 'Well, we received our free tickets for Alton Towers the other day and, if you'd like to come along and use one of them, I could escort you around the grounds myself.' To which she replied, 'Oh, I'm far too old for things like that these days.' Before I could say anything else, she was moved briskly on to the final guest.

Buckingham Palace was next on the agenda. In 2015 I was lucky enough to be invited to the Queen's Garden Party for the voluntary work I'd done on behalf of my profession. There are two podiatry invitations a year, one to a member of staff and the other to a council member. I was fortunate to receive the nomination.

Hazel and I both loved the event. The gardens were decked out in an array of marquees. Sandwiches (without crusts) and miniature battenberg cakes were served. Then the Queen and the Duke of Edinburgh arrived. They walked slowly through two aisles in the crowds, stopping to meet influential guests. We managed to muscle our way to the front and get within a few feet of her.

We were blown away by the whole event and felt privileged to have been invited.

The final honour for me was to be nominated for a long-service award for the commitment and time I've spent supporting both my members and the podiatry profession over almost twenty-five years. It was a great privilege to receive such an award and I felt truly humbled.

Having now been to Clarence House, Buckingham Palace, the House of Commons and the House of Lords on behalf of my profession, I suppose the next place to which I'll be invited will be the Tower of London. Might I have to stay longer than intended?

Chapter 11

Cancer, Quarries and Number 10

'We are sat sheltering under the overhangs of a newly discovered crag (Pen Pych, Rhondda) in thick mist, with squalls of rain drifting in. This was the third attempt to start development, the thirty-minute uphill grind not helped by heavy rucksacks. This time we had the 100-metre static rope and another to extend to hefty pine trees in the forest, so success was ensured. Gary looked at me, "Are we mad, this isn't normal behaviour is it?" "Well Gary," I replied, "we have been doing this for over three decades and I just don't think about 'why' anymore, but, on reflection, I think we are both barking mad."

A pause and a shoulder shrug, Gary stood ... "Ah well, best get set up then and get stuck in," and off he trudged.' Roy Thomas

Catastrophe

Then in the autumn of 2002, catastrophe struck, with the news that Hazel had been diagnosed with cancer. It was a peculiar situation. She'd had a lump on the side of her neck for quite some time and had been referred for an examination to have it checked out.

Strangely, the referral was misplaced, and it wasn't until our return from a trip to Las Vegas with Hazel's parents that she finally got to have a scan and biopsy.

Hazel will tell you that she thought she had cancer all along, although to me she gave no sign of her concern. One Monday afternoon, I came home to find a message on our answer phone from the consultant's secretary, asking us to visit his clinic the following morning. I knew that the consultant was an oncologist, which almost certainly meant Hazel had been diagnosed with cancer. She took it in her stride.

The next morning we both sat in Mr Brunt's clinic, to hear the news that Hazel had been diagnosed with Hodgkin's lymphoma. She would have to undergo four episodes of chemotherapy and a number of radiotherapy treatments. 'When would they start?' we asked. 'Tomorrow,' came the stark reply.

For me, it was one of the most traumatic experiences I'd ever had to encounter. The chemotherapy had a dire effect on her. I witnessed her gradually lose weight, even though she was already as light as a feather. It was an awful experience, but she remained strong, happily coming out to belay me on new routes.

Some may say that I was too demanding of her but Hazel was determined to live as normal a life as possible, so much so that on Christmas day, the day after her last chemotherapy treatment, I had a new route cleaned at Llanymynech quarry, and she was happy to come along and belay me. I remember it vividly. It took her about twenty minutes to get to the foot of the climb, a mere two hundred yards from the car, but she was determined as hell. In keeping with the tradition of the wall, I named the route *I Saw Three Ships*, more as a message of hope than anything else.

Over the following few months, Hazel began to grow stronger as she went through the radiotherapy treatment and began to train for the London marathon. You just can't believe the fortitude of some people! Day after day she would turn up for treatment, and day after day she would do her training. It focussed her on getting better and being back in a routine.

Hazel has always been a good long-distance runner, probably based on her grounded attitude to life, and this marathon, one of twenty-five or so that she has run, was no exception. I say no exception, but it was, it really was. She was very thorough in her training, to the extent that she was looking at a personal best. I remember going down to see her and suggesting that if she saw a news presenter she should go up to them and say hello.

Hazel ran the time of her life. Paula Radcliffe may have been getting all the plaudits for her world record time, but the real hero of the race was my wife. She was brilliant, clocking a time of just over three hours fifteen minutes and beating her previous personal best by quite some distance.

She also managed to get onto television, even though she is oh-so nonchalant. I remember watching as, at the end of the race, she went up to Hazel Irvine, the BBC TV presenter, and said, 'My name's Hazel,' and promptly did an interview. I couldn't fault her. Ever my hero.

Hazel is a very private person; she doesn't seek the limelight and will feel uncomfortable with my account of her illness. Yet it was a defining part of our relationship, which I feel brought us so much closer together. I had been to hell and back with my accident, and Hazel's illness brought a strong realisation to me of just how important our relationship was.

Europe, here we come ...

Together, we agreed to seek some respite from the rigours of Hazel's treatment. When the cancer was in remission, I suggested we take a break from work and plan a trip travelling around Europe in our camper van. We decided on three months, applied through the appropriate avenues at work to get unpaid leave, and planned to set off at the end of January 2004.

Over the autumn months, we upgraded our camper van to a larger, more comfortable specimen, so that we could take along our dog, Lulu, as well.

The plan entailed a quick drive down the west coast of France into Spain and then spending some time with my parents on the Costa

Blanca. Then we would drive back up into France and meet some French friends in Bollène, spend a few weeks in Italy, climbing and sightseeing and, finally, take a gentle ride back home through France. It was a simple idea, yet the whole trip turned out to be a whole new experience, in more ways than one.

We set off at the end of January, in winds of around sixty miles an hour. Prior to leaving, in order to keep ourselves entertained through the dark evenings, we'd bought a DVD player for the trip. However, it had been delivered as part of a box of a dozen. The retailer didn't take long in contacting us to get the others back, and we arranged to meet him at a service station on the M1. In exchange for handing over the said items, we got a bottle of champagne, which seemed like a fine trade to me.

We had a great trip down the west coast of France visiting Biarritz, then northern Spain, searching for crags on the way, to eventually pull up on the outskirts of the capital, Madrid. Hazel had researched the campsites in the area, and we spent three nights in a super quiet spot close to the metro into town. Ironically, one of the railway bridges under which we passed on our way to the metro was bolted for climbing. Now there's an idea.

Our first port of call on the metro would be Atocha station, where we could gain access to the Prado and the Reina Sofia museums. I had always wanted to see Guernica, the famous Picasso painting from the Spanish Civil War. But things never quite work out the way we plan. No sooner had we left the station than Hazel had been pick-pocketed and her purse, together with driving licence and credit cards, had been stolen. Wonderful!

Off to the police station we went, while Hazel cancelled her cards in the hope that nothing would be stolen. Yet within minutes the thieves had extracted money from our bank account. Who says credit and debit cards are safe! The police took little interest in our problems although, after what seemed like a three-hour siesta, they deigned to give us a reference number for the crime. It wasn't a great start to our holiday but, considering the other travails we've had to put up with in our lives, it was nothing more than a passing scratch.

The Reina Sofia was just a few hundred yards up the road, and Guernica proved to be a really magnificent piece of art, even to a heathen like me. After seeing this timeless depiction of the first blitz bombing in history, we decided to have a wander round Madrid in the hope of spotting something else as inspiring.

Sure enough, we found it, although not in any way you could imagine. Just as we passed one of the main thoroughfares, we heard a man shouting his head off at the top of a section of scaffolding on the side of a five-storey building. He was level with the fourth floor.

Now neither of us speak much Spanish; in fact mine doesn't stretch much further than, *Dos cervezas, por favor.* Nonetheless, we quickly worked out that he was going to jump. He must have hollered for around ten minutes before the support services, police, fire and ambulance, finally arrived. Just as we thought they'd talked him out of it, he jumped and landed on the stairwell down to one of the metro stations. We didn't see him move. Ironically, the name of the street was Carrera de san Jeronimo. What a first day to start our break from work!

Over the following few weeks, we toured Spain and met my parents on the Costa Blanca. It was a very mellow time. We went to Italy for a bit of sightseeing, mainly Florence and Rome, before heading back north to the climbing area of Finale Ligure. Here we would meet Brigitte and a number of our French friends for a week's climbing, before starting our journey home. By then we'd been abroad for around two months.

Finale was an absolutely wonderful place, save for the narrowness of the roads. It was fine for the French in their cars, but for us in our outsize van it proved somewhat of a problem. We managed to get around by taking different routes, though, on occasion, it became a little stressful; but we coped.

The reward was some wonderful climbing and the best cup of hot chocolate I've ever tasted. In fact the best coffee I've ever tasted was also in Italy.

Our dog, Lulu, was happy coming along to the crags, sitting at the bottom and enjoying any titbits she was offered. She suffered a little when we took her to Rome and walked her into the Vatican and the Colosseum, but she was able to relax at the campsite afterwards.

The guidebook advised that Silencio, one of the cliffs we climbed in Finale, was a twenty-minute walk; nothing overly stressful, we thought. The only problem was that when we got to top of the crag, the only access down to its base was via a ladder. We decided that the best way to get Lulu down to the foot of the cliff was inside our friend Brigitte's rucksack. We packed her in, loaded her onto my back, and down the twenty-foot ladder we went. She wasn't too happy about it at the time, but, once at the foot of the crag, she quickly forgot about the episode. Unfortunately, the only way out was by the same method.

After a wonderful week, we packed up our belongings from the campsite where we were staying and started to head back. It was a long journey leaving Italy and we were both tired from our exertions in Finale. As we crossed the border into France, it even began to snow in Nice. The journey got progressively more tiresome, to the extent that we decided to pull up in a rest area on the autoroute just to the north of Aix-en-Provence. There were three other camper vans and some lorries parked nearby. We sorted out the stabilising legs on the van, cooked dinner, had the usual glass of wine (when in France ...) and settled down for the night. It was quite early in the evening, but we were bushed.

Then, around 3 a.m., Lulu started to growl, which neither Hazel nor I had ever heard her do before. We'd both been out for the count but when I sat up, I saw that the curtains which we'd drawn across the cabin were wide apart, and a breeze was buffeting the inside of the cab. When I got up to have a look, I found that the side door, which we had diligently locked every night, was ajar. A quarter panel of the door had been removed, and there were two small cans of CS gas or something similar on the grass. Someone had removed the panel to gain entry to our van. Their intentions beyond that? Well, you can imagine ...

We knew we had to get ourselves to somewhere safe, away from the rest area, for the remainder of the night, but, worryingly, we could see the culprits in the woods behind us. In case someone decided to attack us, I handed Hazel the table leg out of the van, while I wound up the stabilising legs. Everybody else had left the parking area and we were the only ones left – except, of course, for our assailants. It was a horrifying experience, but soon enough we were exchanging the parking area for the local police station. Thank goodness for Lulu!

Marathon Man

It would be wrong to suggest that my modus operandi changed as we moved into the twenty-first century. My intentions and drive would always keep me on the same path: climbing new routes and repeating others. There were still a number of places in Britain where I hadn't done any new routes, and, of course, there were always opportunities to visit other countries to sample the delights of their climbing.

I was probably as fit as I'd ever been. I ran on a regular basis, trained and bouldered to improve my strength. I even had spells on a fingerboard – the complete antithesis of how I got into climbing in the first place.

At the turn of the century, I was about to embark upon my fifth marathon. However, unbeknown to me, my whole life was about to be turned upside-down through an extraordinary sequence of events.

I had taken on my third 'football league challenge' at the London Marathon, which gave me free entry provided that I run in the football kit of my chosen club. The starting line was that at which the celebrities started. I'd already met Geoff Banks, Anthony Worrall-Thompson, Steve Cram and a few others at previous London Marathons, but this time I couldn't believe it when man-mountain Frank Bruno walked up to the start line. What a wonderful bloke, huge in stature but friendly and chatty as hell, with the most booming laugh.

Luckily for me I was fighting fit and managed to get round in a good time, well under four hours. Although my target of three hours and fifteen minutes was hampered by a groin strain, I still managed to beat Frank Bruno.

This is my route

'*Gary has a penchant for naming routes: a new routing wordsmith of the modern era. I liked the name he penned for a route he did in Intake Quarry called* Our Kid's Orchid, *which was probably fondly named after my interest in the flora on the quarry floor. Another he did in Huntsman's Leap was called* Little Hunt, *wryly named after the quarrel he'd had with Pat Littlejohn over his ascent of* Witch Hunt.' Phil Gibson

For almost four months we had completely forgotten about Hazel's health problems, and I'd postponed my new routing activity until returning to the UK. However, before we had left the UK, a friend of mine, Ian Milward, had shown me an impressive, undeveloped quarry near to Matlock.

It was time to start cleaning up what I had nicknamed Masson Lees and get stuck into the place, good and proper. However, while I'd been away, others had been having a look at the place. You could see their cleaning efforts on various parts of an overhanging wall which I had my eye on.

One of the culprits was a good friend of mine, Nick Taylor, and another was the indefatigable Pete Clark. Nick had left me some rather unusual messages at the top of the cliff. Written on three separate bits of rock was the barely recognisable message, 'I have cleaned this line'. But there were no bolts, as neither of them had access to a hammer drill. They were relying on me for that.

Over the ensuing weeks and with a few other climbers joining in the fun, we blitzed the place, ticking most of the available lines. Sure it was a bit hollow and dusty, but with a bit of TLC and some glue, the end product was, in my view, one of the best sport venues of its type in the Peak. As usual, I left no stone unturned in my drive for first ascents.

Ironically the last major route to be done was the one that Nick had cleaned before I'd even started work on the place. An even bigger irony was that it was superbly named *Masson Accomplished.*

As is normal for me, I continued to new-route through the summer but wanted another big crag to get stuck into over the autumn and winter months. When I had been looking for new crags a few years earlier, I'd followed Nick and Bill Birch into a huge quarry close to Wirksworth. I've never been one to raid other climbers' developments, except for the odd instance in Cheddar in 1985 and *Too Jugless for Dougless* in Chee Dale, so I left them to it whilst I concentrated on other places. However, in the summer of 2003 I decided to take another look and see what they'd done. To my surprise, there was very little evidence of their cleaning, so, with Hazel and my brother Phil, I developed two good walls and publicised them accordingly. Even so, there was lots of rock still left.

Abide with Me

And then on 21st September 1984 came one of the most devastating moments of my life when I received a telephone call from the local hospital to tell me that my father had died. He had been admitted into hospital for an angioplasty, a relatively straightforward procedure which involved widening the micro vessels around his heart with small stents. He'd got through the procedure but then suffered a massive heart attack and died on the coronary ward of the City General Hospital.

I'd been with him the day before, and he'd been coming out with some very odd statements, asking me to look after my mum, telling me there was enough money for her well-being, as well as a number of other things. He even gave me a big hug, something my dad had never done before.

He didn't want me to come along to the hospital and, on my way home, I knew in my heart of hearts that he knew he was going to die.

He hadn't been well for some time, but the telephone call was like a bullet from the blue. I was full of recriminations on my journey to the hospital, wishing I'd gone with him, and with a load of other things running through my mind.

You know in your life that this day will come, but you can never really be prepared for it. It ripped my whole family apart. It still does, as I write these words almost in tears. You just can't describe it, and I don't want to even try.

The following days were awful, trying to console my mum as well as myself. My only way to deal with it was to go out climbing, my source of comfort, doing new routes and taking my mind away from the stress. I even named a new route after my dad's favourite hymn, *Abide with Me.*

The funeral was a very dignified affair, yet it didn't alter the fact that I'd lost my dad. You just don't realise how close you are until something like this happens. I still miss him so much, at the Vale, having my hair cut and him doing our gardening, even after all these years.

Those Quarrymen

After my dad's death, my climbing efforts became even more focussed and determined. Nowadays I'm most commonly associated with sport routes, but, ironically, it wasn't until October 2017 that the number of new sport routes I had climbed surpassed the amount of new trad new routes that I'd done.

I suppose at the onset of my new routing obsession I had never thought about anything but trad climbing, but, as attitudes have changed, I have become more focussed on sport climbing. It's not that I feel the traditional values, with which I was brought up, should be eroded; it's more that I felt there was a place for all types of climbing, whether trad, sport, bouldering or competitions.

It was inevitable that eventually I would seek every possible outlet for my new routing. As the majority of established crags became more and more worked out, so the search for new routes would have to lead to new crags and most pertinently, quarries.

Today, many people consider my sole contribution to the climbing world has been to develop lots of poor or mediocre routes in crumbling venues, of little real worth to the climbing community. But many of these venues now play host to a large number of medium and lower-grade sport climbers. Just take a look at Horseshoe Quarry, Colehill Quarry and Harpur Hill in the Peak, Trevor Rocks in the Clwyd limestone area and Llanymynech quarry in the Welsh borders, as prime examples.

Although from the very outset of my climbing career I had been climbing in quarries with my brother, I hadn't really considered the almost elitist viewpoint about them until many years later when people started to mock their very existence. I still don't get it. I aim to climb; the aesthetic nature of where I climb comes second or even third, so long as I have had a good day out with my mates, doing what I enjoy doing, climbing and having fun.

And so, as the availability of unclimbed rock on natural crags began to dwindle, I started to focus on the quarries. It became an everlasting obsession, looking for their whereabouts, initially by driving around country lanes and later by the easier use of the internet, via Google Earth and other such applications.

I'd discover a hole in the ground, and my reconnaissance would always be very thorough, whether the quarry company had left or not. Sunday was always a good day. Sometimes I would bump (almost literally, on one or two occasions) into a quarry official. Having to explain yourself was always an interesting experience but provided plenty of fun and one or two interesting stories. It's amazing how quarry officials don't always know where public footpaths go.

On one such occasion, I was trying to develop a wall in a quarry on the outskirts of Wirksworth. This had already been cleaned and equipped by Pete Clark and his son Jon. I'd done a few new routes there, tidying up bits of untouched rock that they had ignored. However, I'd started to develop an area above the large turquoise lake in the quarry which I had christened the Acapulco Walls – not that you'd want to jump in. I'd already done a number of new routes and chose a summer evening to go back and clean off some more lines. Access was no problem; the top of the wall was an easy walk-in and was littered with a line of huge blocks, providing convenient belays from which to abseil.

I ambled into the place, set up my rope and garbed myself with all my usual cleaning kit: harness, brushes, hammers, cleaning tools, bolts, hangers and, of course, my trusty drill on my back.

Just as I was about to lean over the edge to start cleaning, I heard this booming voice, 'What do you think you're doing?' I looked over my shoulder to see two security guards in high-vis jackets staring down at me. My response was somewhat bizarre, 'I'm just going for a walk.'

Well you can imagine the response! I realised the stupidity of my comment, acceded to their demands and trudged out of the place with my tail firmly between my legs. Not that this was going to stop me. I was back two days later and managed another two new routes. I always try to have the last laugh.

A crinoid smile?

I'd been developing a section of cliff with Gordon Jenkin and Hazel on the upper tier of Hall Dale quarry in Matlock. We'd done a number of routes, but I needed to return, to improve the positions of a couple of bolts on one of them. I chose to drop in on a Saturday morning, before going to my local football team's game in the afternoon, so that when I was finished, I could nip off to the match.

Now the great thing about this crag is that I could park in a little lay-by and walk to the top of the routes, which were only about 150 yards away. I wandered along, set up the rope, gathered my kit together, drill and everything, and abseiled in – it wouldn't take long. For some strange reason, I put on my helmet, something that I wouldn't normally do on occasions like this; it was a trifling effort and would soon be sorted.

I placed the first bolt and drilled the hole for the second. Just as I was hammering in the last bolt, a rock dislodged itself from the top and hit me on the head. I tightened up the bolt with the spanner and gingerly abseiled down to the ground. I was about to tuck myself into the rock when another block hit me on the shoulder. I knew instantly that I'd fractured my collar bone; you can just tell these things, when your arm goes numb and free.

Luckily, I was able to stagger back to the top of the crag. But what to do? Then I saw a lady and young child walking across the base of the quarry with their dog. In the loudest voice I could muster, I shouted for help. The lady stopped and asked me what was wrong. I told her that I thought I'd broken my shoulder. She responded by asking me what I expected her to do about it.

In desperation, I wondered what to do. Then, in a moment of inspiration, I realised that I could phone my friend, Denis Vallins, who lived just a few miles away in Chesterfield. I told him what I'd done and asked if he could give me a lift to the nearby hospital. We agreed to meet in the local Sainsbury's carpark, where I could leave my car and my belongings would be safe.

We met about thirty minutes later. As we piled all my gear into Denis's van, we noticed a helicopter circling overhead. I said to Denis, 'What's that doing?', before realising it might have been called out for me. I thought it best to go back to the quarry to see what was happening.

When we reached the quarry entrance, we saw an ambulance, two police cars and two mountain rescue cars parked in the entrance – but no helicopter. Realising all this was for me, I thought it best that Denis and I went into the quarry to let people know that I was safe and sound. At the same time, I appreciated that I shouldn't have been in the quarry in the first place. I needed a credible story.

Sure enough, when we got into the quarry, the helicopter was grounded, surrounded by police officers, ambulance men and mountain rescuers. I had by now decided on my story. I wandered over to the group and explained to the helicopter pilot and policeman that I was the guy they were looking for and that I thought I'd broken my collar bone. But, of course, after taking my details, the policeman wanted to know how I'd broken it. 'I was looking for fossils around the bottom of the cliff and then suddenly a piece of rock from above hit me on the shoulder.' The policeman diligently wrote this down, then asked, 'What type of fossils were you looking for?' Oops! Quickly I retorted, 'Crinoids and ammonites.' 'Oh that's interesting,' said the officer (by this time Denis was in a fit of giggles, about a hundred yards away), 'I collect fossils, and when I'm off duty I'll go and have a look to see what I can find.' 'Be careful that you don't get too close to the cliff,' I cautioned him, 'or the same thing that happened to me may just happen to you.' Such irony ...

Sure enough, after my trip with one of the mountain rescue team to Derby Royal Hospital and a thorough explanation of what had happened, it was confirmed that I'd broken my collar bone.

A few weeks later, I was chatting to an old work mate and climbing friend of mine, Chris Cullen. He told me a tale of a climber who'd broken his collar bone in a quarry near to where he lived and dreamed up some cock-and-bull story that he was collecting fossils. Chris commented that, as soon as he heard the story, he couldn't think it would be anyone but me. What goes around comes around?

The Orangemen

In the quarries, I remember vividly one of the crags that I had decided to develop, now named Slaley Brook. Phil and I had passed this working quarry on the way to Matlock on a number of occasions through the mid 1970s and the early 1980s. One day, in the late 1990s, I was driving along the road from Cromford to Newhaven when I noticed that the quarry machinery had gone, and a new set of gates had been erected at the entrance. I popped in for a peek and saw two good-looking walls, one coated in a superb calcite and the larger, left-hand one plastered in what seemed to be a golden/orange veneer. It was way too tempting not to return, which, in 2000, I did.

I worked only about twenty miles away and chose to start developing the place late on a Friday afternoon in January. I plumped for the right-hand wall first, cleaning and equipping, complete with head-torch, way into the evening. As the evenings began to grow light, I moved over to the bigger left-hand wall; here, my first objective was a thin, sinuous crack running almost the full height of the cliff.

I gave it a thorough clean, spending about four hours hanging on the abseil rope. I cleared off the orange veneer, which turned out to be a fine coating of dust, and equipped the line. At the end of the evening, I was well chuffed, packed my bags and drove off. I hadn't looked at myself in the car mirror.

When I arrived home, Hazel simply burst out laughing. I looked as though I had been tangoed – my face was completely orange. I sat in the bath and washed myself down. When the water drained out, there was about a one-centimetre-thick layer of orange silt coating the bottom of the bath. I think I should have notified the local sewage works before I managed to wash it all down the plughole. The route became known appropriately as *The Orangeman.*

But all this cleaning activity hasn't come without consequences to my health. With all the dust and grime that I've removed, I may well have more Peak limestone in my stomach and lungs than is left in the Peak.

Cops and robbers

When we were developing some of the more recently abandoned quarries, I always knew that one day I might have a full-on confrontation with a quarry owner or one of their cronies. While climbing in Horseshoe quarry, Hazel and I had been approached on many occasions by one of the appointed workmen to advise us that we shouldn't be climbing on land owned and quarried by Tarmac. He would solemnly state it was his duty to inform us that, under the Mines and Quarries Act of 1954, they were under an obligation to keep the area safe. Once we had been duly informed, off he would stroll, having done his work. In fact, it happened so regularly on a Saturday morning, that he would just say,

'Oh, hello, you're back again. You know what I'm going to tell you,' and, with that, he would turn around and wander off again. It seemed he wasn't really bothered if we carried on or not.

Ironically, I knew the law and I knew that this was a civil matter. It would take ten working days to get a writ to remove us and we would be gone by that evening anyway, so what was the point in prolonging the conversation? That's why quarry owners used to have so many problems with new-age travellers and the like.

But I just knew that one day it would come round to a far more aggressive approach from a Tarmac employee – and so indeed it came to pass.

One day I was back, doing some more cleaning at Slaley Brook. As I sat at the bottom, I saw a red-faced quarry workman heading up the hill towards me in a rather aggrieved state.

When he finally arrived and got his breath back, he started to rant and rave at me for climbing on private land and committing trespass. He was going to prosecute me. I told him I wasn't leaving until later that day – it was about midday – and that he couldn't remove me without a civil writ, which would take him ten days to obtain. It was a Saturday, so he couldn't start the process that day, as the courts weren't open.

This seemed to wind him up further, and he started to get even more agitated. Luckily he was much smaller than me, so I think that stopped any physical retribution. He stamped his feet a bit more and said he was going to call the police, which I calmly invited him to do, and off he stormed.

About two hours later, he was back, this time accompanied by the local bobby, complete with uniform and helmet. I smiled rather ironically as they came stumbling up the hill towards me, with the bobby lagging behind. After they finally arrived and the policeman got his breath back – I thought he'd have a heart attack – Mr Tarmac started to rant and rave again, saying this and that and eventually indicating to the policeman that he should remove me.

I calmly (actually by now I was a bit worried) advised both him and the policeman that they couldn't remove me without a civil writ and that they couldn't prove criminal damage etc., despite my having just bolted a route on the cliff above them.

To my surprise, the policeman explained to Mr Tarmac that I was quite right and that he was here to keep the peace, also that he was more worried about Mr Tarmac and his attitude – at which point Mr Tarmac exploded! The policeman duly escorted Mr Tarmac off his own land.

But the story doesn't end here. By climbing in the quarries and cliffs in the Peak and North Wales, I have left myself wide open to attack, mainly for just climbing there but also for publishing details on my website, as well as filling the places with in-situ gear. The criticisms would sometimes come from other climbers but mostly from other quarters.

The most worrying thing about climbing on private land has been the irritation I've caused for landowners. I have never understood why quarries can't be used as leisure facilities after they've been abandoned, but no quarry owner seems to see it that way. They view them as bargaining tools to blow even more holes in the countryside. And that's where the worrying problem comes in. They have the Mines and Quarries Act and the Countryside Act to defend their rights – which places a burden on me as a new router.

Many are the letters that I've received from Tarmac and the Countryside Commissions for Wales and Derbyshire Peaks and Dales, advising me of my wrongdoing. When one of these letters lands on your doormat, it doesn't half put the wind up you. However, by nature I am an anarchist and wouldn't have it any other way. My motto has been, 'Go and climb there and worry about the consequences afterwards,' and I haven't been prosecuted yet.

Hawaii 5-0

One of my major finds (of course one or two other people were also aware of the place) was a quarry on the outskirts of Bakewell. I'd been eyeing it up for a number of years and, once the quarrymen had left, I zeroed in on it. There were two really impressive walls, about four hundred metres long, both with good quality rock and plenty of scope. The only problem was a nesting peregrine falcon. I decided to wait until the end of July 2015 before cleaning a few lines. I'd even promised some new routes to a few mates as well.

I arrived at the quarry one Friday afternoon and set about cleaning a few prospective routes. I thought if I could get about ten cleaned and bolted for the Sunday, we could almost have a party there. I cleaned and bolted two superb-looking lines, both about F6b+ and then started on a third one. At this point, I noticed some people to my right, on the hillside overlooking the quarry. I could see they had binoculars, so I decided to abseil back down to the ground to find out how England were getting on against Australia in the Ashes test.

I sat there for about an hour, but those people weren't budging either, so I decided to leave and come back the next day. I left my rope in place, packed up my gear, walked out of the quarry and down onto the road leading back to my car.

When I got about a hundred yards down the road, I saw a police car hurtling towards me with blue lights flashing and sirens blaring. It just had to be for me.

The car pulled up alongside and the policeman told me that I'd been accused by two people – presumably the ones on the hillside – of stealing eggs from a peregrines' nest and that he needed to search me. He told me to cross the road to a pull-in place where he could do the honours. I advised him that the parking place wasn't good for his car and that there was a better one further up the road. At this point he got a little stroppy and reiterated that I should go and stand where he asked. So I did. As he pulled into the parking place, I heard an almighty screech as his car's sump scratched across the ground. Told you so!

As the policeman had already told me he was going to search me, I decided that the best response was to get ready before he got out of the car. I pulled my trousers down, in preparation. When the somewhat flustered policeman asked what I was doing, I said, 'You wanted to search me,' to which he retorted, 'I meant your rucksack.'

This was all about stealing eggs. I explained to the policeman that I was aware of the peregrines' nest and that the birds nesting there had fledged. I understood that they were a protected species and I'd been at least 200 yards away from the nest. I had absolutely no intention of robbing it and was in no way persecuting the birds.

But he wasn't having any of it. As we started to get into serious discussion, the two chaps who had been watching from the hillside arrived and we went through it all over again. I told them once more that I'd seen the tercel in flight with the fledglings. Things started to settle down a little when they realised that I just wanted to climb in the quarry. It was one of the most bizarre discussions I've ever had with anybody. I tried to dampen their ardour, as well as staying relatively calm.

The discussion then moved on to who'd given me permission to climb here. Of course my answer was, 'No one.' They seemed quite perturbed by that, and hence the discussion became a little more fraught again. I told them that I just chanced my arm and that climbers – well a certain anarchic section of the climbing fraternity – have always done it this way. That shocked them even more. To cap it all, one of them then announced he was a climber.

Things finally calmed down. I gave the policeman my name and address by showing them my BMC membership card. But I also asked the 'wardens' why they hadn't just come down to ask what I was doing, rather than calling out the police. One of them said that I might have had a knife, and I told him, 'Well you could have just shouted across to me.' The policeman then said that I might have had a gun, to which I retorted, 'It's not fucking New York, you know!'

Thankfully sanity eventually prevailed. After all that, the policeman shook my hand, as did the two 'wardens'. They even apologised for disturbing me and said that I could go and get my gear back. It was all very strange.

The cost

My approach to new routes has by now shifted almost completely to sport climbing. The equipment has changed dramatically: stainless-steel bolts and hangers or glue-in bolts. This change came about for several reasons. Stainless-steel gear has become far more readily available than before; a number of climbing-related companies have started to sell it and competition has made the price come down. Another reason was the realisation that stainless gear would last considerably longer. The BMC had set up a committee, of which I was a part, to ascertain which products to use, as well as testing old in-situ gear to prove or disprove its deteriorating nature.

I reviewed my previous in-situ gear where lower grade metals had been used or, indeed, the mixing of metals had accelerated the corrosion processes. I wasn't the only one doing so. To me, the radical solution would be to review all my previous work and, where possible, go back and replace it with more substantial, longer-lasting equipment.

My re-gearing process has spread across a whole range of areas: Chee Dale and many accompanying Peak District crags and quarries, Clwyd Limestone, the South Wales crags, Ban-y-Gor and then on to places such as the Gower. Of course, such actions have a significant cost but, as I am fully committed to the cause, I am quite happy for that.

There was some support. The BMC set up a 'Better Bolts campaign' to help climbers doing exactly what I've described, whilst a number of bolt funds were set up, to which climbers could make donations. Of course I had my own bolt fund via my website but, looking back, in trying to calculate how much I have spent on in-situ gear over the years, I estimate it to be around £70,000 to £80,000. Anyway, I have the view that you pay for your enjoyment in life.

Let me tell you about another little problem. Spending up to eight hours in a harness has an extremely detrimental effect on your legs. It cuts off the circulation and nerve supply for an inordinate amount of time and leads to one of the most painful experiences I have ever had to suffer – the dreaded cramp.

It doesn't come on straightaway; no, it waits for you in hiding. Many times I've returned home and settled down for the night. Half an hour later when I've got up unexpectedly, straight down the inside of the leg my gracilis muscle triggers into cramp. The pain is so intense that you can probably hear my yelling in the houses down the road. A long stretching session follows and eventually it drifts away, only to wait in hiding for another day. Some of us have to pay for our 'art'.

The Craig Arthur controversy

One day, out on a winter walk along the Clwyd Limestone crags with Hazel, I noticed a significant amount of potential on Craig Arthur, a place with a limited amount of sport routes at that time. Here was a prime opportunity to further develop a crag on which I'd done relatively few new routes. I calculated there was scope for around thirty. And so off I set on a mission to fill in the blanks on the cliff, attempting wherever possible not to affect the existing routes.

On the whole, this was quite a straightforward issue but, on the great expanse of the *Nemesis Wall,* it was more complex. Most of its routes wandered around, seeking out the easiest ways and with mostly traditional protection. There was the odd peg or bolt, some of which were remnants of previous aid explorations.

My problem was that this relatively neglected wall had the possibility for some impressive direct lines, which I really wanted to do. My intention was clear – bolt them and, where possible, don't interfere with the existing routes. There were already some terrific routes on it, most of which I'd repeated with my brother Phil and I certainly didn't want to ruin them. I set about developing the place, trudging up straight after work, cleaning until it went dark and returning with Hazel, usually on the Friday, to tick them off.

I was particularly pleased with three routes: *Oblivion,* at E6 6b, a direct line through Pat Littlejohn's *Friday the 13th,* with four bolt-runners on the sections not affecting other routes, *Mercury Rising*, a brilliant 7b running the full height of the wall on its right-hand side and, perhaps the best of the bunch, *Relentless*, 7b, which took a direct line up the centre of the crag.

At no point did any of the bolts on these routes affect the other routes, save for a bolt on *Relentless*, just to the left of the belay on *Friday the 13th*. The problem was that when other people began repeating the routes, it became clear to all of us that *Oblivion* really should have been a sport route. I decided to go back and bolt it, which, of course, did affect Littlejohn's route.

Once these routes had been discovered, it quickly became apparent that I'd fully bolted *Oblivion*. All hell broke loose on social media and other places, condemning everything I'd done on the wall, as well as criticising me for many of the things I'd done elsewhere in the past. There was some support for my action, as well.

Once more, I had courted controversy. Littlejohn removed some of the offending bolts but chose not to return them to me, which I still regard as the theft of my gear. I chose, as I always have done, to stay out of the vitriolic debate which ensued. Whether that was right or wrong, I have yet to decide.

I am a turtle

Roy Thomas and I had been developing a tasty little crag, called Morfa Bychan, on the Carmarthenshire coastline. This was a tidal cliff with two rock ramps at its foot, which tilted down into the sea at high tide. This meant that you couldn't get to the wall we were developing until just before half-tide, unless you abseiled in, of course. We'd spent three days there and prepared a few routes to do on the last day, so that I could get off home as soon as we had finished; it was about a four-hour drive.

On the last day, we took our time getting to the place, as we knew the tide would be in. When we arrived, we sat on the shingle beach biding our time for the tide to recede, so that we could get to the cliff.

As it slowly ebbed, I got an idea; I could climb up the wall below the first ramp and then traverse the second wall, to get onto the ramp below the cliff. I decided to test the theory and, sure enough, after a quick boulder hop above the lapping sea, I could get up the first wall and so traverse the second wall and then onto the terrace.

I dashed back, hauled my huge rucksack onto my back (it contained my drill, bolts, climbing gear and other goodies, plus two ropes) and set off across the boulders. I stabilised myself on the last boulder before the sea and, with the waves lapping at my feet, started to climb the first wall to get onto the ramp. Unfortunately, after only a few feet, a hold snapped, sending me plummeting. The only thought that crossed my mind was that I mustn't get my drill wet. I landed with a thump on my backside, flailing my arms around to stop myself from falling backwards into the sea.

Roy gazed at me as I waded out of the sea, wet from the waist down but with my rucksack still dry. I'd fractured my coccyx, but he was sniggering away. I asked him what was so funny, and his response was, 'It was like watching a turtle trying to get out of its shell.' At that thought, I just couldn't stop laughing either.

I am Superman

'I met Gary for the first time in a long while at Awesome Walls in Stoke a couple of years ago. I had gone climbing with a relative, was obviously out of shape and climbing in hired shoes. After saying hello, Gary couldn't help but jump on the wall in front of me to do a problem I was trying – he hadn't lost that drive to burn someone off!' Derek Beetlestone

I had been walking through Water-cum-Jolly eyeing up the potential of its crags as usual when, as I wandered below Central Buttress, I noticed a number of gaps between the existing routes. In fact, the whole buttress was looking rather tired, with many of its existing routes becoming covered in ivy and vegetation – an issue that, in my mind, had to be rectified. Why let such a wonderful crag go back to nature, when I had such great memories of it?

I decided that I would try to tidy the place up, which not only meant bagging new lines but also, where necessary, cleaning and re-gearing the existing routes, which in itself would be quite a task.

The problem was that the river running directly beneath the cliff is a popular fishing spot and it wasn't uncommon to find someone fishing in the river below the crag, during the afternoon or evening. Due to this, it wouldn't exactly be fair to be knocking rocks off the cliff as the anglers were innocently pursuing their sport.

I decided, therefore, that an early start would be the best solution to this problem and selected a Saturday morning in late August to start my work, after which I could go and see my football team play a match against Wolves, a local derby of sorts. In fact it was the Saturday of the bank-holiday weekend.

I was there nice and early, sorted out my gear at the foot of the crag and wandered around the top with my drill and gear, ready to start cleaning and equipping. I tidied one line, with little consequence; the next line I wanted to clean would be the last before I left.

What I decided to do was abseil in to the place where I proposed to place the lower-off. Then, I would pull the rope down, double it up, so that both ends of the rope touched the ground and abseil off and clean the route as I went.

As I progressed gradually closer to the base of the route, I saw what I thought to be both ends of the rope touching the ground. This meant that I could finish off what I was doing, pull the rope down and wander off back to my car and drive to the match.

As I got about fifteen feet above the ground, I drilled the last hole and placed what would be the route's first bolt. Following this, I decided I could just drop to the base; what I hadn't realised was that only one end of the rope was touching the ground, and the other end was only about a foot below the abseil device I was using. As I let the rope go through the descendeur, it suddenly whipped through the end of the rope, and I was hurtling towards the ledge where I thought the rope ended, which was about fifteen feet from the ground.

As I hit the ledge, I knew I was going to catapult over the edge onto the scree below. So, as I careered head-first towards it, I thought only of protecting my arms by holding them out in front of me, as if flying like Superman – although, unfortunately, my shorts were on the inside of my trousers. Finally, I hit the ground with an almighty crash, head first.

I had banged my leg up rather badly, but my main concern was the blood streaming from my head.

I sat for a short while, maybe about five minutes, and then in true hero fashion, coiled my rope, packed my rucksack and waded across the river to the track on the other side.

As I limped back to the car, about half a mile away, I passed quite a number of people none of whom bothered to ask how I was – I thought I mustn't have looked too dishevelled or injured, which made me feel a whole lot better.

When I reached the car and unloaded all my gear into the boot, a really pleasant chap came up to me and asked if I was alright. I said I was just fine, but he told me that I didn't look it. When I looked in the mirror, I could see that my face was completely covered in blood. I had a huge flapper on the side of my head, poking through my hair, and I had rather badly torn trousers and a severely gashed leg.

Thanks, you lot who passed me by on my walk back to the car, I thought.

When I arrived back at the football club, I decided to go to the St John's Ambulance brigade to get myself checked over. Twenty minutes later, and with some soap and water, I was clean. Needless to say, I needed quite a few stitches and some wonderful TLC before the match kicked off. It might have felt better if we'd won, but we lost, two-nil.

Four thousand

Towards the end of 2013, I realised that I was on a mission to achieve a goal of four thousand new routes. Many people have mocked how many new routes I had done, either due to their lack of quality, lack of line or pure insignificance, but I didn't care. My treasure may have been someone else's trash, but I have loved almost every minute of it, and to achieve such a significant number of new routes was, for me, a major milestone.

I normally do around a hundred new routes a year, with a monthly target of around ten. Having reached the total of 3,900 by the end of 2012, I had worked out that it would be around September before I met my target. Over the winter months I decided, therefore, to recce some new crags in order to accelerate the process. By then, I just wanted it to be over with as quickly as possible.

With a few old crags like Stoney West and Long Tor quarry in the back of my mind, coupled with two new crags, one on Clwyd Limestone and one in the Peak, it wasn't long before I was staring the prospect of my four thousandth new route straight in the face. With so many options, where would I choose the route to be? It really had to be somewhere better than an old, scruffy quarry.

I knew just the place. For quite some time, I'd been looking at the prospect of a new route on the edge of Garage Buttress at Stoney Middleton. With Stoney having been such a historically important place climbing-wise, it seemed to be an ideal choice. My route would also be the closest sport route to Sheffield, which I thought fitted the bill perfectly.

Over a couple of days in July, I cleaned and equipped the line. I circulated an invite to a number of friends to join me for the event. I just wanted my mates to be there and enjoy the moment with me.

And so, on Saturday 13th July (probably the hottest day of 2013, with a forecast of around 95 degrees Fahrenheit), we gathered at the local café in Calver to sup coffee and prepare for the event. Naturally I was nervous, even though the route was only going to be about F6c.

Mick Ryan had come along to photo the route and we wandered around to the top of the crag to select the best position for him to take shots. I was very edgy, as no doubt Mick would testify. I abseiled in to strip tape from the bolts, which I'd put on to prevent anybody else nicking the line, and then I was ready.

I set off with a whole raft of thoughts running through my mind. The crowd below were very supportive, but the pressure was weighing me down, almost as though I was five stone heavier – and I ain't a lightweight, by any means!

I reached the break at two-thirds height relatively quickly. F6c or not, I felt drained by the whole experience. Mick hung around above me, waiting for me to launch onto the most difficult section. I just wanted it to be done before the sun came around; it was very hot. The heat certainly wasn't helping. I could feel myself wilting under the pressure.

Finally, after what seemed like an eternity – but was probably just a couple of minutes – I pushed on and, in what seemed like a blur, Hazel was lowering me back to the ground to applause from my mates. I gave a huge sigh of relief; it was over at last.

As I returned to *terra firma*, Ken Hughes pulled the cork on a bottle of fizz to celebrate. The banter continued at the nearby Red Lion at Litton, where we gathered for a congratulatory pint or two – I actually didn't buy any! The consensus was that I would really achieve something if I got to five thousand new routes. But, when I get there, I know they'll want blood and six thousand.

I look back on that day with just one tinge of sadness. A good friend of ours, Gwyn Arnold, provided me with a video of the event. Sadly, about a year or so later, he passed away from the awful disease that is cancer. You're left with memories of great people and great times.

Who do you think you are?

In 2007, after a series of re-gearing sessions at Ban-y-Gor, Hazel and I were invited down to the Wye Valley guidebook launch in Chepstow. We were to stay with some friends, Yvonne and Carl Jones, in Tutshill. With the event being on the Saturday evening, I decided that it would be a prime opportunity to clean some new routes on a new wall at Ban-y-Gor and then hook up with my good mate Gordon Jenkin, and of course Hazel, Yvonne and Carl, the next day, to climb the routes.

We arrived on a dank and dreary Saturday morning, and, once we'd dropped our gear off at the Jones's, I set off for the crag. I parked up at the usual parking spot and began the long walk in.

Just before I got to the start of the crag, I met a chap walking towards me with his dog and thus ensued one of the most bizarre conversations I've ever had.

We swapped greetings and I asked if the cliff had become any more popular over the past year.

'Oh yes, it's become really popular since all of the routes have been re-equipped,' he retorted.

'That's great; it means all the hard work I've put in has paid off,' I replied.

'Why? Who are you?' he asked.

'I'm Gary Gibson.'

And then it began ...

'You're not Gary Gibson! I know Gary Gibson and you ain't him! He's got red hair and a northern accent.'

'I am Gary Gibson,' I said, defending myself as best I could, in my 'northern accent'.

'I'm not having that,' he shot back. 'I've seen pictures of Gary Gibson, I've even met him a few times and you're definitely not him. Where are you from anyway?' he demanded.

'I'm from Stoke-on-Trent and I've come down here to do a few new routes.'

The conversation then changed tack slightly.

'Huh! You don't look like you could climb the routes that Gary Gibson's done, down here, anyway.'

My sole remaining course of action seemed to be to give him some proof. Luckily I had my work's ID badge in my pocket.

'Look,' I said, 'here's my ID badge. It shows you my name, where I work and what I do.'

He took it from me and gazed at it for over a minute, then handed it back to me, suspiciously. He looked down at his dog, gave it a bit of a tug on his lead and started to walk away. As he wandered off, he muttered to his dog, 'I'm not having that. That ain't the real Gary Gibson!' Of course, the first route we did the following day just had to be named *Who Do You Think You Are?*

Number 10, here I come

In 2008 I had heard a story that the BMC were having a centenary celebration at 10 Downing Street with the Prime Minister in attendance and that around one hundred people from the climbing world would be invited to attend. I had also heard a rumour that I might be one of the 'selected' hundred.

Of course, Hazel would chuckle at the idea when I chatted to her about it, and in my heart of hearts I really didn't think I would be on the list of attendees. I thought there were a hundred more important people than me in climbing and mountaineering who would be more likely to be invited.

As the date of the event drew closer, if we heard the sound of the letterbox at home, Hazel would be there first. I would mockingly ask if my invite had come, never really thinking it would.

Then one day, just a few weeks before the event, the post arrived, and Hazel came in with it, saying that my invite to Number 10 had arrived. I was absolutely stunned, so much so that I just couldn't speak for about forty-eight hours afterwards. I had been invited to meet the

Prime Minister!

I felt humbled.

To pass through the gates of Downing Street, to enter into the home of the Prime Minister and to be treated with such respect, was a great honour for me. The photos on the walls depicted all the prime ministers over the past one hundred years. The occasion was extremely dignified.

At the end of the event, as everyone gathered outside, a photo was taken of Ben Moon, Leo Houlding and Sir Chris Bonington, with me on the end. When the BMC's *Summit* magazine was published in celebration of the event, the photo was on the front cover but they had chopped me off it like the bad guest at a wedding.

Perhaps the story of my life?

And just one more thing?

If I may, I'd like to finish my story (so far) with a tale very much pinched from the annals of Jerry Moffatt's legacy, which intertwines quite well with my own.

Jerry had been climbing in the Shawangunks with a bunch of mates.

John Sherman, he who invented the 'V' grade, was climbing on a route off to the side of Jerry's team when he had a bad fall, ripping out most of his gear and hitting the ground on the stretch of the rope.

Jerry ran over to see if John was OK and whether there was anything he could do to help. John was clearly shaken but declined Jerry's offer, thanking him all the same: 'I'll be OK in a while,' he responded.

It then occurred to John that Jerry seemed somewhat familiar.

'Haven't I seen you somewhere before?' he asked.

'Well you may have seen my photo in the magazines,' Jerry proudly responded.

'Yeah, you're that famous English bloke,' John replied. 'You're Gary Gibson!'

Of course Jerry went on to become the best climber in the world. And me? I just do new routes.

Epilogue

'*JUST AS WELL he's one of life's givers. It just about balances out him being one of the biggest piss takers.*' John Perry

It always surprises me when people publish an autobiography in their twenties or thirties and entitle it 'the story so far'. When writing my story, I was looking for a natural conclusion and the visit to Number 10 Downing Street seemed (almost) appropriate.

I considered ending the story at my four thousandth new route. But that didn't seem quite right either since I doubt I will stop. By now, I've done nearly five thousand new routes and I've started to spread my wings to Kalymnos, to mainland Greece and other countries to satiate my obsession.

Perhaps a more important point is that nowadays, for me, it isn't just about new routing.

(I know – heresy! What would my younger self have said?) But times change and people change (yes, even me). I've increasingly turned my attention to re-gearing existing sport crags, bringing the standard of the equipment up to a higher level and improving its longevity to way beyond my lifetime.

Added to that, I have been trying to bring some of the 'older' and increasingly more vegetated crags back up to a level that makes them attractive again. This has involved painstaking work in cooperation with landowners, in the hope that some of these wonderful crags will regain their popularity of previous years.

My work and efforts won't be finished until I have decided they are.

I have enjoyed almost every minute of cleaning and developing new routes, creating articles for magazines and writing guidebooks, helping out with access agreements and having fun outdoors with my mates, enjoying their company and humour. Long may it continue!